THE DESERTS OF THE SOUTHWEST

A Sierra Club Naturalist's Guide to

THE DESERTS
OF THE SOUTHWEST

By Peggy Larson with Lane Larson

FOREWORD BY EDWARD ABBEY

DRAWINGS BY LYNN LARSON

SIERRA CLUB BOOKS   *San Francisco*

GRATEFUL ACKNOWLEDGMENT is made for permission to reprint material from the following sources: E. F. Adolph and Associates, *Physiology of Man in the Desert* (N.Y.: Interscience Publishers, Inc.). Copyright © 1947 by Interscience Publishers, Inc. / Mary Austin, *The Land of Little Rain* (Boston: Houghton Mifflin Co.) Copyright 1903 by Mary Austin. / Joseph Wood Krutch, *The Forgotten Peninsula* (N.Y.: William Sloane Associates). Copyright © 1961 by Joseph Wood Krutch. / Joseph Wood Krutch, *The Voice of the Desert* (N.Y.: William Sloane Associates). Copyright © 1954, 1955 by Joseph Wood Krutch. / Forrest Shreve and Ira L. Wiggins, *Vegetation and Flora of the Sonoran Desert* (Stanford, Calif.: Stanford University Press). Copyright © 1964 by the Board of Trustees of the Leland Stanford Junior University.

Copyright © 1977 by Peggy Larson. All rights reserved.

Library of Congress Cataloging in Publication Data

Larson, Peggy Pickering, 1931–
   The Sierra Club naturalist's guide to the deserts of the Southwest.

   1. Deserts—Southwestern States.   2. Deserts—
Mexico.   3. Desert biology—Southwestern States.
4. Desert biology—Southwestern States.   I. Larson,
Lane, 1953–   II. Title.
GB616.S68L37   500.9'79   76–24835
ISBN 0–87156–186–7

The Sierra Club, founded in 1892 by John Muir, has devoted itself to the study and protection of the nation's scenic and ecological resources—mountains, wetlands, woodlands, wild shores and rivers. All club publications are part of the nonprofit effort the club carries on as a public trust. There are some 50 chapters coast to coast, in Canada, Hawaii, and Alaska. Participation is invited in the club's programs to enjoy and preserve wilderness everywhere. Address: *530 Bush Street, San Francisco, California 94108*

Series design by Klaus Gemming, New Haven, Connecticut
Maps by Stephen Bahre
Production supervised by David Charlsen & Others
Printed in the United States of America

TABLE OF CONTENTS

FOREWORD

Why go into the desert? That sun, roaring at you all day long. The fetid tepid vapid little waterholes slowly evaporating—full of cannibal beetles, spotted toads, hairworms, liver flukes—and down at the bottom, invariably, the pale drowned cadaver of a ten-inch centipede. Those pink rattlesnakes down in The Canyon, those diamondback monsters thick as a catskinner's wrist that lurk in shady places along the trail, those unpleasant solpugids and unnecessary Jerusalem crickets that scurry on dirty feet across your face at night. Why? The rain that comes down like lead shot and wrecks the trail before you, those sudden rockfalls of obscure origin that crash like thunder ten feet behind you in the heart of a dead-still afternoon. Why? The ubiquitous vultures, so patient—but only *so* patient. The ragweed, the tumbleweed, the Jimsonweed, the snakeweed. The scorpion in your shoe at dawn. The dreary wind that seldom stops, the manic-depressive mesquite trees waving their arms at you on moonlight nights. Sand in the soup du jour. Halazone tablets in your canteen. The barren hills that always go up, which is bad, or down, which is worse.

Why go to Starvation Creek, Poverty Knoll, Buzzard Gulch, Wolf Hole, Bitter Springs, Last Chance Canyon, Dungeon Canyon, Whipsaw Flat, Dead Horse Point, Scorpion Flat, Dead Man Draw, Stinking Spring, Camino del Diablo, Hell Hole Canyon, Jornado del Muerto . . . Death Valley? I think of a home-made sign I once saw at a fork in a rocky road somewhere in the boondocks of western Texas:

Hartung's Road
Take the Other

A good sign. One would have liked to meet Mr. Hartung. But I didn't. I respected his need for privacy. I share that need—as who doesn't these days?

Well then, why indeed go walking into the desert when you could be strolling along the golden beaches of California or camping by a stream of pure Rocky Mountain spring water in colorful Colorado or loafing through a laurel slick in the high blue misty hills of North Carolina?

Sometime ago a friend and I took a walk around the base of a mountain up in Coconino County, Arizona. About half-way around this mountain, on the third or fourth day, we paused for a while—two days—by the side of a stream which the Navajos call Nasja, perhaps because of the strange amber color of the water. (Caused by juniper roots—the water seemed safe enough to drink.) On our second day there I walked down the stream, alone, to look at the canyon beyond. I entered the canyon and followed it for half the day, three or four miles maybe, until it became a gorge so deep, narrow and dark, full of water and the inevitable quagmires of quicksand, that I turned around and looked for a way out. A way different than the way I'd come, which was crooked and uncomfortable and buried. I wanted to see what was up on top of this world. I found a sort of chimney flue on the east wall, which looked feasible, and sweated and cursed my way up through that for an unreasonable distance until I reached a point where one could walk upright, like a human being. Another 300 feet of scrambling brought me to the rim of the canyon. No one, I felt certain, had ever departed Nasja Canyon by *that* route before.

But someone had. I found near the summit an arrow sign, three feet long, formed of stones and pointing off into the north, toward those same old purple vistas, so grand, immense and mysterious, of more canyons, more mesas and plateaus, more mountains, more cloud-dappled sun-spangled leagues of desert sand and rock, under the same old, same true wide and aching sky.

The arrow pointed "into" the north. But what was it pointing at? I looked at the sign closely and saw that those dark, desert-varnished stones had been in place for a long, long time; they rested in compacted dust. I followed the direction suggested and came promptly, within a hundred yards, to the rim of another canyon and a drop-off straight down of a good 500 feet. Not that way, surely. Across this canyon was nothing of any unusual interest that I could see—only more of the familiar sunblasted sandstone, a few scrubby clumps of blackbrush and prickly pear, a few acres of nothing where only a lizard could graze surrounded by a few square miles of more nothingness of interest chiefly to horned toads. I returned to the arrow and checked again, this time with field glasses, looking away toward the north for 10, 20, 40 miles into the distance. I studied the scene with care, looking for an ancient Indian ruin, a significant cairn, perhaps an abandoned mine, a hidden treasure, the mother of all mother lodes . . .

But there was nothing out there. Nothing at all. Nothing but the desert. Nothing but the world.

That's why.

Edward Abbey

Tin Cup Mesa, Utah

CHAPTER I

Rewarding Travel

"REWARDING TRAVEL in an unfrequented land," naturalist–author Joseph Wood Krutch called his journeys through the southwestern desert country. The same reward awaits the explorer of today who approaches the desert with an open, inquiring mind; who comes to the desert with a desire to be a closer, more integral, and harmonious part of the biota; and who also acknowledges, respects, and prepares for the particular conditions to which he or she may be subjected by the unique, noncompromising desert environment.

The desert holds a mystique, a subtle fascination, which is difficult to pinpoint and more difficult to describe. Not all people are so affected by it, but those who have experienced the desert in this way are the richer. Mary Austin—playwright, poet, essayist, novelist—wrote:

> If one is inclined to wonder at first how so many dwellers came to be in the loneliest land that ever came out of God's hands, what they do there and why stay, one does not wonder so much after having lived there. None other than this long brown land lays such a hold on the affections.

This "long brown land" is a land of beauty. But it does not display the traditional concept of beauty imposed upon us by an Anglo-Saxon cultural heritage. Except where drastically changed from its natural state by the introduction of exotic or fossil water, the desert displays no timbered green, no fruited plain, no amber waves of grain. Rather, it reveals bare ground, or shrub- and cactus-studded earth, sand, or rock. And, although the desert may have its mountains, they fall somewhat short of the traditional concept of purple mountains' majesties. Where, then, is the beauty to be found?

The elements of space and openness contribute importantly to desert beauty. Desert air is typically remarkably clear (though unfortunately it grows gradually less so with increasing pollution). Little moisture is held within it, little haze is produced, and under normal unpolluted conditions visibility stretches sixty or more miles. Thus, from an unobstructed location, the human observer can turn full circle, viewing a sixty-mile radius—and in most of the desert, the view is relatively unrestricted. Here and there, mountain ranges rear their rocky masses from the desert's floor, but the view often stretches from the observer to the horizon, where earth joins sky. Nor do large trees or other heavy growth obstruct the vista.

Open space exists not only at eye level; much openness may be found at ground level, as well. With water limited, desert vegetation is sparse and widely spaced. Space and openness in the desert, above and below, result in easy viewing, easy walking, and a feeling of spaciousness—ankle and elbow room, so to speak, an increasingly rare commodity, but one we are learning is basic to human well-being.

Sky contributes to the desert expanse. Little obstructs the extensive view of the sky dome, which in the clear, arid atmosphere appears bluer by day and more brightly star-studded by night than do the skies over many moister regions. Sunsets often tend toward the magnificent, as do sunrises, and the displays of towering, snow-white, black-bottomed, thunder clouds that sweep across the summer sky are spectacular. So, too, are the manifestations of the storms these clouds produce—displays of brilliant lightning, resounding thunder, and occasional drowning deluges in a normally dry land.

The desert's anatomy lies exposed. No complete vegetative cloak covers its naked geology; its geological history is varied, and the composition and relationships of its components are more easily observed and more readily studied and appreciated than those in most other climates. The North American deserts are geologically young; their surfaces have not yet been worn down to monotonousness. Angular, jagged, sharp lines and rough textures—rather than smooth, soft, rounded, cloaked ones—characterize much of the desert's surface. The visible geology, indeed the total visible aspect of the desert, has the character of a handsomely rugged, virile individualist.

The physical components of the desert and the living

things which dwell there abound with texture, form, and color. Much of the variety is derived from the very obvious ground surface—the rocks, sand, gravel, and soil. From the black and reddish volcanic flows which solidified as they once sludged across the landscape, to the occasional greens and blues of mineral deposits, to the beige-yellow sands, the base of the desert displays a wide range of color, as well as of form and texture. The plants exhibit particularly various forms. Unlike other habitats, the desert is seldom dominated by one ecological life form. Shrubs, cacti, bushes, trees, small ground-hugging annuals—to a certain degree all dissimilar from one another in form and appearance—share the role of dominance in the desert, whereas dominance in other habitats is often restricted to a single growth type—for example, conifers, or grasses, or deciduous hardwood trees. The desert's plant variety provides interest in viewing, comparing, and touching. The animals, too, provide variety in color, form, and texture. Consider the patterning, glossiness, and glassy smoothness of the snake's scales; the shine of the beetle's carapace; the flash of the hummingbird's color and iridescent sheen; the coyote's beige-yellow-gray fur; or the black of the feather-slick raven against the summer sky. The color of most desert animals serves to blend into their background of browns and grays. Spots of vivid color do occur in the desert, most of them brief in tenure—flowers, butterflies, some other insects such as beetles, a male lizard in courting display, an occasional bird. For the most part, however, one receives from the desert as a whole a color impression of subdued variations on a theme of gray, brown, black, beige, green, blue, purple, and subtle combinations of these hues.

The desert light, producer of the colors, seems almost a physical entity. Its long rays, warm and almost caressing on an early summer morning, shift to a hard, hot, flat, white glare at noon, then gradually recede to the warm red and pink of the sunset sky; in the waning evening light, cool blues and purples color the distant mountains. Indeed, while much of the coloring of the adjacent desert is in the brown range, the distances are painted in hues of purple. Far mountain ranges in the fluctuating desert light are transposed from a flat-surfaced, grayish-brownish-blue at the sun's daily zenith to sculptured surfaces colored by shades of amethyst and lilac as the sun lies closer to the morning or evening horizons. Particularly at sunset, one may view as many as three or four sets of desert mountain peaks ranged one beyond another, their colors varying from the dark purple of the closest to the lighter shades of the more distant, and all shifting in degree of coloration, minute by minute, as the sun drops. The subtle, constantly changing coloration of the desert is one of its most striking beauties.

The environment of the desert is also harsh and demanding. It does not coddle. Therefore those plants and animals which make it their home often display adaptations of form, function, behavior, or all of these, which allow them to survive and often prosper under the climatic conditions imposed upon them. These adaptations have produced singularly unique and fascinating living things—cacti fifty feet tall, boojums resembling seventy-foot inverted carrots, mice that never drink, snakes that move forward by traveling sideways. The economy of the desert is normally exceedingly frugal, particularly from the standpoint of water. At certain times in the desert, the line between life and death is very tenuous for plants and animals. (For the human species, when unprepared, the line may also prove tenuous.) The desert's nature is open and visible, and its climatic conditions are stringent; probably in no other biome are the relationships of living things to the physical aspects of their environment and to one another so obvious and observable as they are in the desert. A rewarding understanding of the special beauty of adaptation, the tenacity and strength of the force of life, and, by extrapolation, a deeper appreciation of all things living awaits the human desert explorer who looks, learns about, and seriously considers the desert biota.

The deserts represent one of the last North American areas in which large tracts remain relatively uninhabited. The arid wilderness has been slower to "develop" in the usual sense than areas more amenable to settlement and exploitation through agriculture and industry—a magnificent beneficence insofar as desert and wilderness aficionados are concerned. Space between people is one of the desert's most pleasing aspects for those who would explore it.

Surely to meet and enjoy a challenge must be basic to human nature. Adventurers have long accepted the challenge of the mountain, the jungle, and the sea, and tested themselves against them. Fewer have recognized the challenge of the desert; today, increasing numbers are realizing that challenge, wilderness, and rewards also exist in the arid habitat. Just as the mountaineer, sailor, or jungle explorer must recognize the special conditions imposed by the environment he or she seeks to know, so must the desert enthusiast understand desert conditions and how best to cope with them in order to understand and enjoy desert exploration—whether by foot, on horseback, or by winged or wheeled transport. The desert can be a difficult, even deadly land for living things. Many plants and animals have physically adapted to its special conditions over spans of time. Man has not adapted physically, and cannot, but to some extent, as have certain animals, he can adapt behaviorally. Mankind possesses technology and the ability to think on a high level. Common sense demands the use of these two factors for the safe, intelligent enjoyment of the desert in a nondisruptive manner, and the derivation of the many recreational, spiritual, and humanly renewable benefits the desert can afford. Man must understand the components in the desert biome and their interrelationships and the intelligent ways in which the desert lands may be explored and appreciated.

Krutch's travels in an "unfrequented land" rewarded him with a very special feeling for the desert:

> Long before I ever saw the desert I was aware of the mystical overtones which the observation of nature made audible to me. But I have never been more frequently or more vividly aware of them than in connection with the desert phenomena.

In expressing his feelings, Krutch coined an appropriate term; he spoke for a good many of us who experience a deep affection for desert beauty, desert life, and desert wilderness when he readily acknowledged that, indeed, a "desert phenomenon" exists.

CHAPTER II

Define Desert

DEFINE desert. Seemingly, almost as many definitions of the term arise as there are definers. The simplest definition holds that a desert is an area receiving an average of ten or fewer inches of precipitation annually. This definition is far from complete. Some areas receive less than ten inches rainfall annually, yet are called grasslands. Some authorities would place the desert-defining figure at a five-inch limit; however, some areas receiving in excess of five inches precipitation annually are, nonetheless, deserts. Many factors influence the value plants derive from moisture they receive; hence, these factors are instrumental in determining the type of habitat established. A gentle soaking rain benefits the vegetation more than a violent cloudburst, which results in rapid runoff and moisture loss. Several well-spaced showers are more valuable than a single rain, even though the same total precipitation may be produced. Moisture received in summer heat will be more readily evaporated than that received during cool weather; conversely, moisture received in hot weather may be greatly needed by the vegetation for survival in that particular stressful period.

Portions of the North American desert receive very limited rainfall. The record for lowest average annual precipitation for North America is held by Bataques, Mexico, located in the Sonoran Desert, with a fourteen-year average of 1.2 inches. That record is followed closely by the one for Death Valley, California, in the Mohave Desert, with an average of 1.63 inches. Toward the opposite end of the scale lies Tucson, Arizona, considered to be in the Sonoran Desert, yet receiving an average of 11.2 inches annual precipitation.

The figure of ten inches or less annual precipitation, as used in the desert definition, is an *average* figure. However, the erratic nature of its occurrence is a basic characteristic of desert precipitation. For example, Yuma, Arizona, is reported by Dr. Richard Logan, of the University of California at Los Angeles, to have a mean annual precipitation of 3.39

inches. However, extreme annual precipitation records for Yuma include one year of 11.42 inches and another year when a mere .28-inch total was received. An extreme example of the irregularity of desert rainfall is provided by Bagdad, California, in the Mohave Desert, which has an average annual rainfall of approximately 2¼ inches. However, Bagdad holds the record for the longest dry period in the United States, having undergone 767 days—from October 3, 1912, to November 8, 1914—without precipitation!

More than water, or the lack of it, is involved in producing desert. Temperature, too, plays a vital role. High temperatures compound and low temperatures ameliorate the effects of moisture shortage. *Evapotranspiration* is defined as the total loss of water from the soil both by evaporation from the soil surface and by transpiration from the plants growing in that soil. Certainly temperature in conjunction with air movements exerts the major influence on the rates at which evaporation and transpiration occur. Although evapotranspiration rates are not always readily available for many areas, evaporation rates are officially recorded at some government weather stations. These rates are based on the amount of evaporation occurring from water-filled, standardized, four-foot-in-diameter pans. At some of the desert stations in the most arid portions of the United States, these rates reach and occasionally exceed 120 inches of evaporation annually, in comparison to the five or fewer inches of precipitation received annually in these same locations. Yet another definition of desert is that it is an area in which potential evapotranspiration exceeds precipitation.

The high-temperature record for the Western Hemisphere is an impressive 134° F. on July 10, 1913, in Death Valley, California. This temperature is exceeded by only one world record—136.4° F.—reported in 1922 at El Azizia, Libya. Death Valley is also reported to have the hottest summers in the Western Hemisphere, with an average daily (not maximum) temperature of 98° F. And although Death Valley holds the extreme high record for the North American desert, it is not an isolated example; many of the other desert localities report record temperatures in the 120°-plus range. High summer maximum temperatures are often sustained over long periods in the southwestern deserts. Thus Dr. Forrest Shreve, one of the foremost early desert

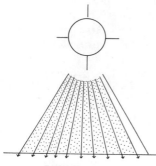 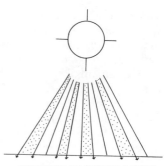

DESERT SURFACE   SURFACE OF HUMID LANDS

FIG. 1. With little atmospheric humidity or plant cover to impede its passage to their surfaces, deserts receive approximately nine-tenths of possible solar radiation, whereas the surfaces of humid lands receive approximately two-fifths.

ecologists, noted that periods of ninety consecutive days with a maximum of at least 100° F. are not exceptional for portions of the Sonoran Desert.

Just as the extremes of precipitation play a very determining role with regard to survival by living things in the desert, so also are temperature extremes important. These extremes are often very great in the desert, where lack of moisture results in air of low humidity and formation of only limited cloud cover. A very high percentage of possible sunlight is therefore received. In one recent year, for example, Yuma, Arizona, received 93 percent of possible sunshine; that same year, Norfolk, Virginia, received 31 percent. With little water vapor in the air and little cloud cover or plant growth to deflect the sun's rays, approximately 90 percent of the solar radiation possible reaches the ground surface and lower air layer in the desert, resulting in very high air and ground-surface temperatures. Official air temperatures are taken in the shade, five feet above the ground. Temperatures at the surface in sunlight often range thirty to fifty degrees higher than the accompanying air temperature. Humid areas receive approximately 40 percent of the solar radiation possible, 60 percent being deflected before it reaches the ground and lower air levels.

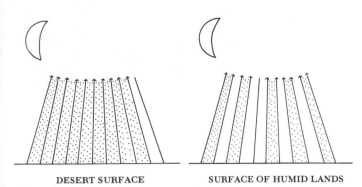

DESERT SURFACE   SURFACE OF HUMID LANDS

FIG. 2. In the desert, approximately nine-tenths of the day's accumulated heat is reradiated back toward the sky; approximately one-half of the day's accumulated heat is lost at night in humid climates. Desert country displays a wide range of daily temperatures; humid lands show a much lesser range.

After sundown in the desert, heat is rapidly and easily radiated back toward the sky, with approximately 90 percent escaping unimpeded. In moister climates, the heat gained at lower levels during the day is less easily lost, with approximately 50 percent of it escaping and the remainder being deflected downward and held by growth as well as by clouds, water, and dust in the air. Thus in moist climates temperatures fluctuate only moderately from day to night, but in the desert the range between daytime highs and nighttime lows is extreme. The difference is often fifty degrees or more. Similarly there is a very great range between the low and high temperature records over the period of a year or several years. For example, Yuma, Arizona reported for one particular year a maximum temperature in August of 116 degrees and a minimum temperature in December of 30 degrees, a difference of eighty-six degrees. This is not unusual for this region. Records over a period of years, as compiled by Dr. R. Logan for Yuma, show an all-time maximum temperature of 123.08 degrees and an all-time minimum of 22.1 degrees, or a difference of approximately 101 degrees.

Snow occurs in the North American deserts, primarily in the more northern parts, but also as far south as Tucson, Arizona, which receives at least traces almost every winter and is occasionally the recipient of 2 to 4 inch snowfalls. Also, incongruous as it may seem, a limited amount of dew occurs in the North American deserts. The amount of water vapor contained in the air at any one time compared to the amount it is capable of containing is known as the *relative humidity*, and is expressed as a percentage. Warm air is capable of holding more vapor than cool air before it reaches the saturation point. Thus although desert air often has a very low relative humidity during the day, as the night air cools rapidly it may reach the saturation point, resulting in excess moisture being deposited on ground and plant surfaces in the form of dew.

In regard to defining or delimiting desert, several mathematical systems using both precipitation and temperature figures to determine climatic classification have been devised. One such system is the Köppen, wherein deserts are characterized as having generally high temperatures and less than ten inches annual precipitation. The Thornwaite system uses formulas which consider temperature and precipitation figures in conjunction with temperature efficiency and precipitation effectiveness. Yet a third system was developed by Dr. Peveril Meigs, former Chairman of the Arid Zone Commission of the International Geographical Union. In the Meigs system, an index of aridity is determined; additionally, seasonal distribution of precipitation and temperature are taken into account.

Under the Meigs system, the most desertic classification is extremely arid. This "E" rating denotes an area that in mathematical computation has a high index of aridity, holds a record of at least one twelve-month period without precipitation, and displays no seasonal distribution of rainfall. Much of the central Sahara, large areas in the Arabian and Takla Makan deserts, and smaller areas in some of the other deserts of the world rank as extremely arid, as does a small area in the North American desert centered near the head of the Gulf of California and stretching northward up the hot, low trough where the Salton Sea and Death Valley are located.

Heat and aridity spawn characteristics typical of deserts. Plants are widely spaced due to lack of moisture. Very occasional areas may be totally without vegetation. Shreve estimated that in the parts of the arid Mohave Desert which support small creosote bushes, only 3 percent of the ground surface was covered. And, in the more "lush" portions of the Sonoran Desert, the percentage of ground covered is considerably higher, although even there much of the desert's surface lies exposed, subject to erosion by both wind and water. Paucity of vegetation results in soil low in humus. Shreve reported humus in soils of the Colorado and Mohave deserts as ranging from 0.25 to 0.65 percent, compared to a range of 3 to 5 percent in soils of more humid regions. Desert soils have acquired relatively large amounts of sodium and potassium salts as well as other water soluble minerals due to the high rates of mineralization in these areas. In more moist regions, minerals present tend to be leached downward through the soil as abundant moisture soaks through it. Not so in the desert, where water is insufficient to soak the soil to any great depth; there, minerals in suspension may even be sucked upward through the soil by capillary action and pulled to the surface to be deposited as the moisture carrying them is evaporated. Depending upon the minerals present and the amounts, desert soils may vary from those exceedingly rich in plant growth to those which inhibit or even prevent it.

Winds are frequent in the desert. These desert winds are caused by general atmospheric patterns, as an accompaniment to storms, or in some cases by local topography. They are also often caused by the rapid heating and cooling of the air near the ground surface. Winds, due to their frequency and to the air they circulate, which is often dry and hot, constitute a powerful evaporative force as they sweep across the soil and over the living things in their paths. They also contribute greatly to erosion of the desert's surface. Winds carrying dust and sand act as agents of abrasion, sandblasting rocks and objects over which they move. The winds also act as agents of deflation and deposition, moving loose material such as soil, dust, sand, and dead plants from one site to deposit it in another.

Steady winds of one or more days' duration are commonplace in the southwestern desert, particularly in the late winter and spring. These winds only occasionally reach or exceed 35 miles per hour in speed, although, due to the openness of the terrain through which they move relatively unimpeded, their speed is often estimated to be greater.

Gusts of wind moving at much higher speeds sometimes accompany storms, particularly in the summer months. *Dust devils,* or whirlwinds—rotating air currents occasionally as much as several hundred feet in height and carrying dust, sand, and debris—are of common occurrence on hot still days; often several at a time may be seen moving across the landscape. These whirlwinds are caused when extreme heating of the ground surface results in columns of upflowing air. Surrounding air rushes into this vacuum and diverts to one side or the other of the rising air, causing a strong, uprising, whirling column. Although dust devils occasionally topple poorly supported block patio walls, they are rarely dangerous in the North American desert. Unlike the potentially very destructive tornadoes—whirling masses of air reaching downward from clouds—the dust devils rotate upward from the ground surface. They can be exceedingly annoying to the person caught afoot or driving through the dusty center of one.

Frequent winds and open ground surface cause occasional desert sand and dust storms. These storms are relatively infrequent; one study determined that in most of the North American desert not more than three or four, and more often a maximum of one to two, occur annually in any one locality. Over most of our desert terrain, winds must reach approximately 35 miles per hour or higher in order to initiate and maintain such storms. Minor storms may last only a few hours; major ones often persist twelve to thirty-six hours. Sand, being heavier than dust, is rarely carried by the winds to any height much greater than three feet above the ground. However, the lighter dust may be carried to heights of many hundred feet in the air. The North American desert has only relatively limited areas of sand, estimated at 1 percent or less of its total area, primarily but not solely limited to the area around the head of the Gulf of California.

Sand storms in the North American deserts are rarely dangerous for human beings, as compared to some of the storms in the Old World deserts, such as the Arabian and Sahara, where much more extensive areas of sand and vast sweeps of open desert contribute to the devastating force. North American sand storms do occasionally damage automobiles, sandblasting paint and windshields, and may also damage other objects, such as wooden power poles. Dust storms in the North American desert can be devastating, however, particularly in conjunction with vehicular traffic; they may suddenly obscure vision, causing serious accidents. Dust storms are intensified where man has removed all plant cover preparatory to planting crops; such areas are often near highways where the mix of dust storm and traffic may prove fatal.

Strangely, however, the most important erosional factor in the desert is not wind, but water. The effects of water are everywhere apparent in this land where the sight of water itself is for the most part a rarity. Precipitation is often received through violent cloudbursts accompanied by rapid runoff. Even when precipitation is received in a less violent manner, its absorption may be somewhat impeded, for much of the desert's surface is rock or gravel, or exhibits other factors of a low or nonabsorptive character. Also, the geologically young North American deserts have many rocky, low, but precipitous mountain ranges which often receive much of the desert's precipitation, but down which much of this water rapidly flows. In the desert the ground surface, more bare than covered, lies vulnerable to these occasional, but highly effective and destructive water forces.

Water, as it falls on the desert mountains, often first runs in a broad, shallow, sheet flow, then collects in normally dry watercourses. It carries with it boulders, rocks, gravel, and finer materials. As the flood debouches onto the lower levels of the hills, its speed diminishes; gradually, the material it carries is dropped, spread out in a fan shape, graded from the heavier material higher up the slope to the lightest at the bottom. A subsequent heavy runoff may follow the same channel, but as the lower levels are blocked by material from the previous storm, its rock-carrying water will be diverted to one side or the other of the blockage to create its own alluvial fan adjacent to the previous fan. A large number of contiguous alluvial fans which eventually coalesce with one another is known as a *bajada*. Desert mountain ranges gradually being buried by debris derived from their upper limits and delivered primarily by water flow to their lower levels are a characteristic feature of the desert.

Much of the North American desert displays a topography referred to as *basin and range*, signifying numerous mountain ranges separated from one another by intermountain basins. The most northern of the deserts is called the Great Basin. Actually, it consists of numerous basins, rather than a single one. Much of the North American desert country, then, gives one an overall impression of generally low, roughly parallel mountain ranges, many of which are skirted at their bases by alluvial fans, or bajadas, which slope gently to low basins, or valleys, between the ranges. The slopes and intervening basins are marked by *dry washes,* or *arroyos*— normally-dry streambeds occasionally carrying heavy, brief streamflow, which drains toward the basin centers. Many of these basin centers—known as *sinks,* or *bolsons*—are un-drained, so that water from a storm not otherwise absorbed into the ground or evaporated before reaching the low point of the basin collects in an ephemeral lake from which it eventually evaporates, leaving behind the minerals carried in suspension. On these *playas,* or *dry lakes,* the buildup of minerals may be extreme, inhibiting plant growth or sup-porting a special vegetative community of plants known as *halophytes* (plants capable of growing in a salty soil). Very occasionally in the desert, sufficient water accumulates to form permanent lakes. These lakes tend to be highly saline, with water constantly evaporating from them, concentrating their mineral content. The Great Salt Lake in the Great Basin Desert is a prime example.

Other basins have the potential for being drained through connections to major streamways. With precipitation se-verely limited, however, this occurrence is often more po-tential than fact. Some rivers do flow, at least part-time, through the desert and eventually deliver water, primarily to the Gulf of California. However, such rivers usually carry water derived primarily from outside the desert; they simply move this water through the arid land, receiving minor contributions during the desert sojourn. One major river which traverses the North American desert and delivers water year-round to the sea is the Colorado, whose water is primarily derived from the Rocky Mountains, and whose remaining water, after man has taken a heavy toll for his use, is finally delivered to the head of the Gulf of California. Similarly, the Rio Grande flows through the Chihuahuan Desert and then far beyond it, finally reaching the Gulf of Mexico. Such rivers as these, crossing the desert but carry-ing water largely derived from sources outside it, are known in the deserts through which they pass as *exotic rivers.*

Dry washes are a dominant feature of the desert land; their rough courses cut into the earth to various depths and are readily visible on the open, sparsely vegetated surface. As recipients of runoff, their borders support a heavier, more extensive vegetation than that of the surrounding area. The wash, or stream, margins may be marked by the heavy growth of large cottonwoods, mesquites, and other species of plants where receipt of sufficient water makes this possible. But even the edges of the smallest washes often display a slightly greener, more favored vegetational aspect, particularly apparent when viewed from the air.

Occasionally in washes, *tanks,* or deep holes, will be worn in rock in the streambed, especially at the base of a sudden drop in the wash. Some tanks are quite large and may hold water for considerable periods following their last flooding. This water serves as a valuable supply for the animals of the area—as it once did and occasionally still does for man. Much of the runoff received by the washes soaks into their beds and may lie rather close to the surface in favored areas. Thirsty animals, such as coyotes, sometimes dig holes in the gravel wash bottoms; into these holes seep small amounts of water—relished by animal excavators and nonexcavators alike.

Flash floods are a desert phenomenon of the rivers and washes. Localized, often violent, rain storms accompanied by thunder and lightning are common in summer in parts of the desert. These storms may produce up to several inches of rain in a brief period of time. Vast amounts of runoff quickly collect in the washes, where, constricted by the banks of the wash and pressed forward by continuing heavy inflow, the water may form an actual wall, or advancing front, varying from a few inches to rarely a few feet in height. This moves with tremendous force down the previously dry streambed, roiling dirt, rocks, and debris with it. Such floods may flow for miles, moving into areas which originally received no part of the storm. The flood may thus startle or even drown the unwary and the unwarned caught in its path. Death by drowning in the desert seems an incongruity but is an actuality each year. Fatalities probably occur most frequently when drivers cross a wash just as the water strikes that point or when they attempt to drive through a flooding wash,

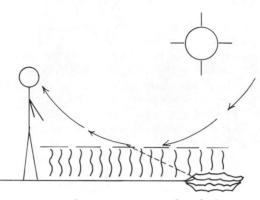

FIG. 3. A common desert mirage is produced when a ray of light, coming from above the horizon, passes through dense cool air, then strikes a layer of hot, shimmering air lying near the ground surface. The light is then bent upward. To the eye of the observer, the image of the sky thus produced appears to be rippling water in the distance.

deceived as to the depth or force of the water, or both, so that vehicle and occupants are swept downstream.

As flash floods sometimes produce water where it is not expected, another phenomenon, the *mirage,* promises water where none exists. Mirages occur in the desert on hot, still days. They are caused by refracted light; light waves from above strike a layer of intensely heated air near the ground surface and are then bent upward into the denser air above. The image of the sky is produced; most often, it appears as distant rippling water, although irregularities in the image may at times produce supposed trees or other shimmering objects.

That *desert* is not easily, specifically defined is apparent. However, certain characteristics of the North American desert can be listed: low and often irregular patterns of precipitation; prolonged high temperatures; extreme temperature fluctuations; low humidity; a high percentage of possible sunlight received; soil high in minerals and low in humus; and extreme erosion of the ground surface by wind and water. Obviously such conditions exert a profound influence on those living things—plant and animal, including the animal called man—who seek to make the desert their home.

CHAPTER III

The Deserts of North America

DESERTS cover approximately one-seventh of the earth's land surface, or about eight million square miles. (Semi-arid lands cover an additional one-seventh, another eight million square miles.) The North American desert, comprising approximately 500,000 square miles, ranks fifth in size among the world's deserts. The world's largest desert is the Sahara in northern Africa, whose 3.5 million square miles stretch from the Atlantic Ocean on the west to the Red Sea on the east. Second in size is the Australian Desert of approximately 1.3 million square miles. The Arabian Desert covers approximately one million square miles; the Turkestan in southwestern Russia claims an expanse of about three-quarters of a million square miles. Smaller than the North American desert are the Patagonian of Argentina; India's Thar; southern Africa's Kalahari and Namib; China's Takla Makan; the Iranian; and the Atacama–Peruvian of South America.

Although all share certain characteristics in common—the overriding characteristic of aridity in particular—each desert is distinctive. Even the four deserts comprising the North American desert are each quite distinctive from one another; their causes, their appearances, their overall characters, and their biotas are pleasingly varied. Indeed, the variations (particularly among the biota) developed in each desert in response to the theme of aridity make the deserts of the world one of the most fascinating of ecological studies.

Deserts are not scattered haphazardly over the earth; the pattern of their occurrence is shaped by the factors that produce them. The major world deserts occur in two discontinuous belts ringing the globe. In both the Northern and Southern Hemispheres, this desert country occurs largely between 15 and 35 degrees latitude. Thus, in the Northern Hemisphere, the desert belt is roughly centered over the Tropic of Cancer; in the Southern Hemisphere, it is centered over the Tropic of Capricorn. Because more land surface occurs in the Northern Hemisphere in the latitudes defined, more desert occurs in the Northern than in the Southern Hemisphere. Centered along the desert belt in the Northern Hemisphere are the North American deserts and the Sahara, Arabian, Indian, and Iranian deserts; somewhat to the north of these on the Eurasian continent are the Turkestan, Takla Makan, and Gobi. Along the Tropic of Capricorn in the Southern Hemisphere are the Australian, the Kalahari and Namib of Africa, and the Atacama–Peruvian and Patagonian of South America; the Patagonian stretches far south of the Tropic of Capricorn.

Desert formation in these particular latitudes is primarily due to complex global air-circulation patterns caused by the rotation of the earth on its axis (so that the earth is moving at great speed at the equator and very slowly near the poles), the seasonal tilting of the earth in relationship to the sun, and other factors. In very general terms, air is heated at the equator, ascends, and is replaced by inrushing air. As the heated air moves upward, it is gradually cooled. Cool air, with a lower saturation point, is capable of holding less moisture within it than warm air. As the air cools, it releases the excess moisture it contains, helping to produce the moist tropics. The ascending air, in the area of low atmospheric pressure over the equator, then flows from that point toward the poles. The air becomes heated as it descends in the subtropical zones of high pressure near the Tropics of Cancer and Capricorn. As the temperature of the air increases, so also does the air's ability to absorb and retain moisture, producing aridity of varying degrees. To the north and south of these desert latitudes, the air once again ascends, producing moisture for the land; finally, over the poles, the air again descends.

Some deserts are caused partially or wholly by mountains; the arid land lies in the *rain shadow* cast by the mountains. In these cases, moisture-laden air encounters a mountain mass and is forced upward. The ascending air is cooled and releases moisture on the windward side of the range. Once over the summit, the air descends the lee side of the range, warming as it does so, and hence increasing its evaporative power. Thus the windward side of the mountain range may support a heavy, well-watered forest, while the lee side and the area far beyond it, robbed of moisture, are occupied by a desert or steppe plant community.

Yet another cause of desert formation is remoteness from oceanic moisture sources. Areas lying deep within a continent may become desert simply because air currents reaching them have already traversed vast land distances; by the time they arrive over the deserts, these currents have already lost the moisture they once carried.

Cold ocean currents flowing from the poles toward the equator, in conjunction with onshore winds, may produce deserts where the currents wash close to shore. Air moving across the frigid currents is cooled to a low temperature; thus the air holds little moisture when it arrives over land, where it may produce mist and fog, but rarely rain. Two of the most extreme of the world's deserts, the Namib and the Atacama, are so influenced; the Atacama is, in fact, the world's most arid desert, averaging less than one-half inch annual precipitation. One site within it—Iquique, Chile—is generally accepted as having the world's record for the longest rainless period: fourteen consecutive years!

All these climatic, desert-producing factors—descending, drying air currents; mountain-produced rain shadows; distance from oceanic moisture sources; and cold ocean currents—are instrumental, sometimes singly, more often in combination, as primary forces producing the four North American deserts or distinctive individual portions of these. Various authorities cut the North American desert into four, or occasionally more, distinctive deserts. To draw precise boundaries for the North American desert in general, or for its individual parts, is often difficult, except in those locations where desert meets mountain, sea, or some similar sharp desert-delimiting factor. Along much of their boundaries, the North American deserts grade gradually into an adjoining environment, desert grassland, for instance, or *chaparral*. In some areas, one desert grades gradually into another. We have chosen to follow the division of the North American desert into its individual deserts as set up by Forrest Shreve, the early desert ecologist.

Desert boundaries certainly bear little or no relationship to political boundaries, and often only partial relationship to geographical features. Shreve therefore delineated the North American desert into four individual deserts—the

Great Basin, the Mohave, the Chihuahuan, and the So-noran—based on their distinctive vegetation. Shreve further subdivided the Sonoran into seven vegetational subdivisions.

A small discontinuous portion of desert country exists in the Columbia River Basin in eastern Washington State. Desert country flows southward from central and eastern Oregon and southern Idaho, covering almost all of Nevada and much of Utah, extends an arm into Wyoming, touches western Colorado, then covers southeastern California and portions of northern, and much of central, southern, and western Arizona. It covers much of the Lower, or Baja, California Peninsula and most of the northern Mexican state of Sonora. The most northern region of this desert country constitutes the Great Basin Desert. The Mohave is located primarily in southeastern California, entering the southern tip of Nevada and touching western Arizona. The Sonoran sections lie in southern Arizona, extreme southeastern California, Baja California, and Sonora.

This one large sweep of desert country is separated from the Chihuahuan Desert by desert grassland on the very low elevations of the southern United States Continental Divide in eastern Arizona and western New Mexico, and increased elevations to the south in Mexico. The Chihuahuan Desert encompasses a small portion of southern New Mexico and a part of western Texas; it then extends far south into Mexico through eastern Chihuahua, over most of Coahuila, then into eastern Durango, northern Zacatecas, western Nuevo León, and northern San Luis Potosí. Small detached areas of Chihuahuan Desert also occur further south in the states of Hidalgo and Puebla.

The most northern of the North American deserts, the Great Basin, is caused primarily by the rain-shadow effect of the Cascade and Sierra Nevada mountains. Lying to the west of the Great Basin, these tall, vast mountain chains wring most of the moisture from the air moving inland from the Pacific Ocean. To the east of this desert lie the Rocky Mountains, a barrier to moisture coming from the east; additionally, the Great Basin lies at a vast distance inland from an eastern moisture source.

The southern deserts lie more directly than does the Great Basin under the pattern of descending, warming

THE DESERTS OF THE SOUTHWEST

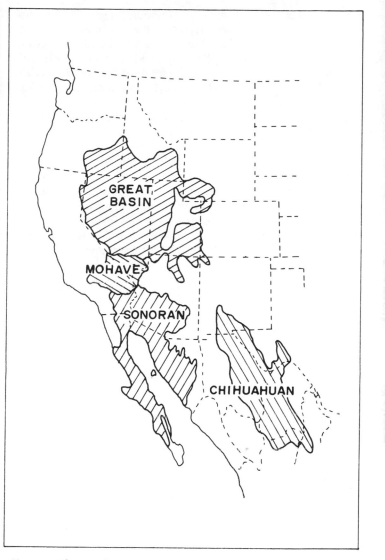

FIG. 4. The North American Desert is composed of four separate deserts: the Great Basin, the Mohave, the Sonoran, and the Chihuahuan.

The Deserts of North America

air—one of the major desert-producing factors. Thus the air-lifting process which would produce moisture is absent or limited much of the time. However, the air circulating over these deserts is not totally lacking in moisture, as is obvious when it meets large mountain masses within a desert or at its borders, is lifted, cooled, and deposits precipitation on the mountain heights.

Additionally the southern reaches of the Sierra Nevadas and other mountains lie to the west of the Mohave and portions of the Sonoran Desert, producing a rain-shadow effect for these areas. This rocky, mountainous backbone extends even into northern Baja California, where on this very narrow peninsula it is a factor in producing an elongated strip of extreme desert between the mountains and the eastern, Gulf-bordering coast of the peninsula.

Off the west coast of northern and central Baja California, the cold California Current flows. In conjunction with onshore winds, this current produces a special foggy, coastal desert of the same general type as the Atacama along the west coast of South America and the Namib on the west coast of Africa.

The Chihuahuan Desert, in addition to being located under the usually inhibiting high-pressure belt characterized by descending air, also lies between two major ranges of mountains which serve to rob it of moisture. Much of the Mexican portion of this desert lies on an elevated intermountain plateau bounded partially on the west by the Sierra Madre Occidental and on the east by the Sierra Madre Oriental.

The figure of a half million square miles of North American desert is an approximation, dependent upon the scientist computing it and the method of determination used. An often-used figure is that of 440,000 square miles. In North America, desert spans approximately 27 degrees of latitude, from about 22 to 49 degrees. This range constitutes an approximate north–south distance of 2,300 miles. The farther one moves either north or south from the equator, the cooler the climate becomes. Obviously, with the latitudinal span of the North American desert, the more northern reaches will be considerably cooler than the southern.

The hottest and driest portion of the North American desert occurs in its more southern and lowest reaches. The hub of this area surrounds the head of the Gulf of California in Baja California and in Sonora, Mexico. It extends into extreme southwestern Arizona and southeastern California, then runs northward up a low trough which includes Death Valley in its northern extremity. Average annual rainfall for this area is five or fewer inches, with the emphasis on fewer. Bataques, Mexico, with the record low annual precipitation rate for North America of 1.2 inches, lies in this area; many other nearby sites report averages of approximately two inches per year. Included, too, in this area is Bagdad, California, with the record for a rainless period in the U.S. In this area, also, the highest sustained summer temperatures occur in Death Valley and the world's second highest maximum temperature has been recorded. Moving outward from this extreme desert core, precipitation gradually increases, with much of the Great Basin and Chihuahuan Deserts receiving five to ten inches precipitation annually.

Temperatures gradually decrease as one moves to the east and north from this arid hub, due to two primary factors: increasing elevation of the desert's floor in these directions and movement into higher latitudes. A general rule is that temperature drops approximately one degree Fahrenheit for each 300-foot rise in elevation. Also, an increase of 1,000 feet in elevation is considered roughly equivalent to a 300-mile move nearer to the closest pole. The altitudinal range of the North American desert as a whole extends from 282 feet below sea level in Death Valley, the lowest point in the Western Hemisphere, to 5,000 feet above sea level, with occasional locations even higher. Thus the more northern desert, the Great Basin, for the most part lies at elevations of 4,000 feet or above; the most eastern, the Chihuahuan, lies mainly above 3,500 feet.

In addition to a general increase in elevation of the desert's surface, mountains rise from the desert base; the desert flora reach to various altitudinal levels on these mountains, depending upon the specific conditions present. Mountains bordering the desert may reach great elevations, as do the Sierra Nevadas; some ranges occurring within the desert may also extend to heights which preclude the presence of desert vegetation on their upper limits. The effects of the mountains on the surrounding or adjoining desert are many and varied. For example, some ranges, such as the Sierra

Nevadas, may cause formation of a rain shadow; others occurring within the desert may cause limited air lifting, resulting in precipitation on their flanks, a portion of which drains into the desert below; or cool air from the upper limits of some ranges may drain down canyons into the desert at their bases, affecting temperature and moisture extremes, and thereby the biota, in these limited locations.

Latitude, in conjunction with altitude, affects temperature extremes, which, in turn, dictate season length. Thus summer in the northern Great Basin Desert may last two or three months, but endure up to seven or eight months in the southern Sonoran Desert. The Great Basin undergoes prolonged periods of freezing temperatures, whereas portions of the southern Sonoran Desert, along the Gulf and Pacific coasts, are frost free.

Large portions of the southern Sonoran Desert border the Gulf of California and the Pacific Ocean. Shreve indicates that more than half of the Sonoran Desert lies within fifty miles of tidewater. Large bodies of water affect, to varying degrees, the land lying adjacent to them—these effects occur in terms of temperature levels, decreased temperature fluctuations, humidity levels, and winds. The Pacific Ocean, with its cold California Current, strongly influences the limited desert land immediately adjacent to it in Baja California in the Sonoran Desert. However, the much more extensive Sonoran Desert area lying like a horseshoe around the upper Gulf of California is only very slightly affected by the waters of this almost land-locked, relatively stable body of water. Shreve states that the Gulf's influence is so negligible as to only slightly lower the air temperature over the land, and then only within 100 meters of the shore during the day. Therefore, the climate of most of the Sonoran Desert, and the climate of all the other three deserts, is of the continental type.

Precipitation patterns over the North American deserts are varied. In general, winter precipitation is the rule in the northern and western portions of the North American desert lands, including the Great Basin, Mohave, and western Sonoran. This winter precipitation is derived from storms from the northwest sweeping in off the Pacific Ocean over the land. Conversely, the eastern and southern desert lands receive most of their precipitation, derived from the Gulf of

Mexico and Gulf of California, during the summer months. Additionally, occasional severe, late summer or early fall storms, known as *chubascos* (Spanish, squalls), strike the southern Sonoran Desert. These tropical hurricanes originate off the west coast of Mexico and move northwesterly. They often move out over the Pacific before reaching the desert latitudes, strike over the Gulf of California waters, or are dissipated before reaching the desert. However, at times they do bring high winds and heavy precipitation to the southern Sonoran Desert.

Thus, the eastern-lying Chihuahuan Desert receives approximately 70 to 80 percent of its precipitation in summer; the northern-lying Great Basin receives approximately 60 percent of its precipitation in winter; and the western-lying Mohave receives almost all of its limited precipitation in the winter. The winter rain pattern overlaps on its eastern margins with the summer rainfall pattern, so that some portions of the most centrally located desert, the Sonoran, receive both winter and summer precipitation. The western Sonoran receives primarily winter rainfall, whereas the eastern and southern portions receive both summer and winter precipitation. Tucson, Arizona, located near the eastern border of the Sonoran Desert, is thus favored with two "rainy" seasons, receiving approximately half its annual average of eleven inches in winter, the other half in summer.

Winter storms tend to produce gentle, soaking, widespread rains, with the storms enduring for several hours or days. In the more northern latitudes and higher elevations, precipitation is often in the form of snow. Summer storms tend to be localized, often violent, brief thunderstorms.

Obviously, no one North American desert climate may be defined nor does a single characteristic desert exist. North American deserts, with their varied causes and the resulting diversity of physical and biotic features, are limited in square miles as compared to such vast deserts as the Sahara, Australian, or Arabian. The pleasing result is that nowhere else in the world is such a concentration of different types of deserts so readily accessible to the desert enthusiast as in North America.

CHAPTER IV

Desert Plants: Adaptations

Facts: (1) Water is the matrix of life, yet (2) the desert's most notable characteristic is shortage of water.

Problem: How does life exist and endure (even thrive) in the desert?

The solutions are numerous, sometimes surprising, and often complex.

Inasmuch as plants are the base upon which all animal life depends, with some animal species consuming plants directly and others occupying higher rungs on the consumer ladder, let us first consider the means whereby desert-inhabiting plants obtain and use the water supplies available to them.

Water is an essential component in all plant tissue; it is a vital ingredient of the basic protoplasm itself. Depending on the plant type, most plants are composed of approximately 80 to 90 percent water. Water not only provides the medium within the plant in which chemical reactions necessary for life take place, and often enters into these reactions, but also provides a transport system to move minerals and other materials through the plant body. The individual plant cells are kept *turgid* (swollen or distended) by the water held within them; water thus provides vital support for the plant. Transpiration of water from the plant cools it by transferring absorbed heat out of the plant. And, finally, water is an essential ingredient in photosynthesis.

In the process of *photosynthesis*, carbohydrates are chemically formed from water and carbon dioxide by the action of chlorophyll through the plant's use of radiant energy. Water is absorbed by the plant, usually through its roots. Carbon dioxide enters the plant from the air through *stomata*—minute openings, often present in great numbers, located in the *epidermis* (superficial layer of cells) of leaves and stems; oxygen, a byproduct of photosynthesis, leaves the plant by way of the stomata. Through the process of photosynthesis, green plants transform a part of the sun's radiant energy into

36   THE DESERTS OF THE SOUTHWEST

a food form—that is, chemical energy—usable by both plant and animal.

Each stoma consists of a pore bordered by two guard cells. When turgid with water, these cells swell and pull apart, thereby opening the stoma. When the water within the cells is insufficient, the cells draw together, closing the stoma. Not only are carbon dioxide and oxygen transferred through the stomata, but water, too, moves through them in the process of *transpiration*—the giving off of water vapor from the plant's surface to the atmosphere. *Stomatal transpiration* is that movement taking place through the stomata; much lesser amounts of transpiration take place directly through the outer surface of the plant in a process termed *cuticular transpiration.* Water is rather constantly circulating upward through a plant from root to leaf, serving various purposes on its journey. Ultimately much of it, up to 98 percent, is transpired, primarily through the stomata, either in the process of cooling the plant or when the stomata are open in conjunction with photosynthesis. As water is lost from the plant to the atmosphere, additional supplies are needed in the leaves; a pressure gradient initiated in the leaves is set up, and water is pulled up through the plant. The amount of water loss from the plant will vary depending upon many factors, including the type of plant, and greatly dependent on environmental factors such as temperature, humidity, air movements, and light intensity.

Plants in general are divided into three groups according to their varying water needs. *Hydrophytes* are plants requiring an abundance of water which grow in water or in soil too waterlogged for most other plants. *Mesophytes* are plants growing under medium conditions of moisture. *Xerophytes* are those plants adapted for life and growth with a limited water supply. Thus we are primarily concerned with xerophytic species as we discuss desert plants. The xerophytes display an astounding array of morphological, physiological, and/or behavioral adaptations to the desert environment.

Let us first survey a category of plants which occur in the desert, but which, through the aspect of time or place, or both, avoid the extremes of desert conditions and are not truly xerophytes. One major group of these plants includes perennial plants growing in locations where water is rather readily available to them. Occasionally, streambeds emerging from canyons which drain higher mountains adjoining the desert may have limited running water several months of the year. In such locations, heavy water-users, such as cottonwood and sycamore trees, may line the stream banks for varying distances, tentatively pushing narrow fingers of green outward from the hills into the desert to the point where the water supply dissipates. Along the few permanent rivers, such as the Colorado, heavy plant growth may occur, but this growth belt extends back from the river only a very limited distance. Although not numerous, occasional oases occur in the desert, around which heavy water-users may cluster. Water in an oasis is often rather high in mineral content; palm trees, unlike many other plants, are capable of using this water and therefore occur in these locations. Tamarisk trees, introduced from the Eastern Hemisphere, are also capable of effectively using mineral-laden water. Since their introduction, tamarisks have flourished near waterways in the Southwest, such as along the Salt River in Arizona—the river's name demonstrates the condition contributing to the tamarisk's virtual takeover in certain areas along its length.

To the casual observer, the abundance of greenery produced in these special locations with permanent or semipermanent water must seem to present the *climax,* or high point, of desert vegetation, in contrast to the surrounding, less abundant, smaller-statured, more drab array of desert plants. Not so, for this abundant vegetation is living in the desert under special, largely nondesert conditions. While pleasant to human observers and often life-sustaining to animal visitors, this type of vegetation is not coping with desert conditions on the same basic survival level as are the xerophytic, truly desert plants growing out on the arid desert plain or hillside.

Thus the cottonwoods, palms, and similar plants take advantage of place—propitious locations—for their growth. So a group of annuals takes advantage of propitious but transitory times, largely in terms of moisture availability, for theirs. These plants, like oases-hugging perennials, never meet the desert head-on, except as seeds; hence, are referred to as *drought-escapers.* The "grasshoppers" of the plant world, these species endure in the desert for months or even years in their durable seed form, but when conditions favorable to their growth occur, they quickly germinate, rapidly grow, blossom, produce seed, and once again enter the long dormant wait. With speed of development an outstanding characteristic common to many of them, the term *annuals* seems almost extreme; hence they are often referred to as *ephemerals*, from the Greek for daily. Although their life span is certainly not limited to a single day, the plants may appear within three days after germination and finish their growth, blossoming, and seeding within a period of a very few weeks.

These ephemerals produce the showy arrays, the blankets of extravagant ground-covering flowers which attract visitors and photographers to the desert, usually in the spring, but only in favorable years. To predict when and where these shows will occur is not always easy, and desert newspapers regularly report the educated-guess possibilities for, and the actual occurrences of, these masses of flowers. Predictability is difficult since more than simple availability of moisture is involved in their occurrence, as was determined through a classic series of scientific investigations regarding these ephemerals conducted over twenty years ago by Dr. Frits Went. Went's experiments were conducted in Joshua Tree National Monument in the Mohave Desert of southeastern California. He concluded that the success of the ephemerals was based on "birth control," and he discovered some of the means whereby the ephemeral species practice this control.

Went found that in order for certain ephemeral seeds to germinate, rain of an amount minimal for the plant's successful growth and development must have fallen. Approximately .4 inch was insufficient, whereas a one-inch fall triggered germination. The seeds obviously had no means of measuring rainfall; Went theorized that the seeds of many ephemerals contained chemical inhibitors which were leached away only by means of sufficient moisture. Such seeds, he found experimentally, could not be tricked into germination by water seeping upward from below by capillary action, for such water movement does not carry the inhibitory substances away from the vicinity of the seed. And if only small amounts of inhibitor are removed by insufficient amounts of moisture, he theorized, the seed replenishes the chemical lost, and the waiting period continues.

Not only the seeds of the ephemerals "plan ahead" hereditarily; many other desert plants use various means to do so. Seeds of the palo verde, ironwood, and smoke trees, which grow along desert washes, have extremely hard coats. These sheaths prevent germination until a strong force cracks their outer coverings. Lying in the bed of a wash, these seeds are caught up in the floods which occasionally move through the washes. Abraded by sand and bashed by rocks during the flood, the seed coat is cracked, germination occurs, and the growth of the plant is initiated under positive moisture conditions. Went reports that seeds of some plants have inhibitors which are removed by bacterial action which occurs only under conditions of prolonged moisture. He further states that some seeds, particularly those of many grasses, delay germination after a rainfall for several days. If after that period of time the soil is still moist, signifying a rainfall of some magnitude, growth is begun. Some plants produce more than one type of seed—a portion of the seed crop is capable of germination soon after production, if favorable environmental conditions are available. Another portion is capable of germination only after the passage of a length of time. Such plants thus accomplish a dispersal of their seeds through time.

Returning to the ephemerals, Went found additional factors which influenced their germination. For example, two subminimal showers of .3 inch each, if they occurred within forty-eight hours of one another, would trigger germination; a torrential rain triggered fewer germinations than a gentle rain, although both produced the same amounts of rainfall; and rain in darkness did not have the same effect as rain during the day. In addition to moisture, Went found the most critical factor to be temperature. In the study area in the Mohave, widespread winter rains provided the major precipitation, but summer convectional storms also occurred in scattered localities. Went found four main groups of annual plant species growing there: (1) summer annuals which germinate and produce seeds following the summer rains; (2) annuals germinating following the winter rains and blooming in the spring; (3) annuals germinating following the summer rains and blooming the next spring; (4) a small group of annuals germinating and growing whenever sufficient moisture was present and temperatures were not too low. All groups required sufficient moisture to initiate germination, but summer-germinating species also required high day and night temperatures; winter-germinating species required cool day and night temperatures. A five- to ten-degree differential separates the two groups; thus summer-germinating species will not be deceived into germinating after the winter rains, nor winter species after summer rains, and only a few species are sufficiently versatile to grow under both extremes of the temperature range.

As a consequence, a general east–west seasonal distribution of the growth and blossoming of the ephemerals occurs in our North American desert, dependent on the seasonal rainfall patterns. Annuals in the Chihuahuan Desert are more numerous in the summer; those in the far western desert areas are more plentiful in the early spring following the winter rains; and the central and eastern Sonoran, which have two rather equal winter and summer rainy seasons, produce two crops of annuals in favorable years, with certain species present in the spring and other species present in the summer.

The season during which an ephemeral grows influences its characteristics greatly. The summer ephemerals tend to have short lives, speeding through their life cycles during the hot time of year. Winter annuals, in lower temperatures, develop slowly and are often small in size. Those ephemerals germinating in the summer and continuing growth through the winter rains tend to be large, since they benefit from both rainy seasons.

A minimal amount of water for probable success in growth, flowering, and seeding often will initiate germination; however, once growth starts, a plant may be further aided by additional showers, in which case it may grow to a large size for its species and produce quantities of seeds; conversely, in some cases a plant may receive no additional moisture and must subsist on that initially present, or die, or it may be submitted to other extenuating circumstances. An outstanding characteristic of many desert ephemerals is their capability to mature very rapidly when necessary, under drought, heat, cold, or other unfavorable conditions, yet produce some seeds, even though the plant has matured at an unnaturally small size—in some cases when only one-thousandth the species' normal mature size.

Whereas the drought-escapers avoid the desert's most extreme aridity, many perennial plant species endure, even prosper, in vegetative form, through moderate to extreme aridity. Their means of doing so are many, far from completely discovered or understood, and somewhat open to scientific controversy. Basically, any plant may suffer from moisture stress if the soil contains insufficient water for the plant's use, if water is being transpired from the plant more rapidly than it can be supplied through the roots, or if the mechanisms regulating water transport and transpiration within the plant are malfunctioning. Regardless of the cause, moisture stress, depending on its severity, causes injury or death to the plant. Stress may ultimately result in direct strain on the plant, such as decrease of turgor, resulting in mechanical injury to the plant as evidenced by wilting. Stress may also result in the disruption of various of the plant's vital metabolic processes, such as photosynthesis, and therefore failure to produce organic materials needed for maintenance and growth. Xerophytes are those species which are drought-resisting, able to avoid water stress or to endure varying nonlethal degrees of it. Their means of doing so are classified as drought-avoiding or drought-tolerating.

Those plants which avoid drought stress are further divided into two major groups—the water-savers and the water-spenders. Water-savers conserve their moisture supply through a variety of adaptations. The stomata of water-savers may be open only very briefly each day and are capable of rapid closure. The stomata of some are sunk below the surface level of the leaf or surrounded by hairs, thought, at least in some cases, to be an aid to moisture conservation. Some saver species have a much lower cuticular transpiration rate than mesophytes. In some cases, leaf modifications are responsible for this reduced rate; for example, some plants have leaves covered with a deposit of lipids, producing a waxy type layer which reduces moisture evaporation from their surfaces.

Water-saving species may cut moisture loss by reducing the surface they expose to the drying, evaporative air, through the shape of the plant body itself or changes in some plant part. Certain plants are capable of moving their leaves so that during the hottest time of day only their narrow edges are directed toward the sun; others roll or fold their leaves, thereby reducing surface area and stomatal exposure. Leaves may be partially or completely dropped during drought, as may entire branches, resulting in a "partial death;" any moisture resources available are then being used to maintain life in the remaining portion of the plant. This physiological independence of one part of a plant from another—that is, death occurring in one part with life strongly maintained in another portion—is a strong adaptation to drought stress.

In some cases the proportion of root to visible portions of the plant is great, supplying water from a large soil area for a relatively small above-ground portion, and some roots develop xeromorphic characters to prevent loss of moisture from root to dry soil. Certain plants, particularly cacti, which have permanent shallow spreading roots, possess the ability to produce small "rain roots" within a few hours after a shower, thereby enhancing their ability to quickly absorb the moisture present.

The cacti and other succulents are outstanding water-savers, storing large quantities of water within the plant

FIG. 5. Prickly pear cacti, *Opuntia sp.*, are among the most common of the cacti and are found in many areas outside the desert. The flattened fleshy stems store moisture. In times of prolonged drought, the water-depleted pads become wrinkled and shrunken. The fruits are edible.

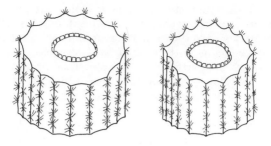

FIG. 6. The saguaro cactus is composed of an inner ring of woody ribs embedded in a fleshy pith. Because its outer surface is accordion-pleated, the saguaro expands or contracts in relationship to the amount of moisture stored within its fleshy interior.

body, either in the trunk or leaves. Cacti (with only a few exceptions) have no water-losing leaves and are covered by an almost impervious epidermal layer, allowing very little cuticular transpiration. Additionally, some succulents, such as the cacti, have developed active dark carbon dioxide assimilation. Most plants open their stomata during the day in order to obtain the carbon dioxide necessary for photosynthesis, but the opening is conducive to moisture loss. Those plants capable of dark carbon dioxide assimilation, however, open their stomata at night under conditions of humidity and temperature far more favorable than diurnal conditions. Due to lack of sunlight, photosynthesis cannot proceed at that time; therefore the assimilated carbon dioxide is stored in the form of organic acids. Later, during daylight hours, the stored carbon dioxide is used to form carbohydrates, while the stomata remain closed.

The water-savers, cautious xerophytes that they are, achieve survival yet pay a price for their safety. With their more frequent and prolonged stomatal closure, extremely moderate expenditure of water, and less expansive surfaces to bear stomata and receive radiant energy, the water-savers, in general, have a very slow growth rate. If the ephemerals are the "grasshoppers" of the plant world, certainly the savers are the "tortoises."

To state that some plants resist drought conditions by expending large quantities of water appears contradictory, yet theirs is a highly successful means. Such plants are able to maintain adequate water contents within the plant body despite high transpiration rates. These xerophytes have the ability, in a set period of time, to extract larger quantities of water from the soil per amount of leaf surface than can nonxerophytes. Therefore the water-spenders, although losing water at a rapid rate, are able to replace it, and photosynthesis with its attendant open stomata and consequent moisture loss can continue during the day when their plant neighbors, the water-savers, have closed down photosynthetic operations.

Various adaptations aid in efficient and rapid delivery of water from roots to leaves in the water-spenders. In some cases, the spenders have a higher proportion per leaf area of veins or water-conducting tissues than do the mesophytes. As with some of the savers, in many cases the spenders exhibit a high root-to-top ratio, thus exploiting the moisture contained in a large soil area for a relatively small amount of transpiring surface above ground. The roots of certain plants may even reach to the water table, as is the case with many mesquite trees in our southwestern deserts. Such water-table-tapping or saturated-zone-tapping plants are known as *phreatophytes*. Many water-spending xerophytes also have the ability to produce and send out new roots into hitherto untapped soil areas even under drought conditions—an ability not found in unadapted plants.

Under certain conditions, dew is deposited in the desert at night; certainly some of this dew condenses on plants. To a very limited extent some plants are capable of absorbing this moisture. However, even if no dew or only very minimal amounts of it are absorbed by the plants, the mere presence of the dew on the leaves in the early morning briefly reduces both the leaf temperature and transpiration from the plant itself. Hence the stomata may remain open to support photosynthesis for a time period ranging from a few minutes to an hour or more longer than would have been economically feasible without this moisture.

The enhanced ability to secure water, as evidenced by the water-spenders, is a primary successful adaptation to desert conditions on their part, but in conjunction with it and contributing greatly to the overall success of the spenders is a second ability: the water-spenders are able to become highly efficient water-savers when certain minimum moisture conditions are reached. Thus the spenders often exhibit xeromorphic structures similar to the water-savers, such as heavy leaf cuticles, yet are extravagant water-spenders when water is available. As a consequence, the water-spenders are able to grow more rapidly than the simple savers yet are able to shut down operations rather completely when necessary for survival. By way of comparison, the spenders under favorable moisture conditions often transpire at an even greater rate than mesophytes, yet once the spenders enter a water-saving regime, they transpire far less than mesophytes. In many ways the water-spenders seem to enjoy the best of two worlds.

Primarily, in surveying water-savers and water-spenders, we have been discussing morphological adaptations (of form) to aridity. Yet another large category of adaptations to aridity exists; these adaptations are physiological in nature. This category includes the second major group of drought-resisters—the drought-tolerating plants. These plants exhibit the ability to undergo drought and yet avoid or tolerate metabolic strain (such as that produced by starvation), or avoid or tolerate direct strain (such as that produced to the plant body from wilting, for example). The adaptations providing these abilities are not so readily apparent as morphological adaptations and are being studied primarily through biochemistry on a cellular and molecular level.

Some plants exhibit the ability to maintain a high osmotic pressure within the cells, thus increasing the plant's ability to absorb water from the soil and to resist loss of moisture to the atmosphere. Some species may produce immature leaves which, due to their makeup—both physiological and anatomical—are more drought-tolerant than the mature leaves, which are shed under drought stress. Rather fundamental changes on the cellular level may be present in some drought-tolerating species, including a small cell size which helps prevent tearing of the protoplasm during dessication and later rehydration. Changes may also occur in the physical properties and strengths of the cell walls. For example, xerophytes wilt only after the loss of 30 to 40 percent of their water content, whereas some shade plants wilt after a loss of only 1 to 2 percent. Even the basic metabolism of various plant species is thought to vary, with some drought-adapted plants having a low rate of metabolism which aids them in

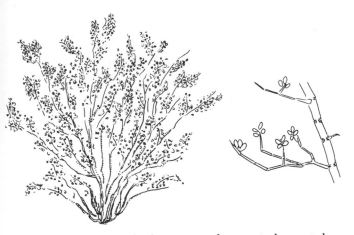

FIG. 7. The creosote bush, *Larrea tridentata,* is the most abundant and widespread shrub of the Sonoran, Mohave, and Chihuahuan deserts. It is extremely drought-resistant and ranges from the southern deserts of North America far south into South America. Growth consists of slender branches arising from the crown of the root.

surviving under a regime of low photosynthetic activity, thus allowing them to keep their stomata closed a large percentage of the time.

An outstanding drought-tolerator is the creosote bush, one of the most common plants of the three warmest North American deserts. During drought its mature leaves are shed, as are whole twigs and branches; however the new, small, partly developed leaves are retained. Robert Chew, of the University of Southern California, and associates, report that these new leaves can survive a reduction in water content to less than 50 percent of their dry weight, and a saturation deficit of at least 77 percent! Yet even at these extremes the leaves are still metabolically active. Therefore when moisture again becomes available, these leaves are able to take immediate advantage of its presence. Chew, et al., also state that these young drought-resistant leaves are 38 to 78 percent smaller than the mature leaves. Such size reduction serves as an aid in preventing mechanical distortion of the protoplasm under stress. Researchers state that the creosote bush is a successful xerophyte, due more to its

FIG. 8. Junco, all spine, or crucifixion thorn, *Koeberlinia spinosa,* is a spreading shrub 3 to 4½ feet in height with rigid, spine-pointed branches. This species is essentially without functional leaves; as an adaptation to aridity, the yellow-green branches have taken over the normal leaf functions.

physiological than to its morphological adaptations, but they also state that the specific nature of many of its physiological adaptations is yet to be determined. Whether or not we completely understand its means, however, the creosote bush is a highly successful, ubiquitous, desert plant growing within a wide spectrum of environmental conditions, including those of extreme heat and drought. For example, it survives even in areas where the daily maximum temperatures are frequently greater then 120°F., and in those areas in which rainless periods of a year or longer are common.

The lines between drought-avoiders and drought-tolerators, and between plants in various subdivisions of these types, cannot be rigidly drawn, as is obvious from the example of the water-spenders which may become water-savers when under stress. Thus the lines are crossed to some extent, but where the higher plants are concerned, Dr. Jacob Levitt of the University of Minnesota, in *Responses of Plants to Environmental Stresses,* concludes that most xerophytes tend to develop mainly avoidance *or* tolerance, rather than displaying an equal development of both kinds of resistance. He also concluded that drought avoidance is a more complete adaptation to aridity than is tolerance, since the avoiders escape the direct and indirect strains produced by water stress, such as wilting or starvation. Drought-tolerating plants, on the other hand, do tolerate the drought but are generally unable to grow during stress due to lack of turgor in the cells; they simply endure, marking time, until better conditions prevail.

When environmental stresses build, animals and man can crawl, walk, run, or fly to reach the most amenable environmental conditions available; not so the rooted, immobile plants which must meet sun, wind, heat, and aridity where they stand. In the desert where moisture supplies tend to be limited and environmental stresses tend to be extreme, the plants, in order to survive, must be capable of operating with a low margin of error where high demand and low supply of water is concerned. Ranging from cacti to creosote bush to boojum tree, those plants that have been successful in meeting this challenge make up one of the most highly adapted, unusual, and interesting of the world's floras. We will consider many of these hardy, desert members of the plant kingdom as we survey individual North American deserts.

CHAPTER V

Desert Animals: Adaptations

LIMITED RESOURCES applied in an economy characterized by parsimony is the theorem of the desert—nowhere else on earth can so little count for so much. This theorem is as applicable to animals as to plants. A few drops of water, a small patch of shade, an underground retreat—all are small things in themselves, but they may provide a life-saving edge for the desert animal which is adapted in some way to make the most advantageous use of one or more of them. Many desert adaptations displayed by animals have to do with handling temperature and moisture stresses. Moisture stresses are often present normally but are compounded by heat stress which, in turn, is ameliorated by increased evaporation of body water, and hence increased moisture stress. Other adaptations for desert life occurring in some species aid them in use of a particular habitat—for example, sand. Some animals have adapted morphologically or physiologically, or both, to desert conditions. Primarily, however, body adaptations consist not of new mechanisms but rather of the evolutionary enhancement and increased development and use of characteristics common to the animal's basic group—that is, quantitative rather than qualitative changes. To an even greater degree, however, most desert animals have adapted to their environment behaviorally.

The so-called desert world is actually a mosaic of smaller worlds, and the environmental conditions present in any one of these small worlds are often strikingly different from those of another area which may be located only a few feet or even inches away. These smaller pieces of the habitat, or *microhabitats,* in general each have their own microclimate. The microhabitat composed of an area under a cottonwood tree growing along an intermittent desert stream often has a cooler, moister microclimate than does the microhabitat under a sparsely leafed creosote bush on a nearby desert plain. So, too, a vast difference is apparent between the small world under an insulating rock on the desert floor and that of the ground surface next to it. A north-facing slope presents different climatic conditions than does a south-facing one. The temperature five feet above ground among the mesquite leaves is considerably lower than that found only a few feet away in the sun at the ground surface. Use of favorable microclimates is one of the very important ways in which animals adjust to desert environmental stresses.

Dr. Knut Schmidt-Nielsen of Duke University reports studies have shown that while summer daytime air temperatures in the desert often are in the 104°-to-113° F.-and-higher range, the temperature of the soil surface at that same time may exceed 158° F. Conversely, at night, if radiation to the sky from the surface is unimpeded, the surface temperature may fall to a level far below that of the night air, and register as much as 122 Fahrenheit degrees lower than the daytime high surface temperature. Due to the insulative quality of the soil, however, temperatures underground are much ameliorated and stabilized. Schmidt-Nielsen states that at a depth of .5 meter (approximately 19.7 inches) in the soil, the daily temperature fluctuation is less than 33.8 Fahrenheit degrees; no fluctuation occurs at one meter (approximately 39.4 inches). Obviously, to prevent being broiled, a low-statured ant, snake, or small rodent must be able to escape such extremes as those found at certain times on the ground surface. These animals and a good many others escape the surface heat by entering underground burrows which provide favorable microclimatic conditions under stressful surface conditions. Such burrows are among the most important means used by the animals to avoid heat and dehydration. Studies of the temperatures of the burrows of a kangaroo rat and of a pack rat determined that the *highest* summer temperature within the two burrows was a comfortable, life-saving 87.8° F.

Some animal groups are, due to their makeup, physically predisposed in many ways to succeed under desert conditions. Certain of the arthropods are included in this group. Some of the arthropod species lose moisture rapidly through their integument and must remain in moist surroundings; they are therefore not well adapted to dry environments. But many of the species, including many insects, are covered by an almost impervious, waxy-layered integument which prevents or greatly impedes desiccation of the body. However, even in these species, small amounts of moisture may be lost from the animal's body through elimination of waste products and by means of the spiracles through which the insect breathes.

Other factors, in addition to the near-impervious integument, can then play a role in effecting a moisture savings. Foremost among these factors is the use of favorable microclimates, primarily those found underground. Thus some arthropods, particularly insects, are especially adapted for burrowing. This adaptation is particularly noticeable among species evolved for life in sand. In some cases their bodies may be flattened and sharp-edged, allowing them to bury themselves quickly in the loose sand with alternate sideways movements. Others may have "fringed" feet, giving them traction on the sand and increased burrowing power. The fringes also may aid them in "sand-swimming"—that is, moving through the sand just below its surface.

Ants, for example, use underground microclimates to great advantage. Even termites, soft-bodied and seemingly totally unfitted for the desert, may be found in large numbers. They provide their own highly favorable microclimate,

F IG . 9. The back feet of the fringe-toed lizard, *Uma notata* (body size without tail 2¾ to 4½ inches), are equipped with lateral fringes of long, pointed scales, an adaptation providing increased foot surface for running on sand and also aiding the lizard in pushing its way under the sand.

either through galleries excavated in the soil or within highly protective, above-ground earthen tunnels of their own construction. Grasshoppers and some other insects have long legs which lift the major portion of the insect's body into a slightly cooler air layer than that found at ground surface. Other insects rest several inches or a few feet above the ground in vegetation. The wings of insects can be a valuable asset. As the winged insect becomes heated near the ground, it can make short vertical flights upward or longer horizontal flights in the higher, cooler, air layers.

Arthropods often employ diurnal or seasonal cycles which favor their desert survival. During the summer, many emerge only at night, when temperatures are lowered and humidity heightened. Some change their daily cycle on a seasonal basis. Thus many desert ants are active at midday under mild winter temperatures; as daily temperatures rise, the same species forages in early morning and late afternoon. Finally in the summer their foraging may be conducted largely at dawn, dusk, and into the nighttime hours as daily heat levels become extreme. Some arthropods may enter seasonal resting stages during unfavorable times. The adults may simply retire underground or to some other protected location and wait out the unfavorable season. Often, the adults may die, and the species endures as eggs, larvae, or pupae in the soil or plants. Some arthropods possess the ability to enter a state of *diapause*—somewhat of a "holding" or resting state marked by a temporary stoppage of growth, reduced metabolism, and often an enhanced resistance to such climatic factors as drought, heat, or cold. Diapause works as a timing mechanism, particularly valuable in an inconstant environment, which the desert often is, allowing the arthropod to wait out unfavorable periods and to take quick advantage of favorable conditions once they again prevail. Arthropods enduring through eggs, immature stages, and diapause are reminiscent in many ways of some desert plants, particularly the ephemeral species which survive unfavorable conditions through the plant's most resistant phase, the seed.

Granted, many arthropods are extremely frugal regarding their bodies' water. But how is the water originally obtained, and how are the small amounts lost replaced? A certain amount of metabolic water is produced by living cells as a byproduct of the oxidative metabolism of food. Also, a percentage—often a surprisingly high percentage—of the plant body is composed of water. Even quite dry plant material absorbs water, such as dew from its surface. Dew itself is sometimes available to arthropods which forage early

FIG. 10. Honey ants represent an adaptation of a few species to aridity and seasonally limited availability of food. Certain members of the colony become "repletes," hanging from the ceiling of their underground nests. These repletes, with their greatly extended abdomens, are living containers of sweet plant juices, which they regurgitate to normal colony members when other food is not available.

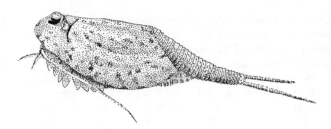

F I G . 11. Tadpole shrimp, *Triops sp.*, a crustacean, is a denizen of temporary rain pools. The species endures in egg form once the pool dries; the young hatch when water is again present. Adult size is approximately 1 inch or less.

in the day and consume the dew-decked vegetation. And many arthropod species are carnivorous; since the bodies of most living animals are roughly two-thirds water, those arthropods consuming animal prey derive sufficient water for their needs.

Additionally, some arthropods have the ability to withstand rather high heat and severe desiccation levels. Certain beetle species seem particularly able to withstand elevated temperatures, and beetles are among the most commonly represented successful desert insects. The eggs of the fairy and tadpole shrimp are outstanding in withstanding desiccation. Some of these small, fresh-water crustaceans are only a few millimeters long; the fairy shrimp are usually more than one-third inch in length and may range up to approximately four inches. These creatures are not restricted to the desert habitat but are found there in temporary rain pools for brief periods as adults. As the water begins to evaporate, these crustaceans produce eggs; the eggs remain in the mud, then finally are preserved in the sun-baked soil of the pool's bottom long after the water is gone and the aquatic adults have perished. Such eggs are known to endure the extreme conditions of the desert's surface for several months; they may endure for as long as twenty-five years or more, until pools once again form in those locations and the cycle is quickly reinitiated.

Not only temperature and moisture stresses must often be endured by desert animals. Food shortages, too, may plague them. Many arthropods, again, score high on their ability to endure such shortages; some are able to survive prolonged fasting. Their small size precludes the necessity for large quantities of food. In the dry desert, vegetable matter is slow to decay or fails to do so altogether; some becomes buried in drifting sand and soil and is later uncovered, or is discovered by subterranean dwellers. In fact, in some severely stark Old World desert areas, a largely subterranean arthropod fauna is thought to survive primarily on plant matter carried there by the winds.

Reptiles are the animal form popularly associated with deserts. True, their species are well represented, but the reptiles are certainly not a special desert creation. Certain species have simply been able to capitalize on particular reptilian characteristics as avenues to desert success.

In mammals the urinary wastes carrying the body's chief nitrogen excretion, urea, must be kept in solution in order for elimination from the body to be achieved. Insects, birds, and reptiles, however, have the ability to precipitate uric acid from the wastes; the birds and reptiles ultimately discharge the uric acid along with the feces as a semi-solid whitish mass. Thus they achieve a great saving in the moisture required for excretion.

Reptiles are *poikilothermic*—that is, their bodies display a variable temperature usually just slightly higher than the temperature of their environment. The reptile at rest in a favorable microclimate maintains a body temperature which needs support only a moderate or reduced metabolic level, demanding only limited water and food. The reptile's temperature during the colder, winter months also drops, and its body has few metabolic demands placed upon it as it endures the waiting period. Additionally, air in an underground burrow, the resting site of many reptiles, tends to have a high relative humidity. If a mammal with a temperature considerably higher than the burrow air temperature exhales warmed air from its lungs into the burrow, moisture is absorbed by the air from the animal's respiratory system and is expelled into the surrounding air, for warm air (that from the respiratory tract) is capable of holding more moisture than cool air (that inhaled from the burrow). Therefore the warm animal tends to lose moisture to the atmosphere. However, for the reptile with a body temperature very close to the burrow air temperature, this saturation deficit is much reduced or does not occur; hence respiratory moisture loss is very small.

Even when maintained at like temperatures, the basic metabolic rates of reptiles are much lower, approximately one-seventh those of equal-size *homeotherms* (animals having a relatively uniform body temperature maintained nearly independent of the environmental temperature).

Most, although not all, desert reptiles are carnivorous, obtaining needed moisture from the bodies of their prey. However, a few subsist on vegetation sufficiently water-filled to sustain them. Additionally, although some moisture is lost through their scale-covered skin, the reptiles' tough outer covering serves to prevent undue moisture loss.

An interesting member of the desert reptile group—a vegetarian, well-protected from dehydration by a heavy skin and shell—is the desert tortoise, *Gopherus agassizi,* which may reach fourteen inches in length and is found even in some of the very arid portions of the Sonoran and Mohave Deserts. Unlike most desert reptiles, which obtain much or all of their moisture from animal prey, this tortoise derives food and water from its vegetation diet, consuming grass, cacti, and other low-growing plants. The desert tortoise often will drink water when it is available, as following a rain; individuals have been recorded to increase 41 to 43 percent in weight by drinking. However, one investigator reported successfully keeping hatchlings for three years without water; when they were at last offered water, they drank very little. Water is stored within the urinary bladder of the

FIG. 12. The desert tortoise, *Gopherus agassizi,* may reach 13 inches in length. These land tortoises are vegetarians; they survive even in some of the very arid North American deserts. They escape summer heat and winter cold by entering underground retreats.

animal; as a water-saving measure, large quantities of waste in the form of semi-solid urates can be stored for long periods in the bladder without ill effect, and the animal is able to endure considerable dehydration. The desert tortoise is active approximately six months of the year during the more favorable plant-growth periods. The remainder of the year is spent in dormancy in long (up to thirty feet), horizontal burrows or dens which the tortoises excavate. During their active foraging months, they retreat to shorter burrows for rest or protection from high environmental temperatures.

Reptiles are not capable of enduring prolonged high temperatures. Reptile species vary in their heat tolerance, with snakes proving less tolerant as a group than the lizards. The lizard *Sceloporus magister*, a desert-dwelling species, has a lethal body temperature of approximately 109° F. An outstanding desert dweller is the desert iguana, *Dipsosaurus dorsalis*, which has a lethal body temperature of approximately 122° F. Lethal body temperatures for some desert snake species considered in one study were approximately 110° F. Although reptiles are able to achieve some evaporative cooling of their bodies through the respiratory tract, they prevent overheating and consequent death primarily through behavioral means. They often retreat to shade or burrows during heat. Active only during favorable seasons and becoming dormant during others, they forage when the most favorable temperatures prevail. Reptile activity is severely reduced or nonexistent during the colder months in the desert. In warmer periods, the lizards tend in general to be diurnal, although they may vary their activity from midday in cooler weather to early morning and late afternoon hours during days of higher temperatures. Snakes tend to be more nocturnal, although diurnal species certainly exist, and some may vary between diurnal and nocturnal activity in response to the environmental temperature.

Even though poikilothermic, reptiles are by no means completely at the mercy of their environment, for many of them actively seek to keep their temperature at a rather stable level when active. Thus they may bask in the sunlight, even flattening their bodies to some extent to expose a larger body surface to the sun's rays and to the warm substratum. When too warm, they may elevate the body by stretching their legs to the fullest extent possible to raise themselves above the warm surface. Certain species have been observed orienting the long axis of the body perpendicular to the sun's rays while warming; later, as their body heat rises, the lizard repositions its body so that its long axis is parallel to the sun's rays. Some lizards sprint over short, hot, sandy areas on hind legs only, with the body elevated. Certain species have the ability, through rapid sideways body movements, to submerge their abdomens a short distance into the slightly cooler area of sand underlying the upper sand surface. Some can dive directly into the sand, "swimming" some distance within it, achieving several purposes— cooling in the lower sand layers, insulative covering, and protection from predators.

The fringe-toed lizard, *Uma notata*, is a prime example of such a lizard. Living only in sandy areas, it is adapted morphologically for that particular habitat. This lizard, with a 2½- to 4½-inch body length plus tail, has toes on the rear feet fringed with projecting pointed scales to provide a "snowshoe" effect on the loose sand. It often runs bipedally at great speed over the sand and literally "dives" into it, rapidly burying itself, moving through the sand some distance, and then remaining still and hidden. To "swim" under the sand, the lizard holds its front legs back against the body, moves its head from side to side, and kicks its hind legs alternately, propelling itself forward. This lizard has overlapping eyelids and ear flaps to prevent the entry of sand into eyes and ears. Its sand-trap nasal passages and nasal valves serve to prevent sand from reaching the lungs as it breathes just under the sand surface. The body form is flattened with a smooth velvety surface, the head is wedge-shaped, and the lower jaw is countersunk into the upper—all features which aid the lizard to enter and move in sand.

Another reptile adapted for sand living is the sidewinder rattlesnake, *Crotalus cerastes*. This seventeen- to thirty-one-inch "horned" rattler, so-called for two hornlike projections over the eyes, is often found in areas of fine windblown sand in the Sonoran and Mohave Deserts. The two "horns" are hinged. When pressure is applied to their tops, they fold down, covering the eyes and fitting neatly into the indentation of scales surrounding them. This protective adaptation is considered valuable for these snakes in

FIG. 13. The fringe-toed lizard, *Uma notata* (2¾ to 4½ inches, snout–vent length), is highly adapted for life in fine sand. Projecting scales on its hind toes provide increased traction on sand. Its flattened body shape, countersunk lower jaw, special nasal valves, and ear flaps aid and protect it, permitting it to plunge into and move under the sand in its habitat.

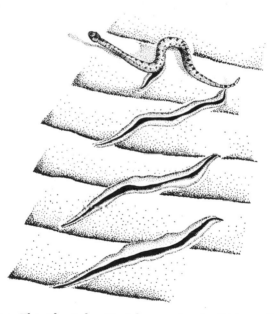

FIG. 14. The sidewinder, *Crotalus cerastes*, is a fairly small (17 to 31 inches) rattlesnake which moves by means of sidewise locomotion. The track left in soft sand is a series of roughly parallel marks.

Desert Animals: Adaptations

hunting rodents in underground burrows where eyesight is of no value but presents a danger to eyes when roots, rocks, loose soil, or sand are present. The sidewinder moves forward with a sidewise locomotion. The snake's body is thrown forward diagonally in a series of loops and the snake appears to be crawling sideways in an S-shaped, flowing curve. The track left in soft sand is a series of unconnected, short, straight lines at a 30-degree angle to the direction in which the snake is progressing. Each line has a J-shaped mark at one end, made by the head and neck. The hooks of the J's indicate the direction of the snake's travel. Sidewinding serves several purposes. The vertical, rather than horizontal, force exerted in this movement is very efficient in moving over a loose surface, minimizing slippage. Sidewinding is a rapid means of locomotion. And it reduces danger of overheating since the amount of contact between the snake's body and the ground is greatly reduced.

For frogs and toads, members of the class Amphibia, the most important means of gaining water is by direct absorption of moisture through the skin. Conversely, moisture can be lost easily by the same means; therefore, to state that numerous species of frogs and toads inhabit the desert seems incongruous although it is true. They are able to live in these areas primarily by avoiding desert conditions. Some live only where permanent water is available. Many others adjust the timing of their life cycle to take rapid advantage of transitory amelioration of desert environmental conditions. Members of this group undergo dormancy underground much of the year, awaiting the arrival of rain during warm periods. Under this stimulus, the adults emerge, gather in the temporary ponds that have formed, and rapidly mate and produce eggs. With like haste, the eggs and tadpoles undergo development, racing to complete these immature stages before their pond waters evaporate.

For example, adult spadefoot toads, *Scaphiopus couchi,* a species widespread in the Sonoran and Chihuahuan deserts, spend ten or more months of the year underground, emerging when the summer rains occur. Their calls are reminiscent of bleating sheep, and these 2½- to 3-inch toads have loud, far-carrying voices which serve well to bring the individuals together in the temporary ponds. Their calls, one of the pleasant sounds of desert summer evenings, may be

FIG. 15. The spadefoot toad, *Scaphiopus couchi* (2¼ to 3½ inches in length), spends most of the year underground awaiting favorable moisture conditions. The "spade" used for burrowing into the ground is shown above as solid black on the hind foot.

heard within an hour or less after the first heavy rain of the season. The eggs of this species have been reported to hatch within nine to seventy-two hours after being deposited in the temporary ponds, and larval life is completed in periods ranging from ten to forty days. As the ponds begin to disappear and dryness resumes, the adults retreat underground into old rodent holes or self-made burrows in the moist soil. *Spadefoot* refers to the presence of a sharp-edged "spade," or projection, on each hind foot of these toads. Using the spades, the animal burrows, backing into the ground, while rotating the body with the hind feet moving alternately in a circular fashion. If rains of sufficient magnitude fail to arrive the following summer, the spadefoot's long rest may continue for another year. At least in some cases, a semi-impervious covering forms around the toad during this waiting period. It is evidently composed of several layers of skin which have become loosened from the body but not completely sloughed off; certainly it must serve to reduce evaporation from the toad's body.

The desert frogs and toads may display other adaptations. Most are nocturnal. The urinary bladder may be used for water storage; the Great Plains toad, *Bufo cognatus*, is capable of storing up to 30 percent of its gross body weight as water in this manner. Many have a special *seat patch*, a ventral region of thin skin through which they can actually absorb water from the ground. Some species are capable of tolerating water with a high level of salinity. The tadpoles of some species are able to endure elevated water temperatures in their often small, solar-heated pools. Certainly one of the most useful capabilities of the desert-dwelling frogs and toads is the enhanced ability to survive a high degree of dehydration. As a group, amphibians are able to tolerate water losses of 7 to 60 percent of their body weight. Additionally, during a moisture shortage, the amphibians are capable of storing large amounts of waste nitrogen in the form of urea within their bodies without ill effect.

Most birds and large mammals do not or cannot use underground escapes to avoid environmental stresses. Additionally, most bird species are diurnally active. These factors do increase the heat-dehydration problem desert birds must face. But birds possess certain positive factors which serve them well in the desert environment—the possession of wings among them. Birds can fly to shade or to resting sites in vegetation in air cooler than that at the ground surface; they may make use of up-flowing air currents to rise hundreds of feet into cooler air where they float with little effort for extended periods. Wings also provide birds with the ability to reach watering sites some distance away, or simply to leave the desert, migrating at certain times of the year to avoid desert extremes.

Many species, however, remain in the desert year-round. Some of these species must live within reach of free water. Others obtain sufficient water from the animal prey they consume; still others are able to survive for at least certain parts of the year on moisture obtained from succulent plant material. Birds can reduce their temperatures through their behavior. They may seek shade, or rest during the hottest part of the day. They may facilitate heat transfer from their bodies by compressing their feathers tightly against their bodies to obtain minimal insulation; they may hold their wings away from the body, exposing the thinly feathered skin in these locations to the air; some species experience increased blood flow to their bare-skinned legs. Birds also reduce their temperature by evaporative cooling, which takes place through the respiratory tract, as they have no sweat glands. For a small animal, however, evaporative

FIG. 16. The roadrunner, *Geococcyx californianus,* is a large member of the cuckoo family, reaching 20 to 24 inches in length. The roadrunner flies short distances but more often walks or runs. It eats insects, lizards, and snakes, including rattlesnakes which are killed by sharp blows of the bird's strong beak.

cooling is expensive in water terms. *Gular flutter,* or the rapid fluttering of the skin on the ventral surface of the throat, is employed by some birds in what is considered to be an energy-saving means of respiratory evaporative cooling.

As earlier noted, birds excrete uric acid rather than urea with a consequent impressive saving in moisture in comparison to mammals. Experimentally, some species of birds were found to endure high levels of dehydration. The mourning dove, *Zenaidura macroura,* survived dehydration until a loss of 30 percent of body weight was reached, whereas one quail species, *Lophortyx californicus,* although it is not a desert-dwelling bird, survived a 50 percent loss. Some species are capable of making use of rather saline water. In one study, mourning doves maintained their normal weight when provided with drinking water that was 25 percent sea water.

The most beneficial factor aiding birds in desert living is a general capability shared with nondesert birds. Normal bird temperatures are considerably elevated above those of mammals, being in the 104°–108° F. range. Thus the bird is much delayed in starting to build a heat load under high temperatures. It may, in fact, still be losing body heat to the atmosphere while the mammal's body is gaining heat from the air. Additionally, the bird's body is capable of storing

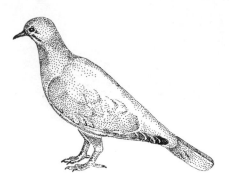

FIG. 17. The white-winged dove, *Zenaida asiatica* (11 to 12½ inches), displays a white wing patch when in flight. Its tail is rounded (unlike that of the mourning dove) and tipped with broad white corners. The harsh cooing of this dove is a familiar sound in mesquite groves and saguaro forests.

heat gained, to the extent of an elevation in body temperature of four to six Fahrenheit degrees, without ill effect. This stored heat can later be radiated back to the surrounding air as temperatures cool at night. This amount of heat gain is therefore dissipated without loss of costly water. With this tolerance of hyperthermia, some birds can endure body temperatures of 113° F. for several hours. Death occurs when their temperatures reach approximately 116.6° F. Evaporative cooling is thus used by birds to keep their temperatures within limits, but these limits are set at a higher level than those for mammals. (Man's critical body temperature lies between 107.6° and 113° F., dependent upon certain variables.)

Body size is an extremely important factor in heat gain. Small animals have a greater surface relative to their weight than do larger animals; hence the smaller ones gain, percentage-wise, more environmental heat. Heat produced in metabolism is also approximately proportional to the animal's surface area. Obviously, the position of the small mammal in the desert with regard to heat gain and loss is precarious, for water must be used for evaporative cooling to prevent death once body temperatures reach certain levels. The kangaroo rat, a small desert rodent, has been found, if exposed to daytime desert heat, to sustain a water loss amounting to 15 percent of its body weight per hour for evaporative cooling. Obviously such an approach to desert living is highly impracticable for the small desert mammals, most of which display nocturnal habits, retreating underground during the daytime.

Some larger mammals, although they cannot enter underground burrows, do live successfully in the desert. Their large body size relative to surface area provides them a benefit in externally received heat gain, and internal heat production is less intense in large mammals than in small. Large-bodied mammals have an enhanced ability to store heat with only a slight elevation in body temperature. The camel, an outstandingly successful Old World desert inhabitant, has been much studied in regard to its adjustments to desert living. The camel was found to store heat in its body during the hot day, unloading it to the environment in the cooler night temperatures. Dissipation of the same amount of heat through evaporative cooling would cost the camel approximately four to five quarts of water daily. While no camels are found roaming in the North American desert today, burros introduced by accident and design have prospered there. They too display the ability to store diurnally several degrees of heat to be lost during the night. Heat storage by some large desert mammals thus reduces the need for evaporative cooling, although evaporative cooling remains an important means of heat reduction, particularly when the upper tolerable limits of gain are approached.

The hair of mammals exposed to desert heat acts as a heat shield, preventing an impressive percentage of possible environmental heat gain from reaching the animal's skin. It allows evaporation of perspiration from the skin, but slows this process, preventing a too-rapid, wasteful evaporation from taking place. In this regard, it acts in a manner similar to man's clothing, which serves the same useful purpose. Within this "heat shield," certain "windows" occur. These more open areas, largely without fur or only lightly haired, are located on the ventral portions of the animal's body, such as those around the mammary glands, on the scrotum, and in the groin. As the animal is standing, these areas are directed downward toward the shade formed by the animal's body; heat is thus lost by convection from these body sites to the shade.

The mobility of large mammals serves them exceedingly well in the desert. They may be able to travel considerable distances to water sources. They also may seek out cool resting areas in which to spend the hottest hours. And their mobility is helpful in obtaining food. As with the other animals discussed, food habits provide aid in filling moisture needs, carnivores deriving most or all of their water from their prey; the large herbivores derive some moisture from their plant food but also need drinking water periodically.

The desert bighorn sheep is one of the large mammals which inhabit our deserts. This animal is successful in dealing with the desert environment. Living gregariously, the bighorn sheep primarily inhabit rugged mountain ranges where their jumping and climbing abilities are impressively put to use. These heavy-bodied animals may weigh 150 to 200 or more pounds, are approximately three feet tall at the shoulder, may be up to five feet in length, and are a pale tan in color. The males have immense, curling horns; the females' considerably smaller horns do not curl as impressively as the males'. The desert bighorns are nonchoosy vegetarians. Living in some of the most desolate and arid of the desert areas, including the stark deserts of Baja California, these animals generally must have access to free water, at least during certain times of the year, but derive a considerable amount of moisture from their diet. Successful as the sheep have been in coping with the desert environment, unfortunately they have not been so successful in their confrontation with man, who has hunted them severely, reduced their access to water sources with agriculture and highways, and released burros which have severely pressured the sheep in terms of water and forage availability.

A few small mammals are active above ground diurnally. The tiny antelope ground squirrel, *Ammospermophilus leucurus*, widespread over the southwestern deserts, may often be seen above ground and is active in hot daytime temperatures. The secrets of its success are several. It displays omnivorous eating habits, partaking of water-filled animal materials in addition to plants. Under extreme heat loads, it salivates or drools; the moisture which wets the fur of its chest provides evaporative cooling at a lower metabolic cost than the alternative of panting. It has, for a small animal, an impressive ability to store heat. In keeping with its size,

FIG. 18. Desert bighorn sheep, *Ovis canadensis* (reaches approximately 4 to 4½ feet in body length and up to 200 pounds), survive in the desert by eating a wide variety of the vegetation available and by visiting waterholes as necessary. The desert subspecies is smaller in size and paler in color than its northern subspecies relatives. Bighorn sheep inhabit rocky, precipitous desert mountain ranges where man and burro threaten their existence.

this heat load must be dissipated frequently, rather than on a daily basis as is done by larger mammals. Therefore, the antelope ground squirrel retreats periodically, sometimes as often as every quarter hour, to its underground burrow to spread out to its fullest extent on the cool substratum, thus unloading its heat gain to the burrow walls. Above ground, too, it often seeks favorable microclimates, resting or foraging in shade, or occasionally climbing up into vegetation.

Jackrabbits are surface-dwelling and heat-enduring mammals. Plant eaters, they cannot subsist on dry food alone, but are able to live on vegetation without free drinking water in some desert areas. They rest in shade during the hot days, seeking food nocturnally. The rabbit's huge, lightly haired, almost bare-skinned ears serve him in the desert. As the rabbit lies resting in his form, a slight hollow in the ground, his ears lie flat, spread along his back. These ears display a high reflectivity to light. The blood vessels in the

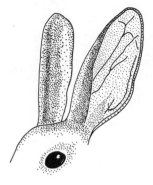

FIG. 19. The large, thinly haired, heavily veined ears of various rabbit species serve to radiate body heat to the atmosphere.

ears are greatly dilated when conditions are propitious for heat loss from the ears to the environment; they are severely constricted when the opposite condition—that is, heat gain from the environment—prevails.

Of the small retreating mammals, the kangaroo rat is an outstanding desert dweller. These animals, and a few others with a similar pattern, are capable of living for their entire lives on a diet of dry plant food and can survive totally without drinking water. The kangaroo rat subsists on the very small amounts of water that may be present in its food, and primarily on water produced by food metabolism. In the bodies of animals, oxidation of 1 gram of starch produces 0.6 gram of metabolic water; one gram of fat yields 1.1 grams of water. The limited water supply thus gained is husbanded by the rat and expended in a most frugal, albeit successful, manner. The kangaroo rat is active nocturnally. During the day it plugs the outside opening to its burrow. The temperature in the burrow remains moderate and the relative humidity remains about two to five times higher than that of the outside air. Thus the rat loses little body moisture while in its retreat. Food stored in the burrow absorbs some of the air's moisture, to be gained by the animal when the food is consumed. The nose temperature of the kangaroo rat is lower than that of its body as a whole. As air is inspired, water evaporated from the rat's nasal passages cools the nasal tissues. In expiration, air leaving the lungs has become

68   THE DESERTS OF THE SOUTHWEST

saturated at the higher body temperature. As this air is expired, it is cooled in its movement over the cooler nasal passage and loses some of the moisture carried from the lungs. A near moisture equilibrium thus occurs. The animal's feces are dry and firm, containing little moisture; additionally, the rat practices *caprophagy,* or eating its own fecal pellets, thereby gaining certain vitamins and some additional water. The kangaroo rat consumes little protein in its diet; thus the need to eliminate urea is reduced. Its kidneys are capable of producing very concentrated urine, approximately four to five times as concentrated as man's.

Many of the small desert mammals enter a dormant period in response to such factors as cold, heat, drought, or food shortage. We are most familiar with winter dormancy, or *hibernation.* A similar summer dormancy is termed *estivation.* In both states, the animal's body temperature approaches within a few degrees the ambient temperature, oxygen consumption is greatly reduced, and the animal is in a deep torpor. This holding action may well help animals to endure unfavorable periods. One desert mammal, the Mohave ground squirrel, *Citellus mohavensis,* becomes dormant during the later summer and remains largely so on through the winter, its state of estivation merging into hibernation. Some small desert mammals are known to undergo daily torpor cycles. In certain desert-dwelling mice

Fig. 20. The kangaroo rat, *Dipodomys merriami,* is one of the most highly adapted desert mammals, able to exist on dry food without need of free water. Several species and subspecies occur in the Southwest deserts; the largest, *D. deserti,* has a body length of 5 to 6 inches and a 7 to 8 inch tail. *D. merriami* is somewhat smaller.

of the genus *Peromyscus*, daily torpor periods of several hours' duration have been found to occur in which the body temperature of the animal drops as much as 50 Fahrenheit degrees, with a resultant drop in energy needs. Such daily torpor cycles are thought to be primarily a response to food shortages.

Adaptations to the desert by the human species will be discussed in later chapters. As one of the desert's large mammals, however, man seldom crawls into burrows; man must wear artificial clothing as a heat shield and to cover exposed, easily burned skin; he requires large amounts of water for elimination of wastes and is incapable of enduring hyperthermia for long; he loses quantities of water in evaporative cooling. His thinking is affected by a water loss equivalent to a 5 percent loss of body weight, and his condition can only be described as critical or dead when this loss reaches 12 to 15 percent. Obviously, man's desert adaptation must be behavioral.

CHAPTER VI

The Great Basin Desert

IN 1776, when momentous actions were underway on the eastern seaboard, Spanish Fathers Garces, Dominguez, and Escalante and their soldier escorts became, in two different expeditions, the first white men to penetrate the great western interior basin of the United States. A quarter-century or so later, fur trappers entered the basin region from the north. Dreams regarding this unknown immense area proliferated in far-away regions. Armchair geographers fantasized, then believed that a river—undiscovered, yet named the Buenaventura—crossed the area and offered a ready route from the great Rockies to the far Pacific.

Jedediah Smith, the Nineteenth Century American trapper and explorer, traveled the area; the first white women and the first wagons entered it in 1841. In 1844, Lieutenant John C. Fremont made the truth known: No mythical kingdom nor river system to the Pacific existed within the region's interior. The area was in reality a basin—a great desert basin. Fremont was soon followed by highly motivated land and gold seekers who traversed the arid land as they pursued their goals to the west.

The outlines of the Great Basin Desert coincide rather well with the outlines of the floor of the Great Basin itself; extensions of the desert environment also reach into adjacent portions of the Colorado and Columbia plateaus. The Great Basin Desert includes a small portion of eastern Washington, central and southeastern Oregon, southern Idaho, much of Nevada and Utah, and a small part of western Colorado, then extends probing fingers into northern Arizona. Dr. William G. McGinnies of the University of Arizona states that the Great Basin itself stretches north to south 880 miles, east to west 572 miles, and includes an area of 210,000 square miles. Northernmost of the arid lands, the Great Basin is known as a cold desert. Most of its vast area lies above 4,000 feet in elevation, and its most northern extensions reach to approximately 49 degrees north latitude. Snow is frequent and winter long; freezing temperatures of a week in duration are common. Precipitation in the form of both rain and snow averages four to eleven inches per year, with up to thirteen inches at the higher elevations and more northern latitudes. Approximately 60 percent of the moisture is received during the colder months, the majority in the early spring months.

The Great Basin, stretching irregularly from the Sierra Nevada Mountains on the west almost to the Rockies on the east (more specifically, some authorities cite its major boundary as the Wasatch Mountains of central Utah), consists of a series of undrained basins, or bolsons, separated by generally north–south-trending mountain ranges. According to

Overleaf: F I G . 2 1. The Great Basin Desert extends the farthest north and is the largest of the four North American deserts. It covers most of Nevada and Utah with extensions into Oregon, Idaho, Wyoming, Colorado, Arizona, and California.

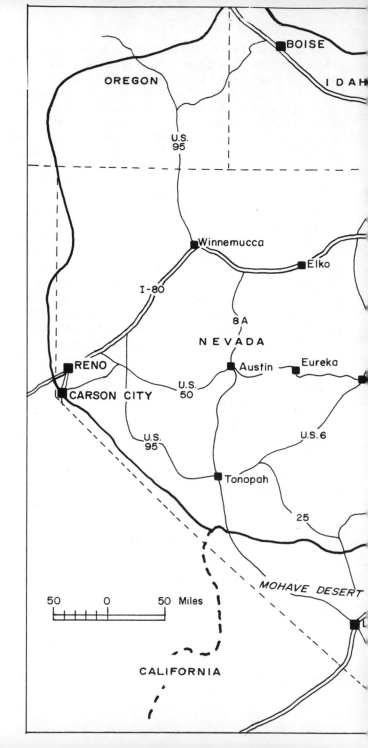

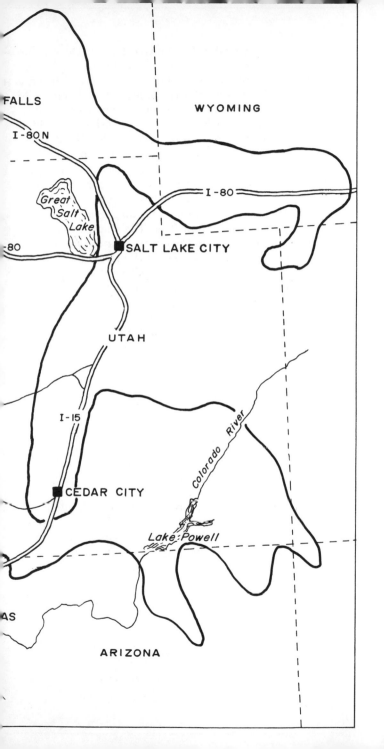

the borders one establishes for the Great Basin Desert, the number of these major bolsons varies, but exceeds 100. Mountain ranges are always in sight in this desert. Most are approximately fifty to seventy-five miles in length and six to fifteen miles in width. Some rise over 10,000 feet in elevation to become islands rising from a sagebrush sea, studded with juniper, piñon, and other conifers. The Great Basin Desert is the classic example of basin and range topography.

Moisture received by the mountains within this giant intermountain basin flows in washes and larger streambeds toward the center of each adjacent basin. Since these basins are without outlet, the water forms *playas;* occasionally, it is contained within a permanent lake. The water evaporates, leaving its mineral burden in the dry playa, or to accumulate in the remaining lake waters. One of the larger streambeds (by desert standards) contained within this closed system is the Humboldt River in western Nevada. A century and a quarter ago, it provided for a distance a welcome watered pathway for wagon-tied, California-bound travelers, until its water disappeared into the Humboldt Sink. After that, the pioneers and their animals faced a grueling, waterless desert before beginning their ascent of the Sierras.

The Great Basin has not always been a desert. It was once a land of lakes, and evidence of these yet remains. During the last ice age, glaciers moved far southward, bringing ice melt and wetter weather to the Basin. Water accumulated, forming lakes in many of the basins. Two spectacularly large lakes were created. In the eastern Great Basin, Lake Bonneville covered much of northwestern Utah, with portions of Nevada and Idaho also included under its approximately 20,000-square-mile expanse. In the western Great Basin, the approximately 8,500-square-mile Lake Lahontan was formed. About 15,000 years ago, the glaciers having retreated, the climate of the Great Basin became arid, and the lake waters began their lengthy evaporative shrinking. Today small remnants of these lakes remain. The Great Salt Lake, the remains of Lake Bonneville, is now approximately 1,500 square miles in extent. Pyramid Lake, in western Nevada, approximately 160 square miles in size, is one of several remains of Lake Lahontan.

Accumulation of minerals over thousands of years in these basins has produced today's highly saline lakes. The Great

Salt Lake is truly salty—its salt content is approximately eight to ten times greater than that of the ocean; the Great Salt Lake is outranked (barely) in salt content by only one other major body of water, the Dead Sea, itself a desert-locked body of water. The waters of the Great Salt Lake are too highly mineralized for human swimmers to sink; its water burns their eyes and salt crusts on their bodies once they come out. It is too highly saline for survival of fish. Life is present, however, for algae abound within it, and tiny, quarter-inch brine shrimp are often present in fantastic numbers. Nesting birds are attracted to the islands which dot the shallow, briny waters. California gulls, white pelicans, blue herons, cormorants, and other seemingly unlikely species flock to the lake. For the most part, these birds derive their food from the fresh waters and marshes feeding into the lake, or even from waters some distance away.

Where the ancient lake waters have completely disappeared, leaving vast dry lakes of mineral residues behind, great level salt flats have often been formed. The Bonneville Salt Flats, west of the Great Salt Lake, extends for miles, its salts undotted by plants. Bonneville Salt Flats—baked solid—is used for car racing; speeds over 600 miles per hour have been achieved on it by rocket-equipped vehicles.

In environments favorable for plant growth, competition occurs between plant species for room, sunlight, and similar factors. Not so in the desert. There, competition is not plant versus plant, but rather plant versus environment. Where desert environmental conditions are adverse, relatively fewer plant species survive. The plants of the Great Basin must survive the extremes of both aridity and cold, in addition to other extenuating factors, such as often highly alkaline soils. As a consequence, flora of the Great Basin Desert is limited in comparison to many other desert areas.

Forrest Shreve classified stands of desert vegetation into three general groups, according to the number of dominant species of plants involved in each. In what he called *simple stands,* only two or three species formed 90 to 95 percent of the plant population of the stand, and coverage was a mere 8 to 15 percent. Such stands, unlike the two remaining classifications, tend to display a uniformity of height. Shreve estimated that about 12 percent of the North American desert consists of simple stands. The second classification, that of *mixed stands,* includes areas in which dominance of the vegetation is held by four to twelve large perennials. Approximately 60 percent of the North American desert supports mixed stands; coverage ranges from 15 to 20 percent. The height attained by these species is not uniform; hence the upper vegetational level is irregular. The third classification is that of *rich stands,* with the dominant and subdominant perennial species totaling fifteen to twenty-five. Slightly less than 30 percent of the North American desert supports rich stands. In these stands, coverage may reach 40 to 70 percent, with the "canopy" again broken into different levels.

Large areas of simple stands occur in the Great Basin Desert. Within the limited number of species capable of surviving in that location, certain shrub or semi-shrub species have been most successful. Best known of these shrubs is the sagebrush, popular trademark of the Great Basin Desert. Trees are not common; cottonwoods and willows grow along some streambeds and, as one leaves the desert to ascend the mountain slopes, piñons and junipers fringe the desert's edge. Ephemerals are limited to a single season—the summer. In some areas, grasses assume seasonal importance. Yuccas occur infrequently. Leafless green plant species are few, represented by *Ephedra*—jointed-stemmed, blue-green, small shrubs commonly called Mormon tea or Mexican tea, which were supposedly once brewed and drunk by these people. Species of cacti are extremely limited; they include small species of prickly pears, such as *Opuntia polyacantha,* the Great Basin cactus. This species of prickly pear forms clumps from one to several feet in diameter, but extends to only a limited three to six inches in height. *Echinocereus,* or small hedgehog cacti, also occur.

Cacti are highly susceptible to damage from cold weather. They are injured if the temperature falls below 14° to 23° F. for a short time or below 28° F. for a longer period. Some prickly pear species range far to the north, but they tend to be small in size, and their pads are rather severely depleted of water content before freezing temperatures occur. For germination, cacti seeds require warm soil temperatures— at least 70° F., or preferably a range of about 80° to 90° F.—and the mature cacti need moisture and warmth con-

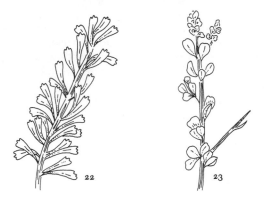

FIG. 22. The sagebrush, *Artemisia tridentata* (commonly 2 to 4 feet, but up to 7 feet in height), a gray-green shrub of the high desert country, is the popular symbol of the Great Basin. The leaves bear three wedge-shaped teeth at the tips, giving this plant a common name—three-tooth sage. Sagebrush is the dominant plant over extended areas, and many animals are associated with it in a variety of ways.

FIG. 23. Shadscale, *Atriplex confertifolia,* is particularly promi-nent in the Great Basin Desert where it often forms almost pure stands on alkaline soils. The plants, compact and rounded, may reach two feet in height and are rigid, spiny, and nearly leafless in winter. Another common name is sheep fat, denoting this plant's usefulness to man.

currently for both growth and moisture replenishment. Therefore, with warm summer temperatures limited in du-ration and more than half the region's moisture being re-ceived during the colder months, conditions in the Great Basin Desert are not conducive to the growth of most cacti species. Other succulent or semi-succulent species are only poorly represented.

Shreve summarized the vegetation of the Great Basin Desert as dominated by a small number of species of gener-ally low-statured shrubs, most of them completely or at least partly deciduous, and as displaying a predominance of sim-ple plant communities, with as much as 95 percent of the simple stand composed of a single species in some cases. The most common dominants are *Atriplex confertifolia,* shadscale, or sheep fat; *Artemisia tridentata,* the sagebrush, or three-toothed sage; *Artemisia nova,* a smaller sagebrush; *Chrysothamnus puberulus,* or rabbit brush; and *Eurotia lanata,* mule fat, or winter fat. Soil conditions are of prime importance in determining where an individual species predominates.

Plants vary in their ability to grow in alkaline soil; the halophytes are especially adapted for growth in soils with a high salt concentration. These plants often occur in the lower levels of the basins; concentric bands of various species of vegetation ring them, with the species makeup of the various bands dependent upon the plants' tolerances to alkalinity. The highly alkaline soils of the playa centers support no vegetation whatsoever. Circling the playa's edges may occur scattered, hardy, often small-leaved, highly adapted, alkali-resistant plant species such as *Salicornia rubra,* or samphire; *Allenrolfea occidentalis,* or pickleweed; *Atriplex corrugata,* mat salt bush; and *Sarcobatus vermiculatus,* or true greasewood. Just above this vegetational ring usually occurs *Atriplex confertifolia,* or spiny shadscale. This species tends to dominate lower basin areas, in which it grows in soil too alkaline for sagebrush. That shadscale is also called "salt bush" indicates its growth ability and usual location. Shadscale is a rounded, compact, woody-stemmed bush which seldom grows more than one to two feet in height, often forming nearly pure stands on the alkaline, heavy soils. During the winter the plant becomes rigid, spiny, and nearly leafless. The shrub ranges from the north-

FIG. 24. The greasewood, *Sarcobatus vermiculatus,* is a salt-tolerant plant often plentiful in the Great Basin Desert. The name greasewood is sometimes incorrectly given to the creosote bush. The greasewood shrub is 3 to 5 feet in height, with numerous branches and somewhat succulent leaves.

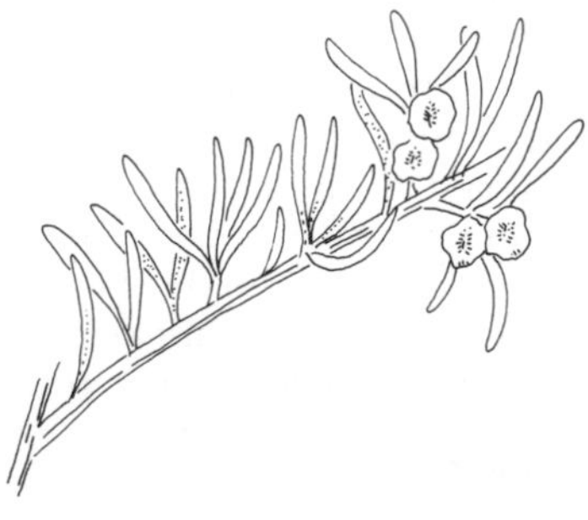

ern Great Basin south into Chihuahua, Mexico, and can be an important browse plant for animals.

One study determined that *Salicornia rubra* and related species were growing in soil with 2.5 percent or more soluble salts. Where the salt content was .8 percent, *Atriplex confertifolia* prospered. With a slight further decrease in salt content and the presence of a coarser soil texture, *Artemisia tridentata*, the sagebrush, was established. Sagebrush in nearly pure stands or mixed with a limited number of other perennial species blankets vast areas of the Great Basin Desert; it also ranges beyond the Great Basin into the xeric woodlands, pine forests, and into the adjoining Mohave Desert. *Artemisia tridentata* is commonly two to four feet in height, but may reach six or seven feet. Soft gray-green in color, *Artemisia tridentata* bears leaves tipped with three short, wedge-shaped teeth. Actually this sagebrush is not a true sage but is a variety of wormwood. Its popular name is drawn from the sweetish, sage odor its foliage bears. When burned, the sagebrush provides a characteristic, pleasingly odored smoke. Because it has figured in so many romantic/ adventure novels, particularly those of Zane Grey, the sagebrush is to many neophytes the universal symbol of desert. In reality, sagebrush is a dominant plant only in the Great Basin Desert; its ubiquitous position is appropriated in the warmer southern deserts by the creosote bush.

Shreve states that nineteen additional species of *Artemisia* are found in rather close association with *A. tridentata* in the Great Basin Desert. Similarly, fourteen additional species of *Atriplex* are associated with the best-known, *Atriplex confertifolia*. He notes additional semi-shrub species of importance in the Great Basin. *Artemisia nova* is similar to *A. tridentata* but is smaller in size and is usually found growing in areas above *A. tridentata*. *Chrysothamnus puberulus*, or rabbit brush, is a compact shrub, usually a foot or less in height, found in the central and northern Great Basin on light or sandy, nonalkaline soils. It blossoms, producing yellow flowers, in late summer. *Grayia spinosa*, or hop sage, is a stiff-branched shrub from one to three feet in height. It has slightly fleshy leaves, and its fruits are enclosed in purple-red bracts. Growing on alkaline soils in both the creosote and sagebrush desert, it ranges from Washington into southern California. *Eurotia lanata*, mule fat, or winter fat, derives its common name from its importance as winter forage. The plant reaches 1 to 2½ feet in height and is conspicuous due to gray-white foliage and white hairs about ³/₁₆ inch long which grow from the bracts of the fruit. *Atriplex nuttallii* is a small salt bush capable of growing in soil with a salt content as high as 3 percent. *Coleogyne ramosissima*, or blackbrush, is a small-leaved evergreen shrub found on higher slopes in the southern Great Basin.

The Great Basin's surface appearance presents an overall effect of linear mountain masses separated by immense, lonely intermountain vastnesses which are partially clothed by shrubs of a rather uniform height and repetitious in form. Some who view the land describe the total as monotonous. To the desert lover, however repetitious its plant growth may be, the Great Basin's expansiveness, loneliness, silence, wilderness, and desert essence endow it with a rugged beauty and character not displayed by man-dominated, treed, or planted lands.

As with plant species, some animal species may range through desert and other habitats. Others may be basically desert species and occur in at least portions of all four of the North American deserts; many others are restricted to one or two of the deserts. Some are so restricted in range as to be found only in a portion of a single desert. Literally thousands of species of living things occur in our North American deserts. Though to know them all would be impossible, we can recognize a broad pattern of organization regarding the habitation in and utilization of the desert by many of the animal species. This study or science of the interrelations between living organisms and their environment we know as *ecology*. Before surveying some of the animals to be found in the Great Basin Desert, let us define and clarify certain ecological concepts.

The place where a plant or animal lives or may be found is its *habitat*, or *biotope*. This area may be large, as is the Great Basin Desert, or even larger, as is the North American desert. Or it may be a small piece of a particular habitat, a microhabitat. A *community* denotes all the populations of living things occupying a given area. A block of nature that includes nonliving substances and a community of living organisms which interact to produce an exchange of materials between the nonliving and the living is an *ecosystem*. In this functional unit, the *biotic* (living) and the *abiotic* (nonliving) are inseparably interrelated and interact upon one another. Within this ecosystem, each species of living organisms fills a particular ecological niche. *Niche* denotes the species' position or status within its community and total ecosystem. The niche filled by an organism depends upon the organism's structural adaptation, specific inherited and/or learned behavior, and physiological responses. Simply, niche may be thought of as the "job," or position, the species fills in the ecosystem. Ordinarily no two species occupy an identical niche in a particular ecosystem, although some may occupy very similar niches, differing from one another in only certain fine aspects—they may be active at different times or use slightly different foods, or the like.

The food used by a species is an important factor in the niche it fills. Within the ecosystem exist *food chains*, through which food energy from plants—the basic source— is transferred, through repeated eating and being eaten, from one to the next in a series of organisms. In each transfer, a large proportion of the potential energy is lost. In most chains no more than four or five transfers, and usually fewer, are involved. The chains are of three basic types. In the *saprophytic chain*, food energy moves from dead matter to microorganisms. In the *parasitic chain*, food energy moves from larger to smaller organisms. The most familiar food chain, and the one we will consider, is the *predator chain*. This chain often moves from the plant base through small and finally to larger animals; for example, plant–insect–lizard–roadrunner–coyote. In this chain, the successive members are larger in size but fewer in total number (for example, coyotes are larger and less numerous than roadrunners, which are in turn larger and less numerous than lizards, and so on). In some cases the sequence may be plants, to large herbivore, to carnivore; for example, plants–deer–mountain lion. The term *trophic level* indicates the consumer's distance from the plant source. Plants represent the first trophic level; *herbivores*, or plant-eaters, the second level; primary *carnivores*, which eat the herbivores, represent the third level; and, if present, secondary carnivores and tertiary carnivores represent the fourth and fifth levels. Consumers which are the same number of steps removed from the plant source are said to be on the same trophic level. Food chains in any ecosystem are interconnected with one another, and the pattern formed is known as the *food web.*

Nature abhors a vacuum, states the philosopher–naturalist. And so living things move in, adapt, and exploit to the best of their ability any opportunities for life that may be provided. The usual end result is that species fill every possible niche in each ecosystem. Some species—for example, the coyote—fill a particular niche in several ecosystems. In some cases, the same species may fill approximately the same niche in similar but separated habitats, with the species population in one habitat genetically differentiated to some degree, as revealed by appearance or adaptation. Such a genetic variant within a species, adapted to a particular environment yet remaining interfertile with all other members of the species, is known as an *ecotype.* Similar or related but not identical species may fill essentially the same niche in similar ecosystems. For example, a particular species of ground squirrel in one desert may not be present in a nearby desert, but a very similar species fills essentially the same niche; the antelope ground squirrel, *Ammospermophilus leucurus,* of the Great Basin and Mohave Deserts is replaced in southern Arizona and Sonora by the Harris ground squirrel, *Citellus harrisi.* Finally, some organisms, often phylogenetically distant from one another, undergo parallel evolution, adapting to similar environmental conditions to fill similar niches in habitats distant from one another. The American sidewinder rattlesnake has adapted to a sandy habitat with sidewinding locomotion. The horned viper of Africa has evolved the same solution to similar environmental conditions. The American kangaroo rat's adaptations to life in an arid environment have been achieved through remarkably similar means by the jerboa of the African deserts. The big-eared American kit fox, especially adapted for a rodent-catching way of life in the North American deserts, is matched similarly by the big-eared, rodent-catching fennec fox of Africa. Organisms which occupy the same ecological niche in similar habitats of different biogeographical regions are termed *ecological equivalents.*

Some generalizations (to which exceptions do arise) may be applied to desert animals. Desert mammals tend to have fur of a lighter color than do members of their species or closely related species inhabiting more humid, cooler climates. The cause of this coloration has not been precisely determined. Ecologists postulate that lighter colors may provide protective coloration against the desert's light, often-faded colors, or that heat and humidity may be involved in the change in hair pigmentation, or both. Desert mammals and birds display a high surface-to-body weight ratio. Under identical conditions, *homiothermal* animals (those having a relatively uniform body temperature maintained nearly independent of the environmental temperature) give off equal amounts of heat per unit of surface area. "Bergmann's Rule" postulates that as temperatures decrease from the equator toward the poles, the body shape of birds and mammals tends to display a lower ratio of body surface to body weight. "Allen's Rule" postulates that over this same temperature gradient, the body extremities tend to become shorter in proportion to trunk size. The end result is a reduction in the surface area from which heat is lost to the atmosphere from the stocky bodies of Arctic animals, and a proportionate increase of heat-radiating body surface in the desert animals. The foregoing rule applies only to birds and mammals. The opposite is true of poikilothermic animals which generally attain larger body sizes in warm climates than they do in cold climates.

A species population, particularly plant, which exerts a major controlling effect on the nature of a community is termed an *ecological dominant,* or indicator. In the Great Basin Desert, two major communities are easily recognized: In the first, the halophytic species, particularly shadscale, *Atriplex confertifolia,* are the dominants; in the second, *Artemisia tridentata,* the sagebrush, is the ecological dominant. Around these dominants and accompanying species, ecosystems are developed. The common names of some species exemplify their presence in and about, and their ties to, the dominant species. For example, inhabitants in the sagebrush community include the sagebrush chipmunk, *Eutamias minimus*; sage sparrow, *Amphispiza nevadensis*; sage thrasher, *Oreoscoptes montanus*; sage grouse, *Centrocercus urophasianus*; and sagebrush lizard, *Sceloporus graciosus.*

The sagebrush lizard is small—2 to 2½ inches in length, plus tail. Gray or brown above, it usually displays blotches or crossbars. It often has a black bar on the shoulder with a rust

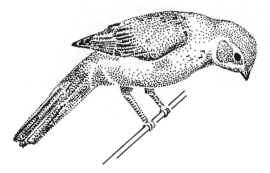

FIG. 25. The sage sparrow, *Amphispiza belli* (5 to 6 inches in length), is a ground feeder in dry brushy habitat, such as the sagebrush plains or open chaparral.

color on the sides of the neck and body, and blue belly patches. This ground dweller is found in the vicinity of brush heaps, rocks, logs, or bushes. It retreats to these areas or occasionally climbs up into vegetation when frightened. The sagebrush lizard prefers open ground with scattered low bushes, requirements met by the sagebrush habitat, although it also ranges into manzanita brushland, pine and fir forests, and piñon–juniper woodland. Its food consists of insects, ticks, scorpions, spiders, snails, and similar animal life.

The sagebrush, or least, chipmunk is a roughly rat-sized rodent with short grayish fur marked by contrasting stripes on the head and the length of the body. Its tail is narrow, round, lemon-yellow or grayish-yellow on the underside, and long—equaling approximately 80 to 90 percent of the head-and-body length. In addition to living in the sagebrush habitat, this chipmunk ranges into juniper woodland. Chipmunks can be differentiated from some similar-looking ground squirrels by the presence of stripes on the sides of their heads. The sagebrush chipmunk hibernates through the cold winter months. It carries food in internal cheek pouches and stores caches of food in its underground burrow for early spring months or for periods during the winter when it may awaken. Chipmunks in general eat seeds and fruits, although the sagebrush chipmunk consumes insects, especially the larvae of Lepidoptera (butterflies and moths) in the spring, becoming more of a seed-eater later in the summer.

Both the sage thrasher and sage sparrow breed in the sagebrush habitat, building their nests in the sagebrush itself and often using fine shreds of the bark as nesting material. The thrasher is almost robin size, and is similar to the robin in shape. Its back is gray, its tail is short with white corners, its breast is heavily striped; it has a straight and slender bill and pale yellow eyes. It often sits atop the sagebrush, voicing its pleasant song and nervously jerking its tail. The sage thrasher is an insect eater and has a habit of often running rapidly from one protective bush to another. This thrasher ranges from Washington and Montana south to southern California, southern Arizona, and New Mexico; it winters in the more southern areas.

The sage sparrow is a small gray bird with a single dark spot on the lighter breast and dark marks on the side of the throat. Its breeding range is throughout most of the Great Basin, reaching into central California. This sparrow winters from the southern edge of the breeding range to the deserts of California, Arizona, New Mexico, and western Texas.

The sage grouse, or sage hen, is one of the very interesting, distinctive inhabitants of the sagebrush community. Individuals of this species are approximately the size of a small turkey; the males average twenty-eight inches in body length, the females twenty-two inches. These birds are gray-brown with a contrasting black belly and spike-like tail feathers. The range of the sage grouse is close to that of the sagebrush, from southeastern Washington and Montana to eastern California, Nevada, Utah, and northern Colorado. The sage grouse are strong runners; they dash through the intervening open areas between sagebrush and the other plants under which they find protection from raptors. Their mottled black, brown, and gray coloration serves as camouflage in their habitat.

The sage grouse is best known for its courtship displays. Early in the spring, the males assemble in special clearings among the sagebrush, called *strutting grounds.* Displays by the males usually take place in the very early morning or late afternoon. Each male chooses a territory, often with a small hillock included. He displays his plumage, erecting a spectacular white ruff about his neck, and spreads, erects, and fans his tail. He begins to beat his wings; he struts stiff-legged and gulps air, filling his lungs and the two air sacs on his breast. The bird arches his wings, contracting the muscles around the air sacs. With his head withdrawn into the white ruff, the balloon-like air sacs protruding from the breast feathers and framed by the wings, and the whole backed by the spiked, spread tail, the male sage grouse is a most unusual apparition, apparently very attractive to the observing females. The finale of each display is provided when the air is released from the air sacs with loud plops which can be heard as much as a half mile away. These displays are repeated many times on different occasions and are accompanied by fighting; eventually, one male becomes dominant and may mate with three-fourths or more of the hens in a particular group. In the winter, the sage grouse live in flocks that may include several hundred individuals. During that period, they feed primarily on the leaves of sage-brush. After mating in the spring, the males break into smaller groups. In the fall the males, females, and young join into the larger flocks.

Another interesting inhabitant of the sagebrush is the pygmy rabbit, *Sylvilagus idahoensis*, the smallest of all rabbits, measuring approximately eleven inches in length. This rabbit is confined to the Great Basin, occurring from eastern California, Oregon, and Washington into southern Idaho, northern Nevada, and western Utah. Even within this limited range, the pygmy rabbit is local in distribution. The young of members of the genus *Sylvilagus* are born naked with eyes closed, in contrast to the precocial young of the hares of the genus *Lepus,* which includes the jackrabbits. The young of *Lepus* species are born with full fur and functioning eyes and ears; they are able to hop about within a few hours after birth. The pygmy brush rabbits occur in patches of dense sagebrush where they live in burrows at the bases of the plants; their food is thought to consist almost entirely of sagebrush.

The black-tailed hare, commonly called the black-tailed jackrabbit, *Lepus californicus,* is widespread in western North America. This large hare, with an average body length of twenty-two inches, sports huge black-tipped ears. Dorsally it is grayish, and nearly white ventrally. The upper side of its tail is black, with the color running up onto the rump;

FIG. 26. The sage grouse, *Centrocercus urophasianus* (males 26 to 30 inches, females 22 to 23 inches), is a resident of the sage-brush habitat, eating the plant's leaves and nesting under it.

below, the tail is buffy-gray. Food of this often-numerous hare is grass and shrubs. These animals are often seen bounding across roads in the Great Basin Desert, and in years of bounty many are seen road-killed.

The few inhabitants of the sagebrush ecosystem we have just surveyed serve as less than a mere beginning in knowing the totality of the literally hundreds of animal species of the Great Basin Desert. In looking at the species inhabiting that desert as a whole, we see certain patterns. Many animals, such as the pygmy rabbit and sage grouse, consume vegetation, as do many insects and other animals. These plant-eating animals may be consumed by predators. Some animals, such as the sagebrush chipmunk, cross lines and eat both plant and animal material. Any community must necessarily include more animals to be eaten than eaters. In this regard, the Great Basin Desert, like the other three North American deserts, has a large insect population, at least seasonally, which provides food for many animals. It also has a huge rodent population which supplies a large food bulk for many predators. As a group, rodents have become well adapted to life in the desert, as exemplified by the kangaroo rat.

Two kangaroo rat species found in the Great Basin are *Dipodomys microps* and *D. ordii*. *D. ordii*, known as the Ord kangaroo rat, has an extensive range from southern Canada south to central Mexico and from eastern Oregon to the Gulf coast of Texas. Pack rats or wood rats occur, including the desert pack rat, *Neotoma desertorum*, which builds its home within stacks of debris which it collects. A multitude of mice occur, including white-footed, *Peromyscus sp.*; harvest mice, *Reithrodontomys sp.*; and grasshopper mice, *Onychomys sp.*, which are unusual in that they have departed from the vegetarian diet, with which mice are ordinarily associated, to become carnivores. Up to approximately 90 percent of their food may consist of grasshoppers and other insects. Kangaroo mice, too, are present; they resemble the kangaroo rats in some ways, but are much smaller. *Microdipodops megalocephalus*, a kangaroo mouse found in the Great Basin Desert, has a tail larger in the middle than at the base, due to an accumulation of fat.

Meadow mice, or voles, usually inhabitants of moister habitats, are represented in the Great Basin by the sagebrush vole, *Lagurus curtatus*. This species is often found in arid sagebrush habitat far from surface water. These animals feed on sagebrush and other vegetation, are active both diurnally and nocturnally, and do not hibernate. The females breed a few hours after giving birth, and the gestation period is a mere twenty-one days, providing a good example of the productive capacity of the smaller mammals to produce food for the larger.

Pocket gophers, also usually associated with more moist areas, occur, with *Thomomys perpallidus* found in the Great Basin Desert. Ground squirrels form a large part of the staff of life for other creatures. These squirrels include members of the genera *Citellus* and *Ammospermophilus*, the latter known as the antelope ground squirrel.

Carnivorous amphibians of the Great Basin Desert include the Great Basin spadefoot toad, *Scaphiopus intermontanus*; western toad, *Bufo boreas*; and leopard frog, *Rana pipiens*. Lizards, primarily carnivorous, which occur in the Great Basin include the leopard lizard, *Crotaphytus wislizenii*; collared lizard, *Crotaphytus collaris baileyi*; western fence lizard, *Sceloporus occidentalis*; side-blotched lizard, *Uta stansburiana*; northern desert horned lizard, *Phry-*

nosoma platyrhinos; western skink, *Eumeces skiltonianus;* and the Great Basin whiptail lizard, *Cnemidophorus tigris.* Among the snakes represented are rubber boa, *Charina bottae;* striped whipsnake, *Masticophis taeniatus;* red racer, *Masticophis flagellum;* Great Basin gopher snake, *Pituophis melanoleucus;* western long-nosed snake, *Rhinocheilus lecontei;* night snake, *Hypsiglena torquata;* and the Great Basin rattlesnake, *Crotalus viridis lutosus.* All of the snakes are carnivorous, preying on a wide variety of animals.

Birds of the Great Basin Desert are extremely varied. Some breed there in the desert habitat. Others breed along the lake shores or on islands in the lakes, such as those of the Great Salt Lake. Still other species are transitory, simply pausing in their migration. In their food habits, as a group, these birds vary from eaters of plant products to insect- and larger-animal eaters to carrion feeders, such as ravens and turkey vultures, *Cathartes aura.* Birds of prey include red-tailed hawks, *Buteo jamaicensis;* Swainson's hawks, *Buteo swainsoni;* prairie falcons, *Falco mexicanus;* Cooper's hawks, *Accipiter cooperii;* sharp-shinned hawks, *Accipiter striatus;* horned owls, *Bubo virginianus pacificus;* screech owls, *Otus asio;* and long-eared owls, *Asio otus.* Several species of sparrows occur, as do the mourning dove, *Zenaidura macroura;* nighthawk, *Chordeiles minor;* red-shafted flicker, *Colaptes cafer collaris;* bullock oriole, *Icterus bullockii;* killdeer, *Charadrius vociferus;* poorwill, *Phalaenoptilus nuttallii;* broad-tailed hummingbird, *Selasphorus platycercus;* western meadowlark, *Sturnella neglecta;* and gray flycatcher, *Empidonax wrightii.*

Larger mammals found in the Great Basin Desert, some of whom occasionally supplement their diet with plant material but who primarily consume reptiles, insects, birds, and smaller mammals, include the coyote, *Canis latrans;* badger, *Taxidea taxus;* and bobcat, *Lynx rufus.*

Among the interesting large herbivorous mammals of the Great Basin Desert are the wild horses, which were introduced, and the native pronghorn. The wild horses, despite persecution by man, prospered for a period in the sagebrush habitat. These small, extremely alert horses roam in bands controlled by the stallion leader. At one point, their population was estimated to be several million; this figure was reduced to an estimated 16,000 less than ten years ago;

currently, it is estimated at something over 40,000. Hated by some ranchers, hunted in vehicles and planes to be sold for dog food, the wild horses have been severely reduced in numbers. Some people, admiring the horses' spirit and seeing them as symbols of freedom, independence, and the will to survive under adverse circumstances, have risen to the defense of the wild horses. Their continued fight for the lives of these horses has made the hunting of them by vehicle or plane illegal on federal land.

The pronghorn, *Antilocapra americana,* is the only living species of its family. Pronghorns were once abundant from southern Canada to the plateaus of Mexico, and from California to the Mississippi Valley. So pressured by hunting did they become that they were virtually eliminated from most of their area. Protected by law for many years, they are now more numerous, although still limited in numbers. Once again, in some states, they are hunted in season. These relatively small herbivores are sometimes incorrectly called antelope. Bucks average approximately 115 pounds; does, approximately 90. The upper portions of the animal are deep tan, and the rump, underportions, and two bands across the neck are white. Both sexes have unique horns. The outer sheath has a forward-projecting prong approximately halfway between base and tip. The sheath is shed each fall; its replacement starts developing from the end of the remaining bony core and extends downward to the base of the core. The pronghorn are well equipped for the temperature extremes of their desert environment, with thick, tubular hair containing large air cells. With their heavy hair layer lying close to the skin in winter, they are well insulated. Each hair, however, can be elevated or depressed as needed. In warm temperatures, the hair can be held somewhat erect, allowing air circulation to the skin.

Pronghorns graze and browse, eating grass and shrubs, such as rabbit brush and sagebrush. They band into large groups in winter and roam about in summer in smaller bands. Animals of the open grassland and sagebrush, they are extremely alert, have an excellent sense of sight, are constantly on guard against enemies, and yet display great curiosity—a trait which contributed to their rapid reduction by hunters. The pronghorns, if alarmed, erect the white hair of the rump patch. The distinctive flash of this white fur

FIG. 27. The pronghorn, *Antilocapra americana* (body length approximately 4 feet; weight 90 to 125 pounds), are grazing and browsing animals once abundant in the sagebrush country and the grasslands. They were practically eliminated from most of their range by explorers and settlers. With protection, the species is gradually increasing.

serves as an alarm for other herd members, and the sight of pronghorns flashing their white signals, bounding across the terrain at speeds up to 50 miles per hour, is one of the many pleasures to be experienced by the fortunate human observer in the Great Basin Desert.

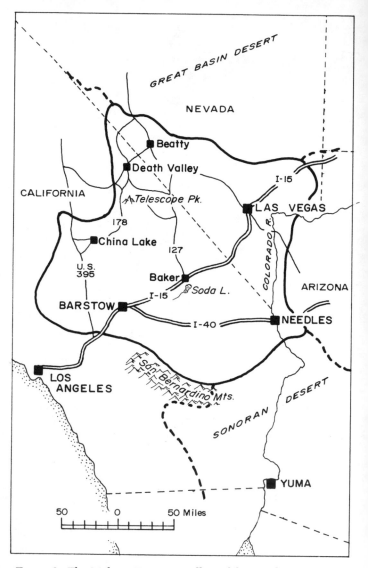

FIG. 28. The Mohave Desert, smallest of the North American deserts, covers southwestern Nevada, a portion of southeastern California, and barely extends into western Arizona. Included within its boundaries is arid Death Valley, credited with the second highest world's official temperature record, 134.6° F.

CHAPTER VII

The Mohave Desert

THE MOHAVE is the smallest of the four North American deserts. It lies primarily in California but also includes the approximate southern quarter of Nevada and projects two small extensions into west-central and northwestern Arizona. Basically it extends eastward from the southern end of the Sierra Nevada Mountains in southern California to the Colorado River on its eastern border, and northward and eastward from the San Bernardino Mountains to the point where creosote bush largely disappears and the Mohave blends into the Great Basin Desert. The western and southern sections of the Mohave, flanked on their borders by mountains, lie at the desert's highest elevations—approximately 5,000 feet; from these high sections, the desert gradually slopes toward the Colorado River at near sea level. The elevation of three-fourths of the Mohave Desert is between 2,000 and 4,000 feet.

For the most part, this desert's topography is of the basin-and-range type; the area contains numerous north–south-trending mountain ranges. A higher percentage of area is covered by mountains in the Mohave than in the adjoining Great Basin. The Colorado River lies along or briefly enters portions of the Mohave's eastern border. Two occasional waterways cut the desert. The Mohave River rises in the adjoining San Bernardino Mountains, flows north–northwest more than 100 miles, and dies in the desert in an alkaline flat. The Amargosa River (Amargosa means "bitter") originates in the desert itself and terminates in Death Valley. Limited amounts of drainage do flow to the Colorado River but, for the most part, the Mohave Desert is a land of undrained basins. This desert, like its Great Basin neighbor, was once, at the end of the last ice age, a wetter, lake-dotted area. At that time, major rivers drained into a series of lakes. One of these lakes, located in Death Valley, received the water from both the Mohave and Amargosa. Even today, populations of tiny pupfish remain in isolated small bodies of water in the Mohave Desert as remnants of the populations that once resided in the plentiful waters.

Precipitation decreases in the Mohave Desert from west to east. The western portions receive approximately five inches annual precipitation; the eastern portions approximately two inches. In some areas, however, rainfall is extremely irregular. Bagdad, California, in the southeastern Mohave Desert, is credited with the United States' record for the longest period without measurable rainfall—767 days. Rainfall is received primarily in the winter months, although in the Mohave's eastern portions, in particular, occasional summer thunderstorms occur in scattered locations. Severe frosts occur only in the western sections; snow may fall in the more elevated portions but seldom lasts for any length of time.

The Mohave Desert is subject to certain generalizations. It is, like the Great Basin, a shrub-dominated desert but is more arid than its northern neighbor. Ephemerals in the Mohave appear primarily in the spring—late March, April, and May—although summer storms may bring the later blossoming of some species. Cacti species are limited, although more are found in the Mohave than in the Great Basin; the cacti species are primarily prickly pear and cholla. Tree species are limited, although the Mohave's most distinguished plant is the Joshua tree. Forrest Shreve described the Mohave Desert as characterized by a limited display of life forms and a simple composition of most communities, and as exhibiting a very strong control of the distribution of its vegetation by the texture and salt content of the soil. Approximately one-fourth of the Mohave's plant species are endemic, restricted to this particular desert.

The averages and generalizations for the Mohave Desert as a whole must be modified to fit its most infamous portion, Death Valley, which is described geologically as a graben. As defined by Webster's, a *graben* is "a depressed segment of the earth's crust bounded on at least two sides by faults and generally of considerable length as compared with its width." Death Valley fits the definition well. It is approximately 190 miles long, from five to twenty miles wide, and banked by mountain ranges on both the east (the Grapevine and Funeral ranges) and the west (the Panamints). The mountains rise rapidly from the valley with practically no

FIG. 29. The cholla cacti, *Opuntia sp.*, are composed of a main trunk which supports branches of numerous cylindrical joints. The joints are readily knocked loose from the plant and, because they are heavily spined, easily become attached to the unwary animal or human passing by.

foothills, only alluvial fans at their bases. In the Panamints the tallest peak reaches 11,045 feet, yet only fifteen miles away, in the trough of Death Valley, the lowest point in the Western Hemisphere—282 feet below sea level—is surrounded by 550 square miles which lie below sea level. In this trough pit, the world's second highest official temperature, 134° F., has been recorded, as has the United States' lowest annual average precipitation, 1.6 inches. Ralph and Florence Welles, collaborators with the National Park Service in an eight-year study of bighorn sheep in Death Valley, found that for the month of July, 1959, the average daily maximum air temperature was 120.1° F. Ground-surface temperatures of as high as 190° F. were recorded in 1958. During the Welles' study, the lowest humidity level recorded was 3 percent. Little wonder that on charts showing expected survival time for man without water, resting in shade and exerting himself not at all, Death Valley ranks as the most extreme area in the United States. Under these conditions, man could expect to survive no more and perhaps less than two days during the month of July.

From its known conditions of heat and aridity, its stark, sere, but geologically fascinating terrain, and its folkloric reputation as the devil's domain, Death Valley is an obvious candidate for the classification of a lifeless desert land. It comes as somewhat of a surprise then to learn that Death Valley National Monument, covering approximately 3,000 square miles, has a total of more than 600 species of native plants, including some, such as the Death Valley sage, *Salvia funerea*, which are found nowhere else. Several hundred major animal species are reported to be present in the Death Valley area. The casual visitor may not see even a small fraction of this number. Some bird species, for example, may be transients or may be present only part of the year; other species may retreat limited distances up the mountainsides during the periods of greatest heat and aridity; and those desert-wise species who brave the desert floor will do so only when optimum conditions for their well-being prevail, as at night or during the winter months.

Sagebrush ranges down from the Great Basin into the Death Valley area. Creosote bush in concert with white bur sage, *Franseria dumosa*, is present. In many areas where the soil is alkaline, salt-tolerant plants such as the familiar shadscale, *Atriplex confertifolia*, grow. The Welles' bighorn sheep study revealed that the sheep, ranging along the lower mountainsides, alluvial fans, and into the valley, fed on at least forty-three different plants. Among those plants grazed or browsed were: galleta grass, *Hilaria jamesi;* evening primrose, *Oenothera sp.;* alkali sacaton, *Sporobolus airoides;* Mohave aster, *Aster abatus;* Mohave thistle, *Cirsium mohavense;* white brittlebush, *Encelia farinosa;* Nevada jointfir, *Ephedra nevadensis;* mallow, *Sphaeralcea sp.;* and desert needlegrass, *Stipa sp.* Occasionally the mesquite, *Prosopis juliflora,* was eaten. The sheep's most dependable food, year-round, was desert holly, *Atriplex hymenelytra.* Desert holly, as a member of the genus *Atriplex,* is one of the so-called salt bushes. Its silvery leaves and large, light green, disk-shaped, succulent fruiting bracts make this plant attractive; obviously, it is of great importance to the bighorn.

The bighorn are among the most interesting inhabitants of Death Valley. This desert subspecies or race of a species, *Ovis canadensis nelsoni,* ranges in small numbers from Canada into Mexico. The bighorn is approximately the size of a small deer, or about four feet in head-and-body length; the relatively small desert subspecies weighs 100 to 200 pounds. The horns of the mature males are gigantic, forming

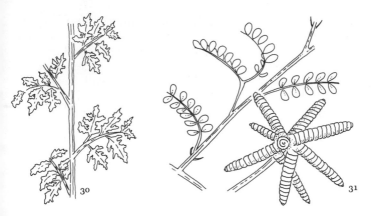

FIG. 30. White bur sage, or burro weed, *Franseria dumosa* (approximately 1 to 1½ feet in height), is a low, bushy shrub associated with creosote bush over vast arid portions of the Sonoran Desert. The plants are low and rounded with numerous branches, the leaves and branchlets whitened by a cover of short hairs.

FIG. 31. The screwbean mesquite, *Prosopis pubescens,* is characterized by tightly coiled seed pods, as compared to the straight pods of the other mesquites. The plant may assume shrub size or that of a small tree, to 30 feet in height. It ranges along desert streams from California to southern Nevada and Utah, into New Mexico and Texas, then south in both mainland and peninsular Mexico.

massive spirals—arched backward, then curved forward. The females' horns are smaller, rarely forming a half circle. The horns are never shed. The animal's color is a grayish-brown with a lighter abdomen. The bighorn is thought to have ranged much more widely prior to modern man's takeover of the countryside. Today these animals occupy the remote mountain slopes and peaks where they have less competition for food and a measure of protection from enemies—primarily man.

The Welles' study determined that the desert bighorn need water the year round, drinking every three to five days in hot, dry weather and every ten to fourteen days in cold weather. They move about in small bands, usually in a family group, often made up of three to five individuals. Infant mortality was high, but of those surviving the first year of life, most lived about ten years. On the basis of their study, the Welles listed some traits of the bighorn sheep which aid in their success in the desert environment: (1) They eat very little of any one plant at a time; since they travel constantly while feeding, they seldom destroy vegetation. (2) They are dispersed widely in small bands, and thus do not exert population pressure on their environment. (3) They are able to subsist for long periods on completely dormant or dead plant material. (4) Green forage is used, when available, to supply at least a part of the sheep's water needs, allowing them to range some distance from surface water sources in their search for food.

The Welles reached the conclusion that predation by wild animals plays very little part in bighorn mortality, at least in the Death Valley area, although possible predators were noted to be present: mountain lions, coyotes, bobcats, and golden eagles. They concluded that the world's supreme predator—man—is the bighorn sheep's greatest danger. Hunting, mining, expropriation of water and range, introduction of disease through livestock, introduction of burros, encroachment of housing, and building of highways across the ranges of these extremely timid, retiring animals—all have taken and continue to take a toll of the bighorn populations. Highways are a major menace, often isolating one mountain range from another, blocking the travels of the sheep which will not approach or attempt to cross the busy roadways. Pushed to the crags, the desert bighorn are now protected on refuges and by law, yet are still hunted by legal permit in some areas. In 1976, one proud hunter, holding the dead head of a magnificent ram, was pictured in a Tucson newspaper. An hour's hunt had netted him a male with thirty-seven-inch horns, sixteen inches in circumference at the base. Arizona Game and Fish officials report that approximately thirty to forty bighorns are killed annually in Arizona, although ten years ago the number was fifty to sixty. The bighorn is now considered a "threatened" species in Arizona, and officials attribute its decline not to limited hunting, which continues, but to deterioration of the sheep's habitat. When the Welles studied the bighorn of Death Valley approximately twenty years ago, the population in that area was estimated at 900. Today it is approximately

550. Monument naturalists attribute the decline in the bighorn numbers primarily to feral burro populations.

Feral burros, offspring of individuals escaped or released by prospectors, miners, and other desert dwellers in the past, are present not only in Death Valley but in many parts of the North American desert. These alert, tough, little animals are extremely well suited to desert life. They are capable of covering long distances in the heat, enduring rather extreme dehydration, and then hydrating rapidly once waterholes have been reached. Additionally they will deign to eat almost any plant available. The end result is pressure on the native wildlife. Donald Jackson in his book *Sagebrush Country* reports that in the ten western states the population of feral burros is 8,000 to 10,000, and the burros are estimated to be increasing at the rate of 20 percent annually. Death Valley National Monument naturalists estimate the current burro population to be over 1,600.

Burros are charged with monopolizing and fouling waterholes, discouraging the shy, quiet-loving bighorns from coming to water as often as needed; consuming water and forage needed by the bighorns; and trampling and killing vegetation around waterholes where it is most needed by the sheep—also thereby destroying habitat normally used by smaller, less obvious, but nonetheless important animal species. The control of burro populations being attempted, at least in certain areas, is difficult—not only because the burros are wily and prolific, but also because considerable amounts of human sentiment are generated in their behalf, often causing problems when their elimination or reduction is proposed. To a limited extent, in Death Valley, where they are rapidly increasing, burros are currently being trapped, then removed and domesticated by California residents who apply to receive them. In one recent year, approximately 100 burros were taken from the valley to homes elsewhere.

The list of Death Valley's pressured animals extends from bighorn to small fish. The approximately two-inch-long pupfish of Death Valley National Monument are a relict population from a moister past. The pupfish live in small, often very saline bodies of water in which temperatures fluctuate greatly on an annual basis, reaching high levels during summer months. Five species of pupfish occur in the

Monument: (1) Amargosa pupfish, *Cyprinodon nevadensis amargosae*, of the Amargosa River; (2) Saratoga Springs pupfish of that springs, *C. n. nevadensis;* (3) Salt Creek pupfish, *C. salinus;* (4) Cottonball Marsh pupfish, *C. milleri;* and (5) Devil's Hole pupfish, *C. diabolis*. The Devil's Hole species is considered endangered, and legal controversies have flared and continue to flare over it. It is found in that single spring at Ash Meadows, Nevada, a body of water measuring approximately fifteen by forty feet. President Truman issued a Presidential Proclamation which added Devil's Hole to the Death Valley National Monument in order to preserve the species. Since that time, private pumping of groundwater for irrigation in the area has caused the water level of the spring to fluctuate, threatening the species. A recent United States Supreme Court decision upheld an earlier ruling stating that the water level in the spring must be maintained at a certain required level. Should it drop below that point, pumping in the area must be stopped.

Death Valley's five species of fish, unlikely as their presence may seem in the United States' hottest, driest area, are joined by three species of another unlikely type—the amphibians: red-spotted toad, *Bufo punctatus;* bullfrog, *Rana catesbeiana;* and tree frog, *Hyla sp.* Thirty-six reptiles, seventeen of them snake species, occur in the Monument, including the Mohave Desert sidewinder, *Crotalus cerastes*

FIG. 32. Approximately 22 species of wood rats, or pack rats, *Neotoma,* are found from northwestern Canada to Central America. These rats vary from about 12 to 16 inches, including tail, and build large nest–homes of piles of debris. Desert species readily incorporate cactus pieces into their nests; they also consume a great deal of cactus which supplies moisture.

cerastes; Panamint rattler, *Crotalus mitchelli stephensi;* Utah black-headed snake, *Tantilla planiceps utahensis;* desert rosy boa, *Lichanura trivirgata gracia;* and western blind snake, *Leptotyphlops humilis.* Over 300 species of birds have been recorded in the Monument, and fifty-three mammal species occur. These include several species of bats; a variety of species of mice; pygmy gopher, *Thomomys bottae;* four species of kangaroo rats, *Dipodomys sp.;* California meadow vole, *Microtus californicus;* pack rats, *Neotoma sp.;* blacktail jackrabbit, *Lepus californicus;* cottontail rabbit, *Sylvilagus audubonii;* ringtail cat, *Bassariscus astutus;* spotted skunk, *Spilogale putorius;* antelope ground squirrel, *Ammospermophilus leucurus;* kit fox, *Vulpes macrofis;* gray fox, *Urocyon cinereoargenteus;* coyote, *Canis latrans;* bobcat, *Lynx rufus;* mountain lion, *Felis concolor;* mule deer, *Odocoileus hemionus;* and wild horses. Despite its name, this valley and its surrounding area appear to hold more life than death.

The Joshua tree, *Yucca brevifolia,* popular symbol of the Mohave Desert, is the object of varying emotions. An early traveler through the Mohave called them "dagger trees," the Mormons christened them "Joshua trees," and Captain John C. Fremont described them as "the most repulsive tree in the vegetable kingdom." Certainly this tree yucca is the distinctive ecological dominant in the area in which it occurs, yet its pattern of occurrence is disjunct. For although the range of the Joshua tree follows rather closely the boundaries set for the Mohave Desert, this plant occurs typically only along the higher edges of the desert. As one moves outward from the mountains to lower elevations, the Joshua trees become smaller and fewer. Eventually, stands of creosote bush, with associated species, become the dominant vegetation. Communities of creosote and bursage, *Franseria dumosa,* reminiscent of large portions of the Sonoran Desert's landscape, actually cover approximately 70 percent of the surface of the Mohave Desert. In the ecosystems dominated by Joshua trees, however, the finest, most interesting development of the Mohave Desert's flora and fauna occurs.

Some of the prime stands of the Joshua tree occur in Joshua Tree National Monument. In this area, the trees, their accompanying plant species, and interrelated animal species have been protected and well studied. The Monument is located in southeastern California, well south of Death Valley, and just east of the San Bernardino Mountains, which form a portion of the edge of the Mohave Desert. The Monument, 872 square miles in area, lies along the junction of the Mohave Desert to the north (of which it is a part) and the Colorado section of the Sonoran Desert to the south. Rainfall averages approximately 4 to 4¼ inches per year over much of the lower area, most received during December and January, with occasional scattered storms occurring from July to October. The Joshua trees require more moisture than this limited amount. They grow at higher elevations where increased precipitation is received and where runoff from adjoining, even higher elevations, reaches them. The range of the Joshua trees was once greater, when moisture in the area of the Mohave was more plentiful.

Although the Joshua tree habitat is of primary interest in this desert area, other dominant plants exist in portions of the Monument and the surrounding desert. Creosote bush belts occur at lower elevations, up to approximately 3,000 feet; yuccas dominate from 3,000 to approximately 4,200 feet; above that lies a piñon belt. A study of the vertebrate animals of the Monument by Alden H. Miller and Robert C. Stebbins of the University of California at Berkeley listed species members of some of these habitats. For the Monument as a whole, including the piñon belt, they recorded a total of 5 species of amphibians, 36 reptiles, 167 birds, and 42 mammals.

The creosote-bush habitat covers expanses of the valleys and alluvial fans of the Monument; regularly occurring animals include the Merriam kangaroo rat, *Dipodomys merriami;* desert tortoise, *Gopherus agassizi;* antelope ground squirrel, *Ammospermophilus leucurus;* and the black-throated sparrow, *Amphispiza bilineata.* Some communities are dominated by Bigelow cholla cactus, *Opuntia bigelovii.* Among the animals Miller and Stebbins listed as occurring in these cactus communities are black-throated sparrows; house finches, *Carpodacus mexicanus;* and particularly wood or pack rats, *Neotoma sp.,* which often incorporate quantities of cholla joints in the exterior of their house–mounds. Along the washes, other communities occur.

F I G . 33. The Gambel, or desert, quail, *Lophortyx gambelii* (10 to 11½ inches) is a plump, chickenlike bird. The body is gray with markings of buff, chestnut, and white; the male has a black throat and belly. A particularly striking slender topknot of dark feathers curves forward from the top of the head. These birds come to water when it is available, but derive much of the moisture they need from green plant foods.

Smoke trees, *Dalea spinosa;* desert willows, *Chilopsis linearis;* catclaw, *Acacia greggii;* and mesquite, *Prosopis sp.,* all grow in this more moisture-favorable environment. Birds are attracted to the tree habitat, including verdins, *Auriparus flaviceps;* phainopepla, *Phainopepla nitens;* roadrunner, *Geococcyx californianus;* Costa hummingbirds, *Calypte costae;* and mockingbird, *Mimus polyglottos.* Occasional oases occur, allowing a growth but of water plants; cottonwood trees, *Populus fremontii;* mesquites; willows; and California fan palms, *Washingtonia filifera.* Many species of animals are drawn to the oases for both water, plant food, and prey. Among these species are the hooded oriole, *Icterus cucullatus;* Bullock oriole, *Icterus bullockii;* song sparrow, *Melospiza melodia;* brown towhee, *Pipilo fuscus;* mourning dove, *Zenaidura macroura;* mountain quail, *Oreortyx pictus;* Gambel quail, *Lophortyx gambelii;* house finch; coyote; mule deer; mountain sheep; and several species of bats.

Despite Fremont's opinion, many people do not find the Joshua tree ugly, though it does differ greatly from the more familiar trees of Fremont's moister home territory. The

Joshua tree is a tree-sized yucca. All yuccas are members of the lily family, though their grizzled exterior would seem to belie the family relationship. Yuccas are shrubs or trees which develop from a *caudex,* or stem base, and are sometimes branched. They have clusters of sharp-pointed, long, narrow, stiff, bayonetlike leaves, which, when dead, may form a *shag,* or "skirt," about the trunk or branch. The Joshua tree normally has a single trunk which often branches a short distance above the ground. The end of each terminal branch is encircled by a mass of leaves. Eventually, a flower cluster is produced at the branch terminus. Following blossoming, the branch forks. Other factors, such as insect damage to the tip, may also cause a branching. In time, the many-limbed yucca assumes tree form.

The Joshua tree may reach thirty feet, or occasionally even forty feet, in height; one has been recorded as having a diameter of four feet. The bark resembles a corky rind, rough and broken by fissures. The trunk interior contains no solid cylinder of wood, hence no growth rings; rather, it is composed of pith, which may eventually disintegrate to some degree, leaving a partially hollow cylinder. Large, branched clusters of blossoms appear in the spring; each individual flower is 1½ to 2¾ inches in length. These blossoms are dull-green to cream in color; they open for a single night, and bear an odor likened to mushrooms. The fruit is a large six-celled pod with compressed, thin, black seeds. The roots extend both vertically (although not to any great depth) and horizontally; new trees often grow from underground runners.

Joshua trees form "forests" in which they are joined by such other plants as sagebrush; creosote bush; desert shrub, *Tetradymia spinosa;* goldenhead, *Acamptopappus sphaer-ocephalus;* and others. Also occurring in the Mohave Desert is another important species of yucca, smaller than the Joshua tree—the Mohave yucca, *Yucca schidigera.* The Joshua trees, as the dominant and tallest species in their habitat, serve in varying ways as bases for animal life. One animal species exceedingly dependent upon these and other yuccas is the yucca moth, *Pronuba sp.*

The fertilization of flowers by insects inadvertently carrying pollen from one to another is a familiar story, but the *Pronuba–Yucca* relationship is deeper. The moth larvae de-

FIG. 34. The Joshua tree, *Yucca brevifolia*, is the largest yucca in the United States. This species' range is confined to the Mohave Desert. Clusters of leaves grow near the end of each branch, where the plant's clustered flowers are also produced. Following flowering on each individual branch, the branch then forks. These trees attain an average height of 20 to 30 feet but occasionally grow taller.

velop within the yucca fruit, devouring a portion of the developing yucca seeds. Through her actions, the female moth instinctively assures that seeds will develop for these young. When yucca flowers blossom, they are visited by the female *Pronuba*. Moving from one flower to another, the female moth gathers pollen which gradually forms into a large ball carried under her head. Moving to yet another flower, the moth climbs part way up the pistil, or female portion of the plant, inserts her ovipositor into the plant's ovary, and lays her eggs. Then she climbs to the top of the pistil and with her head rubs some of the pollen she carries into the flower's stigma. In so doing, she has achieved fertilization of the flower and insured seed production for her young. The larvae eat only part of the seeds, bore their way through the capsule wall, fall to the ground, enter it, and

FIG. 35. The desert night lizard, *Xantusia vigilis* (1½ to 1¾ inches, snout–vent length), is gray, olive, to dark brown, speckled with black. This small secretive lizard is often found under Joshua tree debris, but is also associated with other species of yuccas, agaves, cardon cacti, and occasionally ranges into the piñon–juniper belt.

remain there until the following year, when they emerge as adults to repeat the process. This behavior is indeed remarkable, for the moth collects a material for which she has no direct need and uses this material to bring about a result she cannot perceive. The material gathered and the action undertaken are of no direct benefit to her, yet they benefit the species as a whole. Certainly her action benefits the yuccas also, which appear to be dependent on *Pronuba* for fertilization. This symbiotic relationship is so close that as different species of yuccas have evolved, so also have different associated species of *Pronuba* moths.

Another animal species very closely affiliated with the Joshua tree is the small desert night lizard, *Xantusia vigilis*, often referred to as the yucca night lizard. Only 1½ to 1¾ inches in snout-to-vent length plus tail, this lizard superficially resembles the geckos, the night-active lizards also having a rather velvety-appearing skin. Night lizards are yellow, gray to brown, with black speckling. They occur in desert areas from southern California, Nevada, and Utah to

Sonora and southern Baja California. The night lizard has achieved success in its desert environment by using the microhabitat provided by the Joshua tree. The lizard lives in the spiny branches and in and under the plants' litter or fallen branches. Shade, with attendant reduced temperatures; protection from dessication; protective cover from predators; food—all are provided for the night lizard in its tiny world by the tree, its debris, or the other creatures attracted to these. The lizard feeds on spiders, caterpillars, ants, beetles, crickets, termites, flies, and other moisture-filled food. *Xantusia vigilis* is also found associated with some other species of yuccas and occasionally with other plants, such as sagebrush, but the optimum conditions for this lizard are provided by the bulk of the Joshua tree and

FIG. 36. The Scott oriole, *Icterus parisorum* (7¼ to 8¼ inches), is a handsome bird. The male is lemon-yellow with a black head, wings, and tail; the female is a duller, greenish yellow. This oriole is often found in the Joshua tree forests, where its pouched nest hangs from these yuccas, although it also ranges into oak and piñon country.

FIG. 37. The ladder-backed, or Mexican, woodpecker, *Dendrocopos scalaris*, is small (6 to 7½ inches), cross-barred with black and white on the back, wings, and sides of the tail. The crown of the male's head is marked with red. It is the only woodpecker in the desert with a black-and-white-striped face. This bird drills holes in trees, agaves, and yuccas, including the Joshua trees.

36

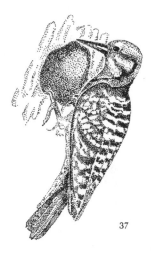

37

FIG. 38. The sparrow hawk, or American kestrel, *Falco spar-verius* (9 to 12 inches) is a small falcon, about the size of a jay. The species is found over most of North and South America. This beautiful bird is brownish, with a black-and-white face pattern; the males have blue–gray wings. Among its nesting sites are cavities in saguaro cacti.

its debris. Most often night active, as indicated by its name, *X. vigilis* is also sometimes active diurnally when conditions are favorable to it.

An interesting Joshua tree–animal association of times past was that of the plant with the extinct giant ground sloth, *Nothrotherium.* Fossilized sloth dung found in Gypsum Cave in 1930 near Las Vegas, Nevada, revealed that approximately 80 percent of the diet of those animals consisted of Joshua tree leaves.

Birds are among the great appreciators of the Joshua trees. The author Edmund C. Jaeger reports that at least twenty-five species of desert birds use the Joshua tree as nesting sites. Among these species is the Scott's oriole, *Icterus parisorum.* These beautiful birds breed from south-eastern California, southern Nevada, north-central New Mexico, and western Texas far south into Mexico. They live and breed in the Joshua tree country in summer, hanging nests constructed of yucca fibers from the Joshua trees. They feed from the flowers of this yucca, eat portions of the fruiting pods, and consume insects—all of which are mois-ture-rich.

The red-shafted flicker, *Colaptes cafer,* and the ladder-backed woodpecker, *Dendrocopos scalaris,* are among the birds excavating holes in the branches of the Joshua trees. Later, their abandoned holes are occupied by a good many other bird species, including the ash-throated flycatcher, *Myiarchus cinerascens;* western bluebird, *Sialia mexicanus;* and Bewick wren, *Thryomanes bewickii.* Other bird species use the Joshua trees as vantage points from which to search for prey. The screech owl, *Otus asio,* perches there by night, and the sparrow hawk, *Falco sparverius,* by day. The loggerhead shrike, *Lanius ludovicianus,* is one of the many species which may seek shade under the Joshua's spiny leaves.

Pack rats sometimes climb the Joshua trees and cut leaves from the plant. These they incorporate into their nests, which are sometimes constructed around the bases of the Joshua trees. Debris under these trees is also used as cover by other creatures—insect, reptile, and mammal.

FIG. 39. Cicadas (approximately 1 to 2 inches in length) "sing" loudly and shrilly by vibrating membranes stretched over a pair of sound chambers situated one on each side, near the base of the abdomen. This noise is often heard midday even on very hot days. Eggs are laid in twigs; the newly hatched young drop to the ground and burrow into it. Underground, the insect feeds on juices of plant roots. Later it emerges, hangs from a plant or object, the skin splits down the back, and the adult emerges.

FIG. 40. Unlike most lizards, the banded gecko, *Coleonyx variegatus,* is active at night, feeding on insects, spiders, and other arthropods. It is occasionally mistaken as the young of a Gila monster. Adult size is 4 to 6 inches.

39

40

FIG. 41. The great horned owl, *Bubo virginianus* (18 to 25 inches with a four-foot wingspread), is the only "horned" large North American owl and ranges from the tree limit in the Arctic to the Straits of Magellan in South America. Extremely adaptable, feeding largely on rabbits and rodents, the species lives in habitats as diverse as forests and deserts.

FIG. 42. The poor-will, *Phalaenoptilus nuttallii* (7 to 8½ inches) is a crepuscular bird (active at dawn and dusk) which catches insects while in flight. Its familiar song is heard at dusk in the desert. The bird's brownish coloring with delicate black markings affords it camouflage as it rests during the day on the ground or horizontally on limbs. Near Joshua Tree National Monument, this bird was first discovered to enter a state of winter torpor, its body temperature and oxygen usage greatly reduced during the period when its insect food supply is greatly reduced.

FIG. 43. The Le Conte thrasher, *Toxostoma lecontei* (10 to 11 inches), is a pale grayish-brown bird with a darker tail and a slender, curved beak. These birds are often found in flat, open desert, and spend much of their time foraging on the ground for insects.

FIG. 44. The verdin, *Aurtparus flaviceps*, is a very small (4 to 4½ inches) gray bird with a yellowish head, resident from southeastern California, southern Nevada and Utah, into New Mexico, Texas, and Mexico. Its enclosed nest consists of thorny twigs and is located in bushes or low trees. Entrance is gained through a vertical passage opening in the side of the nest.

The animal life in the Joshua tree habitat is, in fact, high in species. Miller and Stebbins reported four amphibian species, twenty-five reptiles, fifty birds, and twenty-eight mammals, all occurring in the Joshua tree community within the Monument.

Amphibians include the western toad, red-spotted toad, California treefrog, and Pacific treefrog. In the reptile group the desert tortoise occurs, as do ten species of lizards: the banded gecko, collared, leopard, chuckwalla, zebra-tailed, desert spiny, side-blotched, desert horned toad, night, and whiptail lizards. Snakes represented are the rosy boa, red racer, western patch-nosed, spotted leaf-nose, glossy, gopher, kingsnake, long-nosed, western shovel nose, night, California lyre, Mohave rattlesnake, speckled rattlesnake, and sidewinder.

The bird list is particularly long: the turkey vulture, red-tailed hawk, golden eagle, prairie falcon, sparrow hawk, Gambel quail, mountain quail, white-winged dove, mourning dove, roadrunner, barn owl, screech owl, great horned owl, elf owl, poor-will, lesser nighthawk, white-throated swift, red-shafted flicker, ladder-backed woodpecker, western kingbird, Cassin kingbird, ash-throated flycatcher, black phoebe, Say phoebe, horned lark, cliff swallow, raven, verdin, Bewick wren, cactus wren, canyon wren, rock wren, mockingbird, Bendire thrasher, Le Conte thrasher, blue-gray gnatcatcher, black-tailed gnatcatcher, phainopepla, loggerhead shrike, western meadowlark, hooded oriole, Scott's oriole, Bullock oriole, brown-headed cowbird, house finch, lesser goldfinch, Laurence goldfinch, brown towhee, black-throated sparrow, and the song sparrow are all found among the Joshua trees.

The mammal species represented include: four bats—the California myotis, western pipistrelle, big brown, and pallid; two rabbits—the Audubon cottontail and the black-tailed jackrabbit; the antelope ground squirrel; the Beechey ground squirrel; the pocket gopher; three species of pocket mice; the Merriam kangaroo rat; the western harvest mouse; the cactus mouse; deer mouse; grasshopper mouse; two species of wood or pack rat—the desert and the dusky-footed; the California vole; coyote; kit fox; gray fox; raccoon; badger; bobcat; and mountain sheep.

The list of species is impressively long. Consider though,

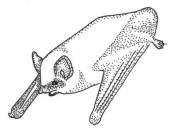

FIG. 45. The western pipistrelle, *Pipistrellus hesperus,* is the smallest bat in the United States and one of the smallest in the world. It has a forearm length of 1 to 1¹/₅ inches; body length of approximately 3 inches. This true desert bat is in some cases the only bat species found over vast creosote-bush areas. It varies in color from pale yellow to gray to reddish brown.

its potential length if invertebrate species also present in the Joshua tree habitat were included. Consider also the complexity of the habitat's food web and of other relationships between its living and nonliving components! Obviously, only the human species interprets the Mohave Desert as the home of both the devil and Joshua. Several hundred other species interpret it simply as home—and a very satisfactory one at that!

CHAPTER VIII

The Chihuahuan Desert

MAPS provide interesting reading, particularly maps of the Chihuahuan Desert where place names in English and Spanish give clues to the type of country and something of its history. Dog Canyon, Grave Pit, Elephant Tusk, Backbone Ridge, Cow Heaven Mountain, and Sotol Vista Overlook appear in English, as do Mule Ears Overlook, Dogie Mountain, Maverick Mountain, Adobe Walls Mountain, and Fossil Knob. Across the border appear euphonious Spanish names, such as Laguna Grande and Bolson de los Muertos (Bolson of the Dead). In Spanish, the word *sierra* often appears, as do the words "mountain" and "peak" in English. Other names indicate the numerous scattered points of higher elevation: Juniper Canyon, Pine Canyon, Lost Mine Peak, Panther Peak. Three dotted lines running north to south through maps of this desert bear perhaps the most ominous labels: the Eastern, Middle, and Western Comanche Trails. Obviously the Chihuahuan Desert was not tame, flat, green land when it was given these names. Nor is it today. Most of this desert lies in Mexico, is difficult of access, and is less familiar and less thoroughly studied than the desert lands of the United States. In this very isolation lies a good deal of the fascination of the Chihuahuan Desert.

The Rockies and associated ranges divide the North American continent, sweeping from Canada through Mexico. The lowest point of this ridge is located in southeastern Arizona and southwestern New Mexico. No majestic peaks loom over this area of high plain, dotted with small mountains. Desert grassland covers it; to the east lies the northern portion of the Chihuahuan Desert. To the west is the Sonoran. This elevated plain is of sufficient altitude to prevent the two deserts from being contiguous, but is low enough to allow certain plant species to make the crossing from one to the other; hence, small areas in southeastern Arizona resemble the Chihuahuan and are indeed often referred to by some authorities as Chihuahuan Desert.

Limited portions of southern New Mexico and southwestern Texas are Chihuahuan Desert. Over 90 percent of this desert, however, is in Mexico, south of Texas and New Mexico. In Mexico, Chihuahuan Desert covers the lower elevations of the states of Zacatecas, Durango, Nuevo León, and San Luis Potosí. The Mexican portion of this desert primarily occupies a vast intermountain plateau. The Continental Divide regains altitude and grandeur south of the United States–Mexico border, forming the great Sierra Madre Occidental range, which extends north to south in western Mexico. A similar range, the Sierra Madre Oriental, flows north to south in eastern Mexico. These immense mountain ranges, each approximately 800 miles in length and more than 100 miles in breadth, have peaks up to 12,000

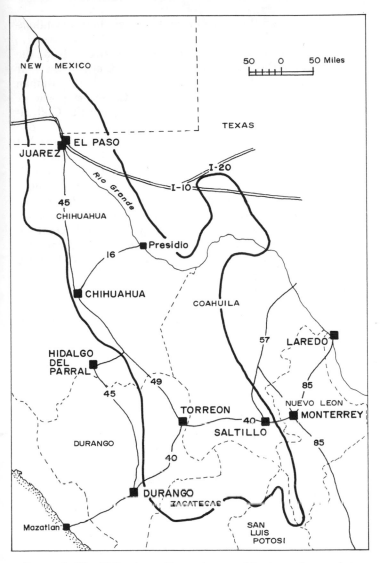

FIG. 46. The Chihuahuan Desert is second in size and extends to the lowest southern latitudes of the four North American deserts. This desert is located primarily in Mexico with small portions extending into New Mexico and Texas.

The Chihuahuan Desert

feet in elevation. Between these two ranges lies the Chihuahuan Desert plateau.

The Chihuahuan Desert is second in size only to the Great Basin Desert and is the most southern of the four North American deserts, extending even further south than the Sonoran Desert's southerly Baja California portions. Due to its plateau location, elevations within the Chihuahuan Desert lie primarily above 3,500 feet. Forrest Shreve outlined the physical conditions of this desert. He states that a small percentage of the desert along the Rio Grande lies below 3,000 feet; nearly half of the desert is above 4,000 feet; some of it extends to over 6,000 feet. Precipitation ranges from three to twenty inches, 70 to 80 percent of this occurring between mid-June and mid-September. Summer temperatures average ten to twenty degrees lower than those of the Sonoran Desert. Winter temperatures may reach low levels, with periods of up to seventy-two hours of freezing temperatures. Therefore, although the Chihuahuan Desert lies at rather low southern latitudes, it is of sufficient elevation and receives sufficient of its moisture during the hottest months when it is most needed to have the "desert condition" somewhat ameliorated.

In addition to the two main mountain masses which outline the eastern and western borders of this desert, numerous lesser mountain ranges with a general north–south orientation jut from the plateau–desert. Notable areas of limestone are found in this desert, and the Sierra Madre Oriental range is composed largely of limestone. Both the limestone and significant deposits of gypsum greatly influence the species of vegetation growing in these locations. The Rio Grande cuts through the northern reaches of the Chihuahuan Desert, providing the most spectacular piece of United States' Chihuahuan Desert in the western Texas Big Bend area—so-called for the lengthy loop in the Rio Grande at that point. This river receives drainage from a portion of the northeastern Chihuahuan Desert; thus water from this desert, unlike that from the other three North American deserts, flows eastward toward the Gulf of Mexico. However, much of the Chihuahuan, like the other three deserts, lacks outlet to the sea and a great deal of the runoff is directed into vast undrained basins, or bolsons.

Summer rain and cold winter temperatures result in a

single growing–blossoming season; in this desert, summer-blooming ephemerals, rather than those which bloom in late winter or early spring, assume prime importance. The creosote bush is a familiar dominant in many areas of this shrubby desert. Cacti are more prominent than in the Great Basin and Mohave deserts, but do not assume the importance they do in the Sonoran Desert. *Opuntia* species are well represented, some barrel cacti are present, and smaller cacti species—such as the hedgehogs and mammillarias—are numerous. Large columnar cacti are found only in the extreme southern portions. Trees are relatively few and small, confined largely to waterways or rocky hills. The mesquites, *Prosopis,* are one of the main species represented. The Chihuahuan Desert abounds in the leaf-succulent plants, such as agaves, and the semi-succulents, such as yuccas.

As the Great Basin has its sagebrush, the Mohave its Joshua tree, and the Sonoran its saguaro as popular symbols, the Chihuahuan is most noted for the agave known as lechuguilla, *Agave lecheguilla.* This agave grows in great masses or mats over the arid mesas and limestone hills; where it occurs in crowded profusion, it constitutes in a good many human minds a pest and one of the "afflictions" of the desert, jabbing legs and ankles of man and beast, causing a sharp, lingering pain, and capable of severely injuring horses' legs and hooves. This character would seem to belie the generic name of these plants, *Agave,* from the Greek word meaning "noble" or "admirable." Common names for various species of agaves include maguey, amole, mescal, century plant (erroneously thought to blossom only after 100 years of growth), and lechuguilla (diminutive of *lechuga,* or little lettuce).

The agaves are succulent-leaved to varying degrees. The leaves are arranged in a basal rosette on the ground around a very short stem, are evergreen, tough, narrow, long, and thick. Each leaf ends in a short, sharp, terminal spine; often lesser spines, prickles, or threads grow along their margins. After a life span of several years, each agave blooms a single time, then dies. At blossoming, a naked, tall flower stalk is quickly produced, which bears numerous succulent flowers in its upper portions. Occasionally agaves are confused with yuccas. Yuccas usually have trunks, whereas the agaves in

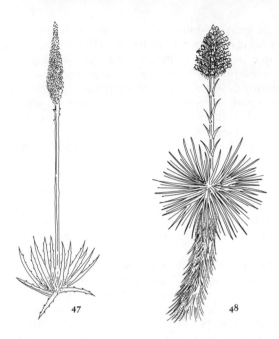

47

48

FIG. 47. The lechuguilla, *Agave lecheguilla,* is the symbol of the Chihuahuan Desert where it is exceedingly abundant on arid mesas and limestone cliffs. The individual leaves are approximately 8 to 16 inches in length, each with a terminal spine. The flower stalk reaches 6 to 13 feet in height.

FIG. 48. *Yucca elata* is a handsome plant with a trunk from 6 to 15 feet high, which may have two or three branches. The leaves are ten to twenty-four inches long, narrow, and thin. When dead, they bend downward to lie along the branch. A panicle of white flowers is produced from a naked flowering stalk.

most species grow at ground level; agave leaves are larger and succulent; and the agaves die after their single blossoming, whereas the yuccas do not. Agaves produce seeds in three-celled capsules, but also grow by means of underground sprouts; hence, where favorable conditions prevail, the agaves may grow in vast colonies, as in the case of the Chihuahua's lechuguilla.

Agaves as a group have long been important to man. The leaves are a source of fiber. Industrial alcohol, as well as such alcoholic drinks including mescal, tequilla, and pulque are derived from them. Soap is made from the stems of some species. Indians of Mexico and the United States prized the central stem, crown, or head of the plant as a food. They buried the crown in a stone-lined, previously heated pit where it baked for many hours before being eaten.

Agaves are prominent plants wherever they occur. The lechuguilla is prominent, not so much because of is size, which is relatively small by agave standards, but because of its numbers. *Agave lecheguilla* has ten to thirty leaves, each approximately eight to sixteen inches in length and 1 to 1½ inches in width. These leaves are armed with spines along the margins and with a terminal spine. The flower stalk, when produced, is six to thirteen feet in height; flowers are greenish- or yellowish-white and may sometimes be tinged with purple. The plant occurs up to elevations of approximately 5,000 feet, and ranges from southeastern New Mexico and southwestern Texas south into Mexico, in an area fairly coincident with the borders of the Chihuahuan Desert.

Yuccas, too, form an important element in the vegetation of portions of the Chihuahuan Desert. Among others, these include *Yucca filfera, Y. torreyi, Y. carnerosana,* and *Y. elata. Yucca carnerosana* is a very large branching yucca, which in some ways closely resembles the Joshua tree. *Yucca elata* is a fairly large yucca reaching to fifteen feet in height, usually with two or three branches. Its leaves are ten to twenty-six inches in length, only ⅛ to ⁵/₁₆ inch wide, thin, and flexible, with the dead ones reflexing and forming a shag along the branches. This species is found in the Sonoran Desert also, and in the desert grasslands. It is notable for its ability to grow in White Sands—the area of immense drifting dunes of gypsum in southeastern New Mexico. *Yucca elata* is a pioneer plant in these areas which are composed of up to 94 percent granular gypsum. Its roots grow deep, and its upper portions often strive to keep head above drifting dune; thus these plants manage to grow in this location; by their eventual death and decay they help pave the way for other plant species, which use the decayed organic material of the yuccas. Gypsum holds moisture well, retaining much that it receives; hence *Y. elata* finds moisture but very little else to promote its well-being in these spectacular dunes, located near Alamogordo, New Mexico, and now protected as White Sands National Monument.

Agaves are members of the amaryllis family, while yuccas belong to the lily family. The lily family also includes a plant similar in appearance to the yuccas, the sotol, *Dasylirion sp.*, sometimes commonly referred to as desert spoon because the base of its leaf resembles a spatula–spoon in shape. Sotol are large plants with a subterranean stem, or one which extends above the ground for only a short distance. The leaves are linear, elongated, ribbonlike, are not spine-tipped, but have prickled edges, and are often numerous, numbering into the hundreds. The flowers are small, whitish, numerous, and produced in an elongate plume atop the flower stalk. This stalk emerges from the center of the leaf cluster and may reach seven to eight feet in height. As with its near relatives, the plant was used by Indians for fibers, and the flower stalks were roasted and eaten, as was, occasionally, the pulp of the trunk. Yet another member of the lily family represented in the Chihuahuan Desert are plants of the genus *Nolina*, in some areas referred to as "bear's grass." These, too, bear a similarity to the yuccas, although they usually appear more grasslike.

One of the interesting Chihuahuan plants is candelilla, *Euphorbia antisyphillitica.* This plant is made up of numerous, pencil-thin, pale-green, waxy stems which contain a milky sap. The stems are practically leafless and closely bunched; the plant reaches one to three feet in height. The wax may be removed from the stems by boiling them in water to which sulfuric acid has been added. The wax, skimmed off the top, can be sold for use in floor waxes and chewing gum; collecting this wax is a part-time occupation of some Mexican citizens.

The guayule, *Parthenium argentatum,* like the candelilla, is a plant of the limestone areas and is yet another distinctive plant of the Chihuahuan Desert. This low-branching shrub with narrow, silvery leaves has stems which yield a high percentage of rubber when processed; the plant was, for a time, cultivated in the United States for that purpose.

Certainly two of the very characteristic plants of the Chihuahuan Desert, also found in other North American deserts, are the creosote bush and the ocotillo, *Fouquieria splendens.* Creosote is the ubiquitous, drought-resistant,

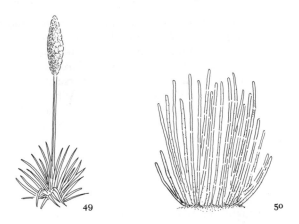

49

50

FIG. 49. Sotol, *Dasylirion sp.*, is a large plant resembling yuccas and species of *Nolina*. Flowers of the sotol are produced in dense panicles.

FIG. 50. The candelilla, *Euphorbia antisyphillitica*, is a plant of the Chihuahuan Desert. The numerous stems from 1 to 3 feet in height are clustered and appear almost leafless. The stems are wax-covered; hence another common name is waxplant.

enduring plant widespread throughout the three southern deserts; the northern line along which it disappears is, in general, the southern boundary of the Great Basin Desert. In Mexico, creosote bush is given the common name *hediondilla*, or literally "little stinker." The name refers to the plant's odor. Particularly when dampened by a shower or when its leaves are crushed, the plant gives off an odor somewhat reminiscent of creosote. Actually, a good many desert-oriented individuals find the odor quite pleasing, often associating it with the arrival of moisture in the desert. Yet another common Mexican name is *gobernador*, or governor, referring to its dominance over vast areas.

The creosote bush has no main trunk, but rather several or many main branches which arise from a root crown. The many branches and their lateral twigs bear numerous small, evergreen, resin-coated, moisture-conserving leaves. Under moisture stress many, but not all, of the leaves are lost. Following rains, the bush produces many small yellow flowers which become white, hairy seed capsules. The plant may reach twelve feet in height under favorable conditions. More often it is three to six feet tall. The bushes are widely spaced, each sucking up moisture for some distance around itself. The intervening spaces are often dotted by one or two smaller plant species. The creosote sparsely covers areas where nothing or little else will grow. When moisture is occasionally available, the plant uses it liberally, but has a remarkably well-developed ability to cut back and simply endure when conditions are not propitious. Under such conditions, its color is a pronounced olive-gray and its normal, ethereal, nonsubstantial appearance becomes increasingly less substantial. Its shade is thin, but nonetheless shade for small creatures; its foliage is relished by only a relatively few animals, but feeds some; its roots help hold the desert earth in place and provide neat, reinforced areas under which small animals may dig their burrows; its flimsy branches provide perches for birds; ground squirrels and lizards climb into it on occasion; small things can hide from birds of prey under it; and, for humans, the desert would be a much duller, more stark habitat without it.

The ocotillos are among the most distinctive plants of the

FIG. 51. The white-footed mice, *Peromyscus sp.* (approximately 7 to 10 inches in total length), are the most widespread rodents in North America, occurring in forests, woodlands, grasslands, and deserts; they live below sea level in Death Valley. They are small to medium-sized mice with soft fur, long whiskers, and a tail not less than one-third the length of the mouse.

FIG. 52. The desert pocket mouse, *Perognathus penicillatus* (approximately 7 inches in length), is one of several species of pocket mice found in the desert. These nocturnal burrow-dwellers store and eat seeds.

51   52

Sonoran and Chihuahuan deserts. The plant consists of numerous stems, often approximately twenty-five to thirty or more. These straight, normally unbranched stems arise from a short crown, and are approximately ten to twelve feet in length, or occasionally longer. The result is a stiff-looking, fanned-out, stick arrangement, the total group forming an inverted cone shape. The stems are dull gray-green and armed with spines their entire length, each spine having developed from the petiole of a shed leaf. Much of the year, the branches remain leafless. However, within a few days following a shower, the plant produces a new crop of small, green leaves; these are borne up and down the length of each stem. When moisture once again becomes scarce, the leaves are quickly shed. Several crops of leaves thus may be produced each year. The ocotillos' orange-red flowers are borne on the upper portion of each stem and are often produced when no leaves are present on the plant. The individual stems have long been used in wattle-and-daub construction in the Southwest and Mexico and are sometimes closely planted to form a living fence. The individual stems root and produce leaves following showers, but never branch to form complete plants.

Two smaller, but widespread plants of the Chihuahuan Desert are the varnish leaf acacia, *Acacia vernicosa,* a spiny, low shrub often found on the Chihuahuan Desert plains; and the tar bush, black brush, or hojase, *Flourensia cernua,* a shrub three to six feet high, common on limestone soils in the Chihuahuan Desert.

The area covered by the Chihuahuan Desert is vast. It is bordered by high mountains on two sides and contains more mountains of considerable height within it. Animals which normally live some distance up the mountains thus often enter the desert to some extent. It is dotted by vast bolsons. Some contain dry alkaline lake beds. Others have water fed by springs; for example, Cuatro Cienegas contains a marsh supplied with gypsum-rich water from thermal springs. Water, or lack of it, or the quality of it, affects the biota greatly. A major river (although now much emasculated by irrigation use) enters the desert, influencing the animal life in that area. The plant life, too, is varied. The habitat possibilities in this desert are therefore exceedingly numerous, and the animal species and possible interrelationships between the

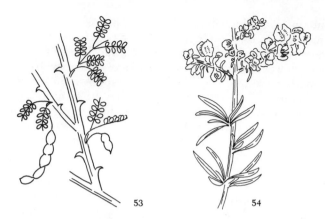

53   54

FIG. 53. Catclaw, *Acacia greggii,* is a shrub or small tree to 23 feet in height and 8 inches in trunk diameter. It is much branched with a broad crown. Fragrant yellow flowers are produced in dense clusters. The spines, which are treacherous and will tear clothing or flesh when they are inadvertently snagged, give the plant its common name.

FIG. 54. The salt bush *Atriplex canescens* is a shrub 3 to 6 feet high which grows on moderately alkaline slopes in both the sage-brush and creosote bush deserts in addition to desert grassland and oak woodland. Its range from eastern Oregon to North Dakota and south into Mexico makes it the most widely distributed species of its genus in the United States.

FIG. 55. Mormon tea, *Ephedra sp.* (often averaging 3 to 4 feet in height), is a low plant with slender, bunched, jointed stems which appear to be leafless; actually, the leaves have been reduced to scales. This primitive-type plant has conelike flowers; female and male flowers grow on different individual plants.

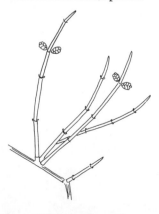

individual animals, the species, and their environments are staggering to imagine.

One area of the Chihuahuan Desert which has been studied and reported upon is that of Big Bend National Park, among the largest of the national parks in the United States, covering 1,106 square miles. Its southern border is the Rio Grande where the river bends first to the southeast, then to the northeast. The confines of the park stretching to the north includes typical Chihuahuan Desert country, as well as mountains rising out of the desert to a maximum elevation of approximately 7,800 feet. Officials have compiled checklists of the animal species which occur in the park. Admittedly, some of these are found in the higher eleva-

FIG. 56. The kit fox, *Vulpes macrotis* (approximately 30 inches in total body length), is well adapted for life in the hot, arid desert. Chiefly nocturnal, it sleeps in shade or underground dens during hot periods. Its yellowish-buff hair blends into the desert background at night, the large ears aid it in locating rodent prey, which provides it not only with food but with much of the moisture it needs; and the bottoms of its feet are covered with long fur as an adaptation to the sandy soil.

tions, yet inasmuch as desert terrain is the primary type in the park, these numbers give a good indication of the richness of the desert life. Ten amphibian species have been recorded in the park, 55 reptile species, 382 bird species, and 75 mammal species. Included among the reptile species are four rattlesnakes: Mohave, *Crotalus scutulatus;* western diamond-back, *Crotalus atrox;* rock rattlesnake, *Crotalus lepidus;* and the black-tailed, *Crotalus molossus.* Only in this one of the four North American deserts does the secretive copperhead, *Agkistrodon contortrix,* dwell.

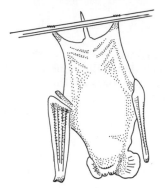

F ig . 57. The Mexican free-tailed bats, Brazilian free-tailed, or guano bats, *Tadarida brasiliensis* (forearm length of 1½ to 1¾ inches; body length approximately 4 inches), live in immense colonies in caves of the southwestern United States. This species is the famous inhabitant of Carlsbad Caverns. Dark brown to dark gray in color, this bat is rather small with long, narrow wings. Its name derives from the fact that the lower half of the tail is free from the interfemoral membrane.

Among the larger mammals represented are those found ranging over at least some of the other deserts and often other habitats as well: coyote, peccary, mule deer, black-tailed jackrabbit, Audubon cottontail, kit fox, gray fox, badger, ringtailed cat, bobcat, bats of several species, and an occasional mountain lion. Bighorn sheep are occasionally reported, and pronghorn, once plentiful in the Chihuahuan, are represented in limited number.

The Chihuahuan is a challenging, interesting, beckoning desert to the admirer of dry lands. Some of us who include ourselves in that group, however, regret that we did not experience it earlier. In the last 150 years in the Chihuahuan Desert, modern man has greatly reduced the pronghorn and bighorn, practically eliminated the wolf, tamed the Rio Grande, and subdued the Comanches. One wonders—what will he be able to achieve for the Chihuahuan and its three related North American deserts in the next century and a half?

CHAPTER IX

The Sonoran Desert

OF THE FOUR North American deserts, the Sonoran is the hottest overall, and holds the North American record for the site with least annual average precipitation. Yet represented within it are more plant life forms, more types of cacti, and more species of plants and animals than in any of the other three. As a whole, the Sonoran Desert represents the "cream" of deserts. A variety of reasons explain the diversity of life within this so-called deserted land.

Lying like a horseshoe around the head of the Gulf of California, this desert is an elongated area spanning eleven degrees of latitude, reaching as far south as 24 degrees north latitude. The Sonoran is a large desert covering 120,000 square miles and is approximately 870 miles long and 400 miles across at its widest point. In terms of political boundaries, it covers extreme southeastern California, southwestern and south-central Arizona, the western half of Sonora, and the lowlands of Baja California. Elevations increase as one moves from west to east across it. Those within the desert are chiefly below 2,000 feet, but range from 235 feet below sea level to 3,450 feet above. Latitude and elevation in varying combinations produce a range of climatic conditions, including areas which receive snow almost every winter to those that are frost-free. Forrest Shreve reports that, not uncommonly, parts of the Sonoran have ninety consecutive days with a maximum temperature of 100° F. Located not far south of Death Valley, portions of the Sonoran Desert share similar extremely high temperatures.

High mountains delineate portions of the desert's borders. Others rise above the desert surface, some to elevations great enough to sustain a mountain-related biota. Such mountains are tall enough to produce orographic lifting, causing rain to fall on their flanks and peaks, a great deal of which eventually drains to varying distances into the desert below. One of the primary factors in producing the range of plant species represented in the Sonoran Desert is the

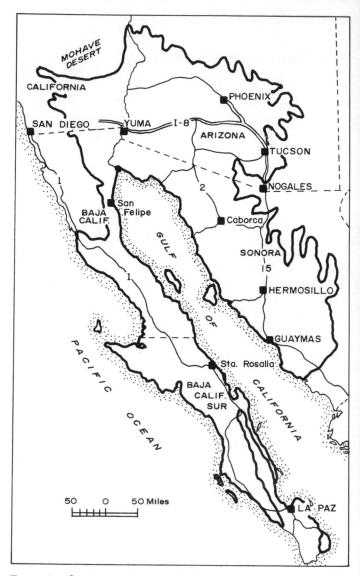

FIG. 58. The Sonoran Desert, third in size of the four North American deserts, covers much of southern Arizona, southeastern California, the Baja California peninsula, and the Mexican state of Sonora.

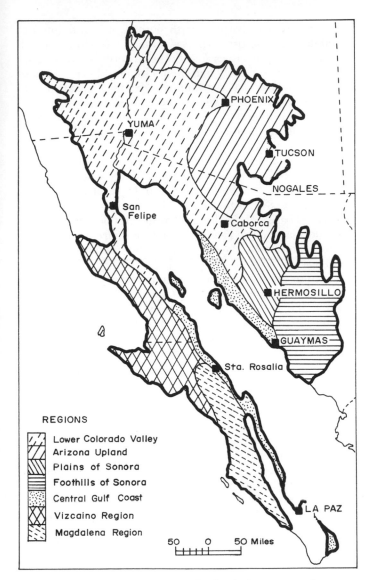

REGIONS

///	Lower Colorado Valley
|||	Arizona Upland
\\\	Plains of Sonora
≡	Foothills of Sonora
∴	Central Gulf Coast
XX	Vizcaino Region
////	Magdalena Region

50   0   50 Miles

FIG. 59. The Sonoran Desert can be divided into seven distinct subdivisions on the basis of vegetation.

biseasonal rainfall pattern, with both winter and summer precipitation. The proportion of summer to winter rainfall increases from west to east, with the eastern desert portions receiving approximately half their allotment in the summer and half in winter. Average annual precipitation varies from Bataques' record 1.2 inches to twelve to fourteen inches on the eastern border.

Much of the Sonoran Desert is within the basin-and-range province; however, this desert, more than the others, has developed a dendritic drainage pattern. The Colorado River bisects it, and several major rivers seasonally flow through it from the western flanks of the Sierra Madres to the Gulf. The Salton Sink, or Basin, is one of the few major undrained basins of the desert. The desert encircles the Gulf of California, and the Pacific Ocean forms part of the desert's western border in Baja California. Both bodies of water influence the adjoining dry land and its biota. With thorn forest to its south, mountains generally on its east and as a part of its western border, and a northern desert-type biota abutting it to the north, this desert presents plant and animal species possibilities of access at its edges; raw material for evolutionary adaptation to this particular desert's conditions has been abundant.

The total result of these many factors has been the development of an arboreal desert—seemingly, but not actually, a contradiction in terms. On the basis of vegetation, this desert is often broken into seven subdivisions. This classification is the work of Forrest Shreve, a foremost ecologist of the North American desert in general, and of the Sonoran Desert in particular. Much of the information we are presenting is available due to Shreve's exhaustive desert work. Shreve first divided the Sonoran Desert, giving each subdivision both a geographic and a vegetative-classificatory name according to the indicator vegetation in each: (See maps) (1) Lower Colorado Valley or *Larrea–Franseria* region; (2) Arizona Upland or *Cercidium–Opuntia* region; (3) Plains of Sonora or *Olneya–Encelia* region; (4) Foothills of Sonora or *Acacia–Prosopis* region; (5) Central Gulf Coast or *Bursera–Jatropha* region; (6) Vizcaino or *Agave–Franseria* region; and (7) Magdalena or *Lysiloma–Machaerocereus* region.

The Lower Colorado Valley is the largest, lowest, hottest,

and driest of the seven subdivisions. It lies around the head of the Gulf, extends northward to Needles, California, westward to approximately Indio, California, and eastward to Gila Bend, Arizona. On the Mexican mainland, one leg extends south along the Gulf coast for a long distance, then juts inland. A long narrow strip flows southward along the Baja Gulf coast to Bahia de los Angeles. The Gila River flows east to west across southern Arizona, terminating in the lower Colorado River, which empties into the head of the Gulf. The Lower Colorado Valley subdivision includes the valleys of the lower Gila and Colorado rivers.

Vast areas of this region consist of gently sloping bajadas, or plains, covered by *Larrea tridentata*, the creosote bush, and *Franseria dumosa*. Due to heat and aridity, these two drought-enduring standbys may form up to 95 percent of the plant cover present over these areas. *Franseria dumosa* is a small, hemispherical shrub approximately one foot in height with a maze of slender stems. The leaves are silvery green, giving rise to one common name, white bur sage. Another name is burro weed, or burro bush—burros are said to be fond of the plant. Often appearing dead, yet alive, white bur sage is the commonest plant—even more common than the creosote bush—in the driest, hottest areas of this part of the Sonoran Desert. Certainly whatever it lacks in appearance is more than compensated for by its tenacity and endurance.

Along dry washes in this region grow small trees. Primary species are mesquites, *Prosopis juliflora;* palo verdes, *Cercidium floridum;* ironwood, *Olneya tesota;* and smoke trees, *Dalea spinosa*. The mesquites are widespread, significant shrubs or trees of the southwestern deserts and semi-arid areas. Their long tap roots reach to moisture. These hardy trees produce long, straight, nonsplitting seed pods relished by animals and historically collected as a basic food source by many Indians. Their wood has brightened many a desert campfire, provided the posts for innumerable fences, and long served for construction in a wood-scarce land. Passed through the intestinal tracts of cattle, the seeds emerge digested only sufficiently to promote immediate germination. Mesquites have thus been ready-planted in often over-grazed rangeland, further deteriorating it and arousing ranchers' ire. To animals, however, the mesquite is a blessing.

The ironwood is a leguminous tree which occurs almost

entirely in the Sonoran Desert, but only in the warmer sections. The gray, rough bark and gray-green foliage make it a handsome, rugged-looking tree. Its blossoms are purple, produced in the late spring. The heart wood is dark and extremely hard—hence the name. It constitutes long-burning desert firewood without equal.

Palo verde (green stick) trees are named for their chlorophyll-bearing, yellow-green trunk and branches. Leaves, when produced during favorable moisture conditions, are exceedingly small and numerous; they are rapidly shed under moisture stress. Photosynthesis is conducted primarily by the trunk and branches. The so-called Mexican palo verde, *Parkinsonia aculeata*, bears long "streamers," portions of the primary leaflets. This species ranges southward to South America and is often planted as an ornamental around homes in desert country. The blue palo verde, *Cercidium floridum*, displays a blue-green color in the branches and leaves. This palo verde grows along the washes, where some underground water is available. In the spring, the tree is covered by masses of yellow flowers which provide spectacular desert scenery. A third palo verde is the foothill palo verde, *C. microphyllum*, its branches more yellow-green than those of the blue palo verde. The foothill palo verde grows above the washes on the bajada slopes. It, too, becomes a mass of bright yellow in the spring. The beans of the *Cercidium* were a food source for desert Indians.

FIG. 60. The handsome ironwood tree, *Olneya tesota*, attains a height of 10 to 30 feet. Its bark is gray, the leaves blue-green, and the peatype flowers are purple. The ironwood is a tree of lower, warmer elevations and occurs in southern California and Arizona, then south in Baja California and Sonora.

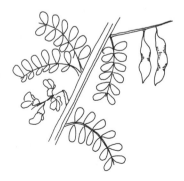

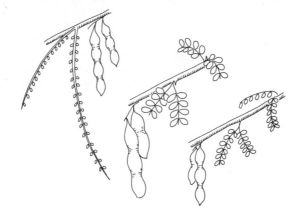

FIG. 61. Palo verde (green stick) trees have trunks and branches, green with chlorophyll, which carry on most of the photosynthesis for the plant. The small leaves are produced only when moisture conditions are favorable. The Mexican palo verde, *Parkinsonia aculeata* (left), is distinguished by its long narrow "streamers." The blue palo verde, *Cercidium floridum* (center), is a tree of the washes in the Sonoran Desert. The foothill palo verde, *Cercidium microphyllum* (right), is the species found on the bajadas and foothills in the same desert. *Parkinsonia* grows to approximately 45 to 50 feet; *Cercidium floridum* to about 30 feet; *Cercidium microphyllum* to about 26 feet.

Smoke trees grow only in frost-free areas of the Sonoran Desert. So adapted to the desert is this shrub or tree as to have practically dispensed with leaves. Much of the year, the plant stands bare of leaves, and its mass of sharp spine-tipped branches, ashy gray in color, gives rise to its similarity to a puff of smoke over a desert wash, and gives it its common name. The seeds of these trees, like those of some other desert-wash species, are extremely tough and must be abraded before germination is initiated. Germination occurs when moisture conditions are propitious for the plant's growth, as the seeds are tumbled about among the rocks and gravel of the wash during floods. The smoke tree blossoms with deep purple flowers in late May and June.

In the desert, as one ascends rocky slopes or bajadas away from the more level intermountain plains, the vegetational cover often reveals a change in character. The upper elevations, with more rock, provide better anchorage for plants

The Sonoran Desert

and better opportunity for water penetration. In the Lower Colorado Valley, as one leaves the *Larrea–Franseria* plains, palo verdes, ironwoods, ocotillos, barrel cacti, and other cacti species are found. Another plant which often occurs is *Encelia farinosa,* or brittlebush. This handsome plant is a hemispherical shrub usually one or two, occasionally three, feet in height. Its light green, oval leaves are produced twice a year following the two rainy seasons. The large yellow flowers, too, are borne twice a year on long, bare, projecting stems which display the flowers at their tips some distance above the outer limits of the remainder of the plant's vegetation. The green foliage, bright flowers, and composition of the plant as a whole make it most attractive, particularly against the dark lava rocks where it frequently grows.

An outstanding plant found in particular locations in this area is the fan palm, *Washingtonia filifera.* These palms grow in colonies of a few trees in isolated desert canyons in southern California, Baja California, and Mexico. A single colony exists in western Arizona in the Kofa Mountains. Palm trees must have quantities of water for survival, but can tolerate alkaline water well. They are found growing near springs in desert oases. The fan palms are large trees, attaining a height up to fifty feet, or occasionally more, with a trunk-base diameter up to 3½ feet. In the fan palms, the leaf blades are nearly circular in outline, and the divisions or splits in the blade extend half or two-thirds of the way to the base. The result is a palmate arrangement (unlike that of the date palm, a plant introduced and cultivated in southern California, whose leaf blade is elongated and pinnately arranged, divided all the way to the midrib). Old leaves of the fan palm hang downward along the trunk forming a heavy thatch. The tree produces small white male and/or female flowers in June which develop into a hard, blackish fruit. The leaves have long been useful to man who has used them for thatched roofs and walls; the fruit is edible. Certainly these trees and the accompanying springs or seeps serve as important gathering points for birds and other animal life which visit them.

In the Colorado Valley, vast carpets of ephemerals occur in favorable years. These displays primarily follow winter rains and are often outstanding, particularly in the sandy areas.

FIG. 62. The California fan palm, *Washingtonia filifera*, is the only palm tree native to the United States, although additional species occur in Mexico. This species may reach 50 or more feet in height. The leaves are fan-shaped; once dead, they hang in a thick thatch against the trunk below the green, living leaves. Palms grow only where water is available to them, but are tolerant of alkaline water.

The Lower Colorado Valley subdivision of the Sonoran Desert is particularly noted for its areas of sand dunes and its volcanic fields. The dunes occur near the head of the Gulf and in the area a short distance to the north, near Yuma, Arizona. Those near Yuma are known as Algodones (Cotton) Dunes; they extend approximately fifty miles in length and are about five miles wide. The other major group of dunes lies just to the east of the upper Gulf in Sonora. They bear the fitting and descriptive name El Gran Desierto. Most outstanding of the little eroded or degraded volcanic areas is the one surrounding Pinacate Peak, just east of El Gran Desierto. Both the dune and volcanic areas are extremely isolated, stark, beautiful desert.

The Arizona Upland is one of the very interesting subdivi-

FIG. 63. The saguaro cactus, *Cereus giganteus,* is the largest cactus found in the United States, reaching up to 50 feet in height, weighing as much as 8 to 10 tons, and living 150 to 200 years.

sions of the Sonoran Desert and one of the best studied. It includes the eastern half of Arizona's portion of the Sonoran Desert and extends well into northern Sonora. To the west and south, it abuts the Lower Colorado Valley subdivision. To its north and east lie mountains. With higher elevations, increased precipitation, and a more favoring biseasonal distribution of rainfall, plant growth is more diversified and plentiful in the Arizona Upland than in the Lower Colorado Valley region. The two genera with which this area is designated are *Cercidium,* the palo verdes, and *Opuntia,* genus of the prickly pear and cholla cacti. It is also referred to as a stem-succulent desert, acknowledging the important presence of these plants, particularly the saguaro cactus.

Saguaros, *Cereus giganteus,* are the symbol of the Sonoran Desert, although they do not occur throughout this desert. The range of the saguaro is primarily the confines of the Sonoran Desert east of the Colorado River and south into northern mainland Mexico. Only a few specimens occur in California, just across the Colorado River. This massive columnar cactus may reach forty feet or exceptionally more in height. It consists of a single, pleated, cylindrical trunk which throughout its length is spine-adorned along the ridges. When the plant reaches a height of approximately fifteen to twenty-five feet, it branches, often producing five or more "arms." These arms grow outward from the trunk briefly, then turn upward. A mature plant may weigh seven or eight tons, with three-fourths or more of its weight being water content. Flowers with white petals and yellow centers ring the tips of the individual arms and trunk in the spring. Each flower is pollinated by birds, bats, and insects on the single night and following day that it is open. A fruit is formed, which splits open to reveal a bright red pulp with one or two thousand tiny black seeds. Saguaros may survive for 150 to perhaps 200 years. Certainly each saguaro represents an important focal point around which the lives of many animal species revolve. So important did the Papago Indians find its fruit that their annual calendar started the new year with the Month of the Saguaro Fruit Ripening. The fruit was eaten fresh, cooked into a jam, or dried for later use; the seeds were ground for flour; the juice was fermented for an alcoholic beverage used in the dances and celebrations held partially as a measure to bring the summer rains. Today the Papagos continue to collect the saguaro fruit, although they arrive in the saguaro forests in automobiles or pickups rather than by horse or afoot. The best stands of these giant cacti are the forests protected by national monument status just outside Tucson, Arizona.

The Arizona Upland section of the Sonoran Desert contains numerous low mountain ranges and vast bajadas. Between these, on the flatter, gently sloping, lower plains, creosote bush and *Franseria sp.* dominate. But as one ascends the bajadas and hills, a richer mixture of vegetation prevails. Saguaros predominate due to their size. But the ocotillos, barrel cacti, prickly pear and cholla cacti, mesquites, palo verdes, and brittlebush are also present. In one small northwestern section where the Arizona Upland plant species meet and briefly mix with those of the Mohave Desert, saguaros and palo verdes grow beside Joshua trees, junipers, and oaks.

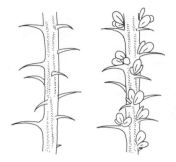

FIG. 64. The numerous straight, usually unforked branches of the ocotillo, *Fouquieria splendens*, arise from a short crown and resemble a stick bouquet reaching 8 to 12 or more feet in height. This plant rapidly produces leaves following a moderately heavy rain. Despite the spines, these plants are not cacti.

The Plains of Sonora subdivision joins the Central Gulf Coast and Lower Colorado Valley subdivisions on its western border, the Arizona Upland to the north, and the Foothills of Sonora subdivision to the east and south. Its species designation is *Olneya–Encelia*, or ironwood–brittlebush. This subdivision is dominated by trees and shrubs. In addition to ironwood, foothill palo verde and mesquite are important. Here a different species of palo verde is also found, *C. sonorae*, as is another species of ocotillo, *F. macdougalii*. Organ pipe cactus, *Lemaireocereus thurberi*, occurs. This large cactus has no main trunk; it branches with five to thirty-five branches at ground level. The plant may reach ten feet in height. The fruit is red, spine-adorned, about the size of a small tennis ball, and tastes a little like watermelon—it is eaten by man and animal. A second common name for this cactus is *pitaya dulce* (sweet pitaya). Also present is a similar-appearing cactus, *Lophocereus schottii*, known as old man cactus, or senita. This plant, too, branches at the ground and has several erect arms, but the arms are thicker-ribbed than those of the organ pipe; additionally, many coarse, hairlike spines around the tips of the stems give the old man a bearded look. The plant grows to twelve feet and produces bright red, practically spineless fruit.

The Foothills of Sonora constitutes the subdivision of the Sonoran Desert's mainland portion which extends the farthest south. So, too, it is the desert's easternmost extension. Called a tree desert, this area is labeled by Shreve as *Acacia–Prosopis. Prosopis* designates mesquite; *Acacia* refers to *Acacia cymbispina,* or espino. This acacia has a flat crown; the foliage is sparse. Also present are the Sonoran palo verde, ironwood, ocotillo, and torote blanco, or elephant tree—*Bursera odorata.* The comb cactus, *Pachycereus pecten-aboriginum,* is a large member of the plant community, more at home, really, in the thorn forests to the south, yet found in the Sonoran Desert. This cactus is heavy and columnar, up to forty feet in height, with many ascending branches, somewhat similar in form to the saguaro. The heavily spined fruits were used as combs by the natives; hence the plant's scientific and common names.

The Central Gulf Coast is a subdivision located on opposing portions of the Gulf coast, one on the mainland, the other on the peninsula. Both elongated strips share common vegetational characteristics. This subdivision is noted for its trees with trunks of large diameter and is designated by Shreve as the *Bursera–Jatropha* region.

F IG . 65. The organ pipe cactus, *Lemaireocereus thurberi,* is a large plant composed of numerous columnar branches 9 to 20 feet in height. This species barely enters the United States in southwestern Arizona. It ranges south in Baja California and Sonora.

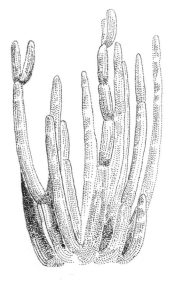

Bursera microphylla is the distinctive elephant tree, or torote. These trees have disproportionately thick trunks and main branches in relationship to their height, which is often six to ten feet and occasionally greater. The outer layer of the trunk's bark exfoliates in very large, curling pieces, exposing fresh yellow bark beneath. The foliage is dark green and evergreen. Another species of *Bursera* is also present and important in the vegetation—*Bursera hindsiana,* or copal, a shrub or small tree to ten feet in height.

Jatropha cinerea, or lomboy, is an abundant shrub or tree which may reach twenty feet in height. A member of the Euphorbiaceae, or spurge, family, lomboy has limber, smooth-barked branches. Its leaves are grayish green and are quickly produced following rain, then shed when dryness prevails.

The most distinctive plant of this subdivision is the boojum tree, or cirio, *Idria columnaris.* Cirio refers to the plant's similarity in appearance to a candle. The term "boojum" comes from Lewis Carroll's reference to a strange mythical plant growing on far-away shores. The boojum is a member of the family Fouquieriaceae, as is the ocotillo, and in many ways it closely resembles a single gigantic ocotillo branch. The boojum is a polelike tree, most often unbranched, which tapers in diameter toward the upper tip and may reach a height of seventy feet. Along the entire length of the trunk are many pencillike, tiny, short branches which bear the small leaves. As with the ocotillos, the boojum's leaves are produced following rains, and several crops a year may be grown. Occasionally some individual plants may branch, often near the top, serving only to increase the plant's bizarre appearance; occasionally, the tip of one bends back down to the ground to form an outlandish arch. Small tassels of tiny white flowers grow at the tip of the trunk or the branches. Great forests of these plants provide the strangest of desert landscapes. The boojums' range is exceedingly restricted; they are found only in Baja California; on Isla Angel de la Guarda, an island in the Gulf; and in one small location on the mainland across the Gulf from the main stands.

A good many of the species widespread over the Sonoran Desert, including creosote bush, ironwood, ocotillo, mesquite, palo verde, and brittlebush, are also present in the

FIG. 66. The boojum, *Idria columnaris*, is one of the most unusual plants of the desert. Related to the ocotillo, this plant consists of a single, stout column which occasionally forks near the
top. Along its trunk or main branches occur many very short, pencillike branches The plant may reach a height of 70 feet. It occurs
only on the Baja California peninsula and in a single small location
on mainland Mexico.

Central Gulf Coast region. Various species of cholla cacti are
abundant. The most distinctive cactus of this region, however, is the cardón, *Pachycereus pringlei*. This huge cactus is
similar in form to the saguaro, but more massive. The cardón
may reach sixty feet in height and weigh ten tons. Its many
arms, from five to thirty, branch from the trunk at a point
closer to the ground and are directed upward at a sharper
angle than those of the saguaro. Cardóns are thought to live
occasionally to be 200 years of age. Like the saguaro, the
cardóns are often present in large numbers and are the focal
point in terms of food, lodging, and even narrow bands of
shade for innumerable animals.

Between the mainland and peninsular Gulf Coast sections
are numerous Gulf islands. Most lack fresh water. They are

covered by vegetation typical of the Gulf Coast subdivision. The animal life on them is varied; the species present on these isolated islands vary from one island to another and are influenced by evolutionary forces working in isolation. The islands are host to many species of sea birds which nest or rest in the extreme desert habitat but live off the Gulf's exceptional bounty. Biologically these islands provide some of the most intriguing, although not exactly typical, areas of the Sonoran Desert. Some hold great forests of cardón and bats which live among the rocks and fish for their food with their feet in the Gulf water while in flight. Rattlesnakes on one or more islands have dispensed with their rattles, or are in the evolutionary process of doing so.

The Vizcaino region occupies the central third of the Baja California Pacific coast. This portion is extremely arid, receiving strong winds from the Pacific Ocean. Though the winds have a high humidity level, they contribute little moisture to the desert. Although much of this region is stark desert, several distinctive plant species occur within its boundaries. Shreve defined it as an area of leaf-succulent plants, and he applied the designation *Agave–Franseria*.

Franseria in this case applies particularly to *F. che-nopodifolia*, or bur bush. Several species of agaves are represented, including the most common, *A. shawii* and *A. deserti*. The root crowns of these plants formed a very basic and important food source for the Indians of the peninsula. *Yucca valida*, or datilillo, is a plant somewhat resembling the Joshua tree; it may grow to a height of twenty feet. The boojum tree is an important plant of this region, as are the cardón and peninsular ocotillo, *Fouquieria peninsularis*. Another plant commonly called elephant tree is found in this region. *Pachycormus discolor*, or copalquin, is a squat, very heavy-trunked tree, found only in Baja California. It too displays curling sheets of exfoliating bark. Copalquin, as well as other plants, is sometimes seen covered with dodder—a parasitic, orange plant. Also found growing on cacti, shrubs, and trees is ball moss, or *Tillandsia recurvata*, which resembles a mass of straw or twigs and grows high above the ground attached to another plant. This plant is not a moss, but rather an *epiphyte*—that is, a nonparasitic plant that grows upon another plant or object and derives its moisture and nutrients from the air, rain, and debris that may accumulate about it. *Tillandsia recurvata* is found growing in areas which receive coastal fog; it is similar to the Spanish moss found in the southern United States.

The Magdalena region is comprised of the southern portion of the peninsular desert bordering the Pacific coast and extending into the central and east–central portions of the southern peninsula. To the north, it adjoins the Vizcaino and Central Gulf Coast regions; to the south and east, it abuts nondesert regions. Shreve designated the Magdalena as a tree and stem-succulent desert, or the *Lysiloma–Machaerocereus* region.

Lysiloma candida, or the palo blanco, is a lovely straight-trunked tree. It has a spreading crown of branches and bright green leaves which contrast with the silvery-white, smooth bark. This light, airy-appearing tree may reach thirty feet in height.

Machaerocereus gummosus, pitaya agria, or galloping cactus, forms vast thickets of its sprawling and/or erect branches. The plant, its ridged branches armed with long spines, may reach a height of three to ten feet. Its famous but far less abundant relative is *M. eruca*, or creeping devil. This cactus is composed of thick, spined, ridged stems which grow across the ground surface, the growing tip often slightly elevated above the ground. The stem roots as it grows, and eventually the older portions die. The end result is a cactus that does "creep" or advance across the landscape. The stems, up to fifteen feet in length, growing at various angles to one another, their "heads" elevated, resemble gigantic, alert worms advancing across a science fiction landscape. The cardón grows in this region, and cholla, mesquite, peninsular palo verde, peninsular ocotillo, lomboy, and organ pipe cacti also play an important part in the vegetation of this region.

For the most part, animals—particularly birds and larger mammals—are less closely tied to specific type habitats than are plants. Thus a good many of the animal species in any one of the vegetational subdivisions of the Sonoran Desert is likely to be found in one or more of the others. Again, we find the same pyramid of vast numbers of insects and rodents supporting larger and less numerous species, which are themselves often prey to yet larger and even less numerous ones. As the Joshua tree is a dominant species in one habitat,

FIG. 67. Stink beetle, or Pinacate beetle, are two common names for these large (about 1 inch long), black, shiny beetles of the genus *Eleodes*. When disturbed, these insects often elevate the rear portion of the body and may give off an offensive odor.

supportive of many animal species ranging from insect to reptile, bird, and mammal, so the dominants in other habitats serve as a focal point for animals. Outstanding examples are the saguaros, cardóns, chollas, and others. The variety of habitats and microhabitats available to animal species in the Sonoran Desert is particularly great, and animal life is rich in numbers and varied in species.

For example, in Saguaro National Monument near Tucson, Arizona, a checklist of species reported from the desert and foothill areas, in which the saguaros and related desert vegetation occur, lists 8 amphibian species, 4 of turtles, 19 lizard, 29 snake, 124 bird, and 69 mammal species.

By no means is the following list of the species of animals in the Sonoran Desert complete, but it provides an indication of some of the important species occurring in that desert, or in certain portions of it.

Of the amphibians found in the Sonoran Desert, three examples include: Couch's spadefoot, *Scaphiopus couchi;* red-spotted toad, *Bufo punctatus;* and the Colorado River toad, *Bufo alvarius.*

Reptile species include the desert tortoise, *Gopherus agassizi,* and many lizards: Gila monster, *Heloderma suspectum;* chuckwalla, *Sauromalus obesus;* banded gecko, *Coleonyx variegatus;* desert iguana, *Dipsosaurus dorsalis;* zebra-tailed lizard, *Callisaurus draconoides;* Colorado Desert fringe-toed lizard, *Uma notata;* leopard lizard, *Crotaphytus wislizenii;* collared lizard, *Crotaphytus collaris;* desert spiny lizard, *Sceloporus magister;* long-tailed brush lizard, *Urosaurus graciosus;* side-blotched lizard, *Uta stansburiana;*

FIG. 68. The zebra-tailed lizard, *Callisaurus draconoides* (snout to vent length 2½ to 3½ inches), is a slim-bodied, long-tailed, long-legged lizard adept at running at high speed. The undersurface of the tail is white with black crossbars. When running the lizard curls the tail up over the back displaying the "zebra" tail. This lizard is found in the Sonoran, Mohave, and portions of the Great Basin deserts.

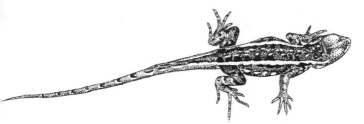

FIG. 69. The side-blotched lizard, *Uta stansburiana* (1½ to 2⅓ inches, snout–vent length) is brownish with a blue or black spot on the side of the chest behind the axilla; hence its common name. This lizard is one of the most widespread and abundant of the arid areas, being found in all four North American deserts.

desert horned lizard, *Phrynosoma platyrhinos;* and flat-tailed horned lizard, *Phrynosoma m'calli.*

The snake species represented are exceedingly numerous. Some of them are: western blind snake, *Leptotyphlops humilis;* rosy boa, *Lichanura trivirgata;* spotted leaf-nosed snake, *Phyllorhynchus decurtatus;* red racer, *Masticophis flagellum;* desert patch-nosed snake, *Salvadora hexalepis;* gopher snake, *Pituophis melanoleucus;* glossy snake, *Arizona elegans;* kingsnake, *Lampropeltis getulus;* long-nosed snake, *Rhinocheilus lecontei;* western ground snake, *Sonora semiannulata;* western shovel-nosed snake, *Chionactis occipitalis;* banded sand snake, *Chilomeniscus cinctus;* night snake, *Hypsiglena torquata;* Arizona coral snake,

Micruroides euryxanthus; Sonora lyre snake, *Trimorphodon lambda;* black-tailed rattlesnake, *Crotalus molossus;* tiger rattlesnake, *Crotalus tigris;* western diamondback, *Crotalus atrox;* sidewinder, *Crotalus cerastes;* speckled rattlesnake, *Crotalus mitchelli;* and the Mohave rattlesnake, *Crotalus scutulatus.*

A very few of the very many bird species include: the roadrunner, *Geococcyx californianus;* phainopepla, *Phainopepla nitens;* verdin, *Auriparus flaviceps;* cactus wren, *Campylorhynchus brunneicapillus;* elf owl, *Micrathene whitneyi;* Arizona crested flycatcher, *Myiarchus tyrannulus;* caracara, *Caracara cheriway;* turkey vulture, *Cathartes aura;* Gambel's quail, *Lophortyx gambelii;* Gila woodpecker, *Centurus uropygialis;* gilded flicker, *Colaptes chrysoides;* white-necked raven, *Corvus cryptoleucus;* Leconte's thrasher, *Toxostoma lecontei;* white-winged dove, *Zenaida asiatica;* mourning dove, *Zenaidura macroura;* curve-billed thrasher, *Toxostoma curvirostre;* western red-tailed hawk, *Buteo jamaicensis;* Nuttall poorwill, *Phalaenoptilus nuttallii.*

Mammals of this desert are for the most part represented by others of their own or related species in the other deserts. These include the pocket gopher; deer, pocket, cactus, and

FIG. 70. The cactus wren, *Campylorhynchus brunneicapillum,* is a large (7 to 8¾ inch), light brown bird with a heavily spotted breast and a white stripe over the eye. This bird builds numerous large enclosed nests and is adept at constructing and entering these nests from a side entrance even when they are placed in the extremely spiny cholla cactus.

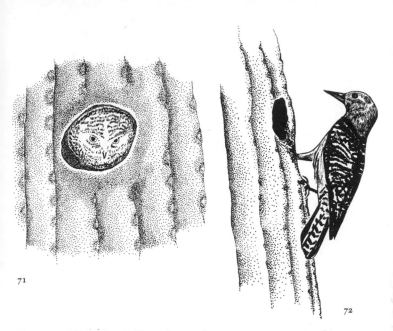

71

72

FIG. 71. The elf owl, *Micrathene whitneyi*, is sparrow-sized (5 to 6 inches) and the smallest owl in the world. It is often associated with the saguaro cacti, living in holes hollowed in these or other trees by woodpeckers. Where the owl occurs, its call is a familiar one at nightfall in the early summer.

FIG. 72. The Gila woodpecker, *Centurus uropygialis*, 8 to 10 inches in length, is fawn colored with a black-and-white barred back, wings, and tail. The male sports a round red cap. These birds are prime excavators of holes in the saguaros which are later used by other bird species.

grasshopper mice; desert shrew; pack rats; kangaroo rats; various ground squirrels, such as the Harris, antelope, and round-tailed; rabbits, including the desert cottontail, blacktail jackrabbit, and antelope jackrabbit; skunks of various species; gray fox; kit fox; coyote; ringtail cat; coatimundi; badger; bobcat; peccary; mule deer; mountain lion; bighorn sheep; and pronghorn.

Webster's gives one definition of desert as "desolate, sparsely occupied, or unoccupied." Obviously Webster never visited the desert known as the Sonoran.

FIG. 73. The Harris ground squirrel, *Citellus harrisi,* is very similar to its California relative, the antelope ground squirrel, *Ammospermophilus leucurus.* Both are approximately 6 inches in length, with a fluffy tail 2 to 4 inches long which is usually carried curled over the back. The underside of the tail of *A. leucurus* is white; that of *C. harrisi* is gray. These animals are active even on hot days and occasionally climb into vegetation to obtain seeds or foliage.

FIG. 74. The round-tailed ground squirrel, *Citellus tereticaudus,* is 5 to 6 inches in body length with a 2 to 4 inch tail. It is readily identified by its pencillike, nonbushy tail. Its color is a pinkish-cinnamon, slightly lighter on the belly. This ground squirrel lives in burrows in the Mohave and Sonoran deserts. The animal is diurnal when active and hibernates during the colder months.

FIG. 75. The blacktail jack rabbit, *Lepus californicus,* occurs in all four North American deserts. Body length of this rabbit is approximately 18 to 20 inches; ears measure 6 to 7 inches. Vegetation-consuming and largely nocturnal, this rabbit often rests during the day in slight hollows in the soil called forms. This species is marked by black ear tips and a black streak on the top of the tail.

FIG. 76. The ringtail, or cacomistle, *Bassariscus astutus,* is approximately 15 inches in body length with an additional 15 inches of tail. This shy animal inhabits rocky canyons and foothills. It is nocturnal and carnivorous and ranges in favorable habitats from southeastern Oregon to southern Mexico. Pale brown in body color, the ringtail has a bushy tail ringed with alternating black-and-white rings.

FIG. 77. The coatimundi, coati, or chulla, *Nasua narica* (body length of 16 to 24 inches, with a tail approximately the same length), lives basically in Mexico but is extending its range northward in Arizona and New Mexico. Primarily, these animals live in wooded areas and are seen most often in the desert mountains. They travel over the ground or through trees in troupes. The long tail serves for balance and to some extent for grasping.

FIG. 78. The badger, *Taxidea taxus* (body length of 20 to 24 inches), ranges from southern Canada to central Mexico. Flat-bodied, a grizzled gray to brown in color with a white abdomen, black-and-white face markings, and a white stripe extending from the nose to approximately the shoulders or further along the back, these animals weigh approximately twenty to thirty pounds. They are powerful diggers, devouring rodents and reptiles which they often dig out of the earth.

THE DESERTS OF THE SOUTHWEST

FIG. 79. The bobcat, *Lynx rufus*, is approximately 25 to 30 inches in body length. It is reddish brown, marked with darker spots, and has lighter underparts. The tail is short, approximately 5 inches, and black-tipped; the backs of the ears are black with a white stripe. Throughout their range from western Canada south through Mexico and Central and South America, bobcats are important predators.

FIG. 80. The collared peccary, javelina, or *Pecari tajacu* (3 feet in length; 20 to 24 inches high) ranges from southern Arizona, New Mexico, and Texas to South America. It is approximately three feet in length and covered with coarse, grizzled gray hair. These animals travel in bands and prefer brushy areas. They are legally hunted in some areas.

CHAPTER X

Planning Desert Exploration and Enjoyment

INTELLIGENT PREPARATION and common-sense execution often provide the difference between an enjoyable and a miserable desert exploration. They may occasionally provide the difference between life and death. Many books have been written on camping, hiking, and backpacking equipment and techniques, and others are being added to the list. In this book, we are concerned primarily with factors of particular significance to desert exploration and enjoyment. We concentrate on the two most extenuating factors associated with the desert environment; heat and aridity. Cold weather can also occasionally provide the desert outdoor enthusiast with difficult problems—including snow and freezing temperatures—particularly in the higher desert regions such as those in the Great Basin Desert. Numerous publications present information on how to cope with cold weather stress, and thus this problem will not be our primary concern.

All degrees of desert exploratory activity are possible. They range from simple sightseeing in the family vehicle along desert highways and in parks and monuments to back-trail reconnoitering with four-wheel drive to backpacking, where the hiker must depend upon two feet and the equipment and water he or she carries. Equipment suggestions vary with the type of activity. Remember, however, that by means of a wrong turn and mechanical problems even a simple summer sightseeing trip may conceivably become, rather rapidly, a serious survival problem.

Clothing

Clothing is a matter of personal choice, but remember:
1. Although daytime temperatures may be high, the des-

ert cools rapidly after the sun sets. A sweater, sweatshirt, or the like sometimes, but not always, feels comfortable in the late evening, even in the summer. In winter and during periods of moderate temperatures, coats or jackets will be needed at night and during some days. A very cold wind may whip across the desert in winter; when it does, some sort of head covering—a stocking cap, sweatshirt hood, or the like—will feel extremely comfortable.

2. Long pants are advisable for the hiker, even in summer. They provide a degree of protection against cactus spines, dehydration, sunburn, scrapes and scratches from brush and rocks, and rattlesnake bite (a loose, denim pants leg may help foil or lessen the force of a rattlesnake strike).

3. You may prefer short-sleeved shirts or blouses during warm temperatures, but remember that long sleeves can be valuable, particularly in preventing sunburn or where possible dehydration is a problem.

4. A hat which provides shade for the head and allows some air circulation is a valuable asset. For summer hiking, it may be considered a necessity. One of us, caught in an emergency situation, exposed to 100° F.-plus temperatures in desert sun from dawn to dark without any head protection, now attests that the giddiness, fuzzy thinking, and other problems which develop from partial dehydration with hot sun beating on one's head and neck all day underscore the need for a hat, or at least for an emergency substitute.

Footwear

Whether you are out for a half-day hike or a two-week backpack into one of the remote desert regions, proper footwear is one of the most important pieces of your equipment. Remember that a hiker with painful feet is more than an unhappy hiking companion; he or she is a liability to self and group. Such individuals have been the downfall of many an outing, for no group is much better than its poorest member—or the feet of its poorest member. Wear sandals in the desert only if you plan to stay inside, on city sidewalks and well-maintained paths, or are prepared to face the circumstances from venturing away from these. In many regions, tennis shoes and similar footwear may be fine for hiking; however, in the desert where one encounters cactus spines, shrubs, sand, and sharp rocks, tennis shoes are not entirely practical for hiking. In addition, these shoes readily conduct heat from the ground surface to the feet. (Remember the temperature of that surface may register 160° F. or more on a hot day.)

Boots—*well chosen, well broken in*—can be of great value to the desert hiker. Among their advantages are: 1. support for the foot and ankle in rugged, often rocky, ankle-twisting terrain, 2. insulation from desert heat through the boots themselves and the fairly heavy socks worn with them, 3. protection against sand, gravel, and the like entering the footwear and rubbing against the skin, and 4. protection from cactus spines and rattlesnake bite (a high percentage of rattlesnake bites occur on the ankle and lower leg).

In choosing desert wear, consider boots which: 1. reach at least to your ankle bone, or preferably higher, 2. are of fairly tough leather to withstand spines and sharp rocks, 3. have soles of tough design which will provide good traction, such as those of a rubber lug type, and 4. are as lightweight and cool as possible while fulfilling the foregoing criteria.

When shopping for boots, observe these rules:

1. Don't buy boots that don't feel at least fairly comfortable when tried on in the store.

2. Stand on an incline of about thirty-five to forty degrees to determine if your toes slide down and hit the front of the boot—if they do, your feet are going to hurt on downhill hiking.

3. Make sure the boot laces tightly enough so that the foot does not wander inside it.

4. Try the boots on with a good pair of thick socks or with two pairs, one heavy and one light, depending on what you plan to wear with them in the field.

Break your boots in before your trip by wearing them around home daily for increasingly longer periods. Treat your boots, once in use, with respect. Take proper care of them.

1. Keep boots clean by brushing off deposits of mud and dirt after your return home.

2. Treat them with leather conditioner and/or waterproofing conditioner. (Determine at the time of purchase the proper means of care for your particular boots.)

3. Protect boots from too-intense campfire heat. If they become wet on a trip (as is possible in the desert) be very careful not to overheat them while drying them near a fire. Touch the inside of the boot's leather; if it feels uncomfortably hot to the hand, the boot is too hot.

Socks

Personal preference plays a role in choice, but a good many hikers prefer the two-pair method; they wear a light- or medium-weight cotton or nylon inner sock and an outer, thicker, wool sock—yes, even in the desert! Carry extra socks to provide a change when yours become wet or compacted. Also, remember that your feet will perspire heavily during hot weather hiking.

Sleeping Bag

For many years a bedroll, consisting primarily of a good wool blanket, was considered standard for the hunter, camper, cowboy, or other individual sleeping outside. Sunset seldom signaled an enjoyable, beautiful, star-filled night, but often marked the start of a dreaded time of chill and shivering. Following World War II, a wide portion of the outdoor public was introduced for the first time to lightweight, down-filled, warm bags at reasonable weight and price levels. Since then, the sleeping bag industry has displayed a rapid series of modifications in design and materials. Today, a wide choice of sleeping bag types is available over a varying price range. You tend to get what you pay for. In purchasing a bag, consider how you will be using it and the criteria to be met to fill your particular needs; then buy accordingly.

To stress the need for warmth in a sleeping bag may appear incongruous in a discussion of desert camping, but it is not. Over much of the North American desert country, nighttime temperatures often drop below freezing, snow falls, and strong cold winter winds are common during part of the winter. In warmer weather, nighttime temperature lows usually drop far below daytime highs, and even following the very hottest summer days, an outdoor sleeper seldom does not want at least a lightweight covering during the predawn hours.

The purpose of a sleeping bag is to maintain body heat. The bag does so by layering materials around the body which trap air pockets. The air in these pockets is heated by the body to near body temperature. These dead air pockets have the attribute of being very good insulators by being poor conductors. The warmth of a particular bag depends on the filler or insulating material, the bag's design, the closures, and the material which holds the insulating material in place.

Various types of fillers are used in bags. Currently, the best all-around one is down, the very tiny, fluffy feathers growing next to the skin of waterfowl. Goose down is now accepted as the top of the line, and sells for top dollar. Some bags are stuffed with duck down, which is not a bad insulator; superior duck down will insulate better than a poor grade of goose down. Some companies mix down from ducks and geese, producing a waterfowl down which is a good insulator and less expensive than the 100 percent goose down-filled bag. Although not inexpensive, down is a very popular filler; it is very warm; it can be stuffed into a small bag for compact packing, it is very lightweight, and a small amount will expand greatly to produce the dead air pockets. Of products currently available, down has the greatest warmth-to-weight value.

Bag fillers of synthetic fibers are also available, popular, and often less expensive than down. Although down does have the greatest warmth to weight ratio under ordinary conditions, wet down fails miserably. For this reason in addition to several others, the recent synthetic fillers are gaining great popularity. Polyester synthetic fibers are not new insulators. Although some synthetics have been around for some time, it is the second generation polyester fibers which are modifying the sleeping bag market at such a rapid rate. In 1971 two polyester fibers were introduced. These fibers, Dupont's Dacron Fiberfill II and Celanese's Fortrel PolarGuard differ only slightly. The fibers in PolarGuard are cut to approximately 100 inches or longer in length. They are resin coated to stabilize their position. Dacron's Fiberfill II is composed of two-inch fibers which are stabilized in position by a backing of Tyvek. The fibers are lubricated allowing the fiber to slide and hence to maintain loft.

Although these differences exist, both of these fibers essentially serve the same purpose—that is, they are less expensive and boast the fact that they are warm when wet, unlike down. Bags constructed with these insulators resist moisture very effectively. The fiber absorbs less than 1 percent of water by weight. These springy fibers do not flatten out like down and this provides better ground insulation. Even when wet these fibers lose only about 10 percent of their loft. Another factor of importance to some people is the fact that these synthetic fibers are nonallergenic and can be washed often.

When considering buying a bag remember that although down is more expensive, it is warm for its weight. On the other hand, the synthetics may be heavier, but they are more economical, plus they provide 70 to 75 percent the insulation of down and, unlike down, will keep you warm even when wet.

In buying, check the construction of the bag:

1. A baffle should be sewn on the inside of the bag the length of the zipper so that body heat does not escape through the small spaces in the zipper. Such a baffle also prevents the sleeper from rolling against the cold metal zipper and suffering the resulting shock on a cold winter night.

2. The method used to hold the insulating material in place can be very important in maintaining warmth in the bag and in preventing cold spots. Several methods of sleeping bag construction are common. Simplest of these and most likely to produce cold spots is the sewn-through method. In this method, the seams extend through both cloth layers and the insulating material. More protection is afforded by a sewn-through bag which has an additional outer shell covering added. Styles with offset seams provide better protection from cold spots but in some cases increase the weight of the bag.

3. Zippers should be sturdy. If bags are bought to be zipped together, make sure the zippers mate correctly and that the zipper baffle tubes are on opposite sides.

4. The material used for the lining and outer shell of the bag varies in quality. A synthetic fabric, such as nylon, is

most often used. Check for durability, care required, and weight.

Once you have chosen and purchased a bag, care for it to prolong its life. Follow the manufacturer's directions for cleaning and care. Keep the bag out of the dirt as much as possible and away from fires—most bags have a nylon-type covering which is easily damaged by flying sparks from a campfire. When you are carrying a bag on your back, guard against ripping and tearing the bag's covering with thorns, spines, and sharp rocks—especially in the desert. If the bag is to be used on the ground, clear the area of such sharp objects before rolling out the bag. If you are sleeping on the ground, the use of some sort of protection under the bag is advisable (for the sake of both sleeper and bag). Some type of foam pad is best; air mattresses tend to be easily punctured when used in the desert.

Shelter

One of the most beautiful experiences the desert can offer is the view of its fantastically clear evening sky with infinite numbers of stars bright against the blackness. Lying back and integrating oneself into the desert at such times is an experience that will be remembered forever. For this reason, many desert campers feel that to sleep in a tent on such a night is a waste akin to sleeping in a cheap hotel when far better accommodations are available. Beautiful desert nights should be enjoyed; however, at times the desert can be a harsh place in which to camp. It rains in the desert occasionally and blows rather frequently. The person without protection gets just as wet, cold, and windblown in the desert as he or she does in many other environments. Therefore a tent or shelter of some sort is often an asset. Personal considerations, such as price, size, anticipated uses, transportability, ease of use, weight, and the like, must all be evaluated when purchasing a tent.

Some people prefer to sleep in a tent in the desert for a reason other than weather. Summer nights are the most active period for much of the desert fauna. Snakes and scorpions represent probably only a relatively small risk to the person sleeping on the desert's surface but, in spite of the old horsehair rope trick—which certainly does not work—nothing can guarantee that these small creatures will not inadvertently make their way into your camp. (Consider the more likely possibility that you are in *their* camp, and that they are even less enthused about your presence than you are about theirs.) If the camper worries about the presence of these guests (and admittedly, at times, one should), this concern detracts from the trip. Some modification can be made. A small, zippered, floored tent is one possibility. (Make sure it provides for plenty of air circulation for warm summer evenings.) Another possibility is the use of small, compact, lightweight cots to elevate the sleepers a few inches above the "intruders." Hammocks may occasionally be useful in some areas, such as along washes where larger trees grow. During the winter months, cold temperatures keep snakes and scorpions inactive at night and reduce the need for vigilance.

Packs

Once you have done some hiking in the desert environment, you may very likely decide to go farther and stay longer. For these longer journeys, the hiker must be able to carry a quantity of food, water, and various equipment. A backpack is the answer. As with sleeping bags, backpack design has improved and production increased over the last two decades. Backpack styles are numerous but can be briefly categorized.

First, the small frameless rucksacks or day hikers supply space to carry enough gear for a good day's hike. The load hangs directly from the shoulders. Also available are larger frameless backpacks of approximately the same design, used widely by climbers and skiers. When compared to frame-supported backpacks, these frameless models exhibit a number of drawbacks. The gear must be carefully arranged within the backpack so that sharp articles are not constantly poking the carrier in the back. Additionally, the load tends to work its way to the bottom of the bag, resulting in an uncomfortable arrangement and a poor distribution of weight. Another disadvantage applies not only to the frameless rucksack but also to a majority of framed rucksacks (yet another type of backpack); they tend to bulge out when stuffed full. The carrier's back prevents excessive distribution of load toward the front; thus the load is directed backwards. This shift causes the center of gravity to be moved back with respect to the hiker. In order to offset this imbalance, the hiker must lean forward. This compensation does move the center of gravity of the main mass forward over the feet but also tends to give the leaning backpacker a backache.

Not until the "contour frame pack" was developed were these problems greatly reduced. Most leading packs today are of this type, which employs for the frame light, strong, magnesium or aluminum tubes bent to follow the curvature of the back. These pack frames not only have shoulder straps but also have a waist band, which carries the majority of the weight. The waist strap is fastened directly to the steel frame by means of clevis pins, rivets, or some similar attachment. This band can be adjusted so that the major portion of the pack's weight rests on the hips, the strongest portion of the body. The shoulder straps, once the main load carrier, now have as their major function the balancing of the load, which pivots on the hips. When the pack is adjusted correctly, one should be able to slip a finger under the shoulder straps with no difficulty. The contour pack directs the load upward, not outward, by keeping it close to the body. Thus only a slight inclination of the body to adjust the center of gravity to the proper position is required. The sleeping bag can be tied onto the frame of most models, leaving the bag and its various compartments for smaller items.

The frames usually have some arrangent of backbands which run horizontally from one bar to the other. This strap conformation provides a comfortable area for the carrier's back to rest against. On some packs, these bands are fixed; caution must be taken to buy the correct size. On most models, they are adjustable. A few models have crossbands of cotton; most use nylon. In the desert, the back will sweat profusely where a solid crossband rests against it. To improve this situation, some backpacks offer a nylon mesh backband which affords some ventilation to this area. Solid backbands need not always be avoided; however, backpack frames which have a solid backband extending nearly the entire length of the frame are not as suitable for warm weather desert hiking as are those which allow more air circulation.

The backpack is your home when you are in the wilderness. When you are ready to buy one, research your purchase carefully:

1. Consider the type of design you want and need in the bag. Determine the type of hiking or climbing you will be doing. Personal preference, too, will affect your decision. Most packs are divided into compartments and usually have small pockets on the sides. If, for example, you are a photographer, you may want a certain arrangement of small pockets.

2. Consider the size needed. Remember, you may want to widen your range of perspective. You may begin on simple weekend trips into the desert country, then find you enjoy backpacking so much that you will go on an extended two-week trip on your vacation. Allow room for expanding horizons.

3. Consider the pack construction and the conditions to which you will be subjecting it. Check small things like zippers. Are they sturdy, with large handles which are easily grasped? Check the buckles. Are they solid? Does the waist buckle have a quick-release feature? It should, in the event you have to jettison your pack in a hurry. Are the strain points sufficiently reinforced? Is the bottom sturdy? Check to be sure the straps are sufficiently wide and are padded to avoid irritation.

4. Consider the fit. Choose the pack that feels comfortable. Then put thirty pounds of weight in it and test it. (The outing stores usually have sand bags for this purpose.) If the pack does not feel comfortable, be assured it will certainly feel considerably more uncomfortable after you have been wearing it for a day. *Make sure the pack is comfortable.*

Additional Items

Where you go, how you get there, what you plan to do, how long you will spend, how fully you plan for the unforeseen, your preferred style of desert exploration—all play a part in what you take with you in your desert exploration. Make your own checklist, and add to it as experience dictates. Don't lose it between trips. Refer to it before you leave home. You can easily grow confident and careless, with subsequent regrets in the field. The following items are definitely, or very possibly, of vital significance to you:

1. **Water.** Even if you are simply auto-exploring on established roads, you should carry some water with you. You may well need it for passengers or vehicle. Simply driving in hot weather, one consumes liquids far beyond normal, and one should be prepared for this change, plus an overheated radiator, plus the possibility of a mechanical breakdown or wrong turn, which would prolong one's stay in the desert environment.

In camping carry plenty of water. In hot weather, consider *a gallon and a half per person minimum for drinking,* adding what will be used for washing, cooking, dishes, and so on. This minimum is for a resting or only moderately active person. The truly active individual will require considerably more. In backpacking *consider very carefully the water that will be needed.* (See Figures 75–77 and Tables 1 and 2 in Chapter XI) Backpacking is strenuous physical exercise, and the backpacker's body requires a great deal of water even when temperatures are moderate; certainly very large amounts are needed for exertion in heat. *Do not depend for your water on waterholes, wells, tanks, and other sites marked on your maps* unless you positively know they have water—and then doubt them. Remember that a gallon of water weighs approximately 8.3 pounds. The amount of water you can carry is definitely limited. *Plan your water supplies for desert backpacking very carefully.* Nothing else is so important.

In all degrees of desert exploration, from car to backpack, the wisest course is to determine the amount of water you think you will need, then take considerably more. You may never need the extra, but the one time you do, you may need it desperately.

2. **Water containers.** The explorer who travels by vehicle may wish to use various types of water containers. Campers often prefer five-gallon metal or plastic cans. However, even if your base in desert exploration is a vehicle, remember you will probably take hikes away from it. Be prepared when leaving your water supply to carry water with you in canteens or other containers. (Plastic and

aluminum canteens are available, plus lightweight plastic and aluminum water bottles.) When choosing containers for hiking, and particularly for backpacking, choose durable, sturdy, tough ones; those of polyethylene plastic are not only durable but lightweight and semi-transparent, allowing quantity determination. Do not use glass bottles for water transport; before the advent of plastic bottles, some desert travelers died when their last glass bottle of water shattered. For backpacking, smaller containers should additionally allow for efficient packing and be versatile so that punches or the like can be mixed in them.

The hiker engaged in summer backpacking in areas where water is scarce and separated by long distances (an activity to be recommended only for the experienced, well-conditioned desert backpacker, and only after intensive planning), may find it necessary to carry several gallons of water (remember that three gallons of water will weigh approximately twenty-five pounds). To transport large amounts of water while backpacking, collapsible poly-ethylene jugs are most appropriate; they will shrink in bulk as the water supply diminishes.

3. **Snake bite kit.** This compact item should be carried. It should contain a sharp blade, antiseptic, a lymph-constricting band of a type that can be applied using only one hand, and one or more suctioning devices, thereby provid-ing the means for administering first aid for poisonous snakebite. In the absence of such a kit, or where hikers are scattering to some extent and each hiker does not have his own kit, each person can easily carry in his pocket a new, wrapped, single-edge razor blade which can be used for cutting the site of a poisonous snakebite; suctioning can then be done by mouth.

4. **First aid kit.** A first aid kit should always be available. Its contents will be discussed in Chapter XIII.

5. **Compass and maps.** Both compass and maps are extremely important and should be carried. Buy a compass of some degree of quality—if you need one, you'll need one that works. An oil-filled rather than an air-filled compass is recommended. Check to see that the base has an edge long enough to make drawing a line easy (for taking a bearing on a map). The United States Geological Survey topographical map series is excellent; these maps may be based on 15-

minute quadrangles (covering 15 minutes of both latitude and longitude, or roughly 1 inch to a mile); or on 7½-minute quadrangles. These maps are carried by map stores and by many outing stores. Also available in many outing stores are maps of local hiking trails which may prove valuable. Maps are interesting reading. Buy them, study and enjoy them, and take care of them—no doubt you'll use them over and over.

6. **Signaling mirror.** A lightweight, metal signaling mirror should be carried. It is an invaluable, powerful aid in signaling. Its use will be discussed in Chapter XIV.

7. **Knife.** One of the handiest items to be carried is a knife, which need not be fancy; a useful style is one fashioned after a Boy Scout model. The knife should have a good strong main blade for general cutting and a smaller very sharp blade which may be used for removing spines and splinters and for delicate cutting. If necessary, it can be used in the absence of a snakebite kit for the cut-and-suck method of rattlesnake-bite first aid. The knife should also contain a can opener, but knives with many more utensils are not necessary.

8. **Flashlight.** A flashlight may prove to be a more important piece of equipment than one might judge. It is often used for searching in one's pack at night; it may prove to be helpful in signaling at night; and it serves a very important purpose in summer nighttime camping. You should use a flashlight when walking in the desert on warm nights—on your bedtime bathroom retreat, for example. The light may prove a valuable aid in preventing you from stepping on or unduly upsetting a prowling rattlesnake. Be sure to take sufficient batteries on your trip. Beware of the light switch being inadvertently pushed to the "on" position while the flashlight is in a pack, thereby wasting batteries. The batteries may be reversed in the light after use to prevent this accident, or a piece of adhesive tape may be placed over the switch when the light is not in use.

9. **Whistle.** A whistle is useful for signaling; its use is particularly advisable on longer hikes and backpacks, especially for children. A whistle can be worn around a child's (or adult's) neck for use in case he or she becomes lost, hurt, or frightened. Its sound carries farther than the human voice, and blowing a whistle is much easier and less costly physiologically than continued shouting.

10. **Matches.** Always carry matches, in a waterproof container. If you become lost, you have a means of signaling and keeping warm.

11. **Rope.** Rope has numerous uses, ranging from pitching a tent to making a clothesline to emergency and first aid requirements. Parachute cord which is about 550-pound test is the best. The weight of a little extra cord is well worth the uses you will find for it.

12. **Plastic sheet and tube.** A six-foot square of clear or almost clear plastic and a four-to-six-foot length of plastic tubing can be used for construction of a solar still under emergency situations. The still and its use are described in Chapter XIV.

13. **Dark glasses.** Some people feel that dark glasses detract from the desert's scenery and its total effect. However, for many people, dark glasses are very comforting for the eyes. Certainly the daytime desert environment offers a great deal of bright sunlight and glare. Excessive exposure to this glare without the protection afforded by colored glasses tends to impair distant vision and retard adjustment of the eyes to nighttime conditions.

14. **Toilet articles.** Toilet items will be those of personal preference. Don't forget toilet paper. Other items that are particularly helpful in the sunny, dry desert are sunburn lotion, a tube of lip salve, and drops for dry eyes.

15. **Pocket comb.** You may want to comb your hair, but primarily a comb can be an invaluable aid for removing cactus joints from body and clothes. See Chapter XIII.

16. **Repair kit for equipment and clothing.** When the outdoorsman takes off a pack and drops it only to see one of the joints separate, or is sleeping by the campfire when the wood pops and sends an ember through the outer covering of a sleeping bag so that the heretofore contained down starts flying, he or she will be thankful for a repair kit. Recommendations include a few ounces of such specific repair equipment as ripstop nylon repair tape for repairing bags and coats; needles and safety pins of various sizes; thread—a few lengths of assorted weights; clevis pins and steel wires for repairing pack frames; and other items suitable for your specific equipment.

Before You Leave Home

1. *Always notify someone as to your destination and the date you expect to return from a desert trip.* Give yourself a little leeway as you set the time for your return. Let it be understood that someone should come to your aid if you have not returned at that time. Notify your contact when you do return home. If you change your plans as to destination or return, notify your contact. If you are in an area where you do not have personal contacts to fill this role, notify the local sheriff's office of your plans. If you are flying, the same rules apply; you must also *file a flight plan and stick to it or change it officially.* One of us, involved in a plane crash in Baja California on a flight which did not follow the flight plan, can testify to the vital importance of this rule. The other, waiting at home for the plane's return, can testify to the anguish caused to the person responsible for the search and the waiting. Breaking these rules can be deadly for the hiker, flyer, or backpacker who has developed a problem. It can also prove time-consuming, expensive, and even dangerous to other people—the searchers—when search and rescue services, including vehicles, airplanes, and helicopters, must be employed. When such services are needed, they are invaluable, and no price tag can be placed on them. But when a hiker, flyer, or the like has changed plans, failed to notify contacts, and been delayed beyond a deadline, the mistake can be costly, both in money and emotional upset, as well as in terms of survival.

2. Obtain maps of the area where you will be hiking. Study these maps ahead of time to learn something about the country.

3. Prepare yourself to be a good outdoorsman. A course in first aid may prove invaluable. Learn some basic survival skills and practice them. Learn to use a signaling mirror. Learn about the plants and animals of the area you will be visiting. Learn to use a compass and to read topographic maps before you get into the field. Learn to camp effectively, efficiently, and enjoyably, not only by doing it but also by reading some manuals which provide you with ideas. Learn some of the simple mechanics of your vehicle, if you are not already knowledgeable in that regard.

Camping Sites

If you are choosing a camping site away from established campgrounds, remember:

1. Do not camp in a dry wash. A sandy-bottomed, tree-lined wash is an inviting location for a camp. Such a site is, however, subject to a flash flood. Flash floods are infrequent but can be exceedingly powerful when they do occur. Remember that such floods may occur in your area under clear skies; the rain which caused them may have fallen some distance away. Enjoy the washes by camping above them and hiking down into them or building your campfire in the wash bottom.

2. Avoid camping directly next to piles of debris, abandoned buildings, pack rat nests, masses of rocks, or the like, as these are potential rattlesnake areas. To sleep away from such areas is certainly wise.

Camping Manners

The desert is a particularly delicate ecosystem. Any scars on its surface will remain for exceedingly long periods; garbage consigned to it will endure, and endure, and endure. *Leave no sign of your desert sojourn behind upon your departure.*

1. Take all of your garbage that cannot be completely burned—*all of it*—home with you. If you do burn paper, be sure it is completely burned and the ashes buried. Carry out all cans, aluminum foil, pop-top can lids, and every other nonburnable item. Do not bury such materials. The desert is dry; breakdown of such materials may never occur. Besides, animals almost invariably dig up any buried garbage. Remember the rule: If you can carry it in full, you can certainly carry it out empty.

2. If you are camping away from areas with toilet facilities, bury human wastes deeply. If no camp toilet has been set up, keep a regular shovel or hand shovel available in camp, and establish and enforce the rule that anyone leaving camp for bathroom purposes is to take and use the shovel. To burn waste toilet paper before covering the "cat sanitation site" is wise, also.

3. *Do not:* molest animals or their homes; damage plants; deface rocks or ruins; roll boulders down hillsides; leave rocks overturned, thereby destroying the habitats of living things; collect or remove from their sites Indian artifacts (these artifacts are protected by law, and stringent penalties are given for infractions; additionally, you may be destroying archaeological evidence of importance); target practice, unless you have set up your range carefully, are positive no one else is in the vicinity, pick up your empty cartridges, and never use animals, plants, signs, rocks, or similar items for targets.

4. *Do:* close gates after opening them; respect waterholes, the land in general, and the living things who make their homes there; look, explore, enjoy, and leave things as you found them, or better. No law prohibits picking up and carrying out garbage left by a slob camper who preceded you—and you may gain considerable righteous pleasure.

Special Considerations for Exploring Desert Country in Mexico

Some of the most interesting and isolated of the North American desert lies in Mexico. Visitors from the United States are generally welcomed; however, certain additional considerations should be kept in mind when traveling in Mexico.

1. Good manners are imperative. When in Mexico, you are a guest in a foreign country. Do not forget that you are a guest; do not abuse the privilege of visiting. Respect the culture of the area, and do not demand that conditions and services be identical to those in the United States.

2. A Mexican Tourist Card is required; this card can be obtained at the border when you enter Mexico or at offices of the Mexican Ministry of Tourism located in many cities near the border. Proof of citizenship and identity such as a birth certificate or passport, is required. Individuals 17 years of age or younger, not traveling with their parents or legal guardians, are required to present a notarized letter, signed by both parents, which grants permission for that individual to travel in Mexico with another adult.

3. You will need to purchase special vehicle insurance through your insurance agent or from an office at the border. Your regular insurance does not cover your vehicle in Mexico, except within a specified distance of the border (usually only a few miles). Despite the terminology on your policy, even within this limited distance your United States insurance may not be valid, for in many cases American insurance companies are not licensed in Mexico, and the Mexican government may refuse to recognize them in connection with any accident you may have.

4. As you enter Mexico, you are required to show the registration slip and obtain a permit to take your vehicle into Mexico.

5. *Never* have illegal drugs in your possession. Cars are subject to search. To take firearms into Mexico is illegal unless a special permit has been obtained. *Drug and firearm violators are prosecuted, and Mexican jails and prisons are definitely not to be recommended as places to spend your vacation.*

6. In many respects, Mexican law differs from that of the United States. In practice, burden of proof of innocence may be yours, rather than the prosecution bearing the burden of proof of guilt. When possible, beware of becoming entangled in legal disputes in Mexico.

7. Before entering Mexico check on the advisability of taking your citizens band radio. At the time of this writing the attitude of Mexican officials toward these radios fluctuates. Some travelers have found them useful; others have had their radios confiscated.

8. Established camping facilities are relatively few in Mexico, although their number is increasing.

9. At the time of writing, the highest grade gasoline in Mexico is No-Lead. Using nonleaded gas in an engine designed for normal gas can have drastic effects. Although the lower grade gas has a very low octane rating and sometimes produces engine knock, it may prove the lesser of two evils. Some veteran Mexican travelers add a very small amount of diesel to low quality gas to retard detonation (the very quick explosion of gas vapor that causes knocking). Gasoline additive in low grade fuel also helps performance.

10. Take precautions with food and water obtained in Mexico. If you have doubts about the water, purify it. Just

because water comes out of a hydrant or faucet does not necessarily mean it is pure. Ice, too, may be contaminated. If possible, purchase purified water. "Montezuma's Revenge," or intestinal upset, can be a problem for American tourists; avoid foodstuffs that may be contaminated.

11. Driving is more difficult in Mexico than in the United States. Highways are often narrower. Bridges are sometimes narrower than the highway on which they occur. Directional signs are often few or lacking, requiring inquiries as to the route. Night driving, if it can be avoided, is best not done in Mexico. Highways are usually not fenced, and many traverse open rangeland. Watch for cattle and horses on the road, particularly at night when they are very difficult to see. Also, particularly in rural areas, some Mexican vehicles are in need of repair—beware of those being driven at night without taillights. In some cases, road shoulders are narrow or lacking; beware of disabled vehicles stopped on the road itself.

Desert Driving

The desert possesses one unique quality—its accessibility. Due to the desert's relative starkness and openness, roads are built or created quite easily. Such roads are welcome in that they provide access to desert areas. Conversely, as increasing numbers of people take advantage of the areas opened, in some cases abusing the privilege, accessibility is contributing to rapid deterioration of large portions of the desert. Many individuals show disrespect for the living plants and animals. Pressure of this sort is very damaging in the fragile desert ecosystem and may cause problems which will endure forever. Additionally, the land surface is being irreparably scarred. With the popular onslaught of cycles, four-wheel-drive vehicles, and dune buggies, the deserts are rapidly becoming crisscrossed with myriad trails and off-road tracks. On most of the desert surface, tracks are, for all intents and purposes, permanent. A single set of tracks may conceivably endure twenty-five years; well-worn tracks last much longer. *When at all possible, drive on established roads and trails.* This rule cannot be stressed strongly enough. If and when you leave the established road, consider carefully the damage you may create, both by leaving your own tracks and by encouraging future drivers to follow them, causing increasingly permanent damage. Strive to prevent as much damage of the desert as possible. Remember that permanent tracks carved on the desert's surface by vehicles are an unneeded and unwanted legacy for future generations.

Certainly all degrees of desert vehicular travel exist, ranging from interstate freeways, back roads, and trails to cross country. The vehicle and equipment needed will depend on the type travel you plan. Rules for all types of desert travel include the following:

1. Have your vehicle maintained in good condition for desert travel. If your car is in mediocre or poor condition for city travel, it certainly is not ready for the desert.

2. Service stations are often long distances apart in the desert—even on major highways. Fill up on gas and water when opportunities are presented.

3. Carry a tool kit and extra vehicle parts (see checklist at the end of this chapter for suggestions).

4. Use common sense when preparing for a trip and when driving in the desert. Be sure the radiator is clean and unclogged. Coolant added to the radiator water is an aid to prevent overheating. If your car becomes overheated, check the radiator (carefully! avoid being burned). If the water is at the proper level, drive in a lower gear in order that the motor's rotations per minute will be higher, and the water pump will move the water through the radiator at a higher rate. If you continue to have problems, avoid driving in the heat of the day, and drive at night or during the cooler parts of the day. Remember, too, that your tires are rapidly rotating on the desert's surface, which may be superheated. This heat certainly provides added stress on tires and possible attendant difficulties.

5. In certain areas, particularly in southern California, sand storms may be severe. On major highways, electrical signs advise travelers if blowing sand is extreme, and travel should be delayed until the storm abates. Not only may driving be dangerous at such times, but wind-blown sand is highly damaging to vehicles' paint and glass, efficiently sandblasting them—very often to the extent that a new paint job and replacement of windshield and windows are needed.

6. In parts of the open desert, strong winds may occur with or without accompanying sand and dust. These winds may pose a hazard for taller, lighter vehicles, such as campers. At such times, warnings may be issued, via electric signs and/or local radio, to high-profile vehicles, advising them to delay travel until the wind lessens.

7. Dust storms and vehicular traffic on highways can be lethal. Along some highways, fields have replaced desert growth. When these lie bare at certain times of the year, a strong wind may pick up the soil in such quantities as to completely obscure the vision of highway drivers. Some roads, such as the one between Phoenix and Tucson, Arizona, have a system of electrical signs which are activated at the scene, or remotely, to warn drivers of impending danger. Cautions, particularly for high-profile vehicles, may be given first. If the storm intensifies and the dust problem becomes serious, drivers are warned that travel is no longer safe, and the highway is closed. The Arizona Drivers License Manual states, "The reddish brown cloud varies in density and will, at times, limit a driver's vision to only the interior of the vehicle he or she is driving. Drivers may react violently to this situation by panic—stopping their vehicle in the traffic lane. The results are rear-end collisions." The manual advises the following action, "It is suggested that if you are engulfed by a dust storm you immediately reduce the speed of your vehicle and drive carefully off the traveled portion of the highway. Stop your vehicle as near the Right-Of-Way fence as possible. Turn your vehicle's lights off and wait until the dust storm has passed." Two points are very important: *Get as far off the road as possible; turn off all lights, including flashers.* That lights be turned off immediately is important, for following vehicles may think you are still moving, may attempt to follow your taillights, leave the road, and in the dense dust hit your car before realizing it is stationary. *Never stop your car on the highway. Get off the roadway before your ability to do so is blocked by increasing impairment of vision. Always obey warning signs and radio announcements regarding dust and sand storms.*

8. Beware of flash floods and of crossing flooded washes in your vehicle. The depth and force of water in these washes can be very deceptive. Each year in the deserts, a number of people drown as a result of such accidents. Remember that

flood water may move rapidly from the area where it was received into areas where no rain or only small amounts have fallen. A wall of water may hit a car crossing a wash. More often, a driver misjudges the water's depth and attempts to cross. The vehicle may be swept away by the force of the flowing water, or the motor get wet, causing the car to stall, whereupon rapidly rising water then tumbles the vehicle downstream. Passengers and driver may drown in the vehicle, or if they are able to escape from it, may often still drown in the turbulent waters which carry smashing boulders, logs, and other debris. Floods in washes, like sand and dust storms, usually dissipate within hours. Wait them out, if necessary, rather than risk lives for the sake of a few hours' time.

As one leaves the highways and main desert roads, additional considerations are necessary with regard to road conditions and driving techniques.

1. It is always safest to travel with a second vehicle when entering remote areas.

2. Your vehicle should be capable of the type of travel you are planning. People who do a great deal of back-country desert driving usually have pickups and/or four-wheel-drive vehicles, which provide the necessary power and high ground clearance.

3. Tires should be sturdy and chosen for the type of traveling to be done—that is, heavy-duty, wide-track tires are needed for rugged trail or sand driving. Sharp rocks, cactus spines and other thorns, and sharp vegetation are tire hazards. For this reason, some people prefer tubeless tires for desert driving, as these reduce air leakage from minor punctures.

4. Carry a rather extensive array of tools and spare parts. (See the checklist at the end of this chapter.) Know how to use them.

5. In turning your vehicle around on desert roads, remember that the road shoulder is often soft. Maneuver your car back and forth on the roadway itself, cutting your wheels sharply and reversing their angle each time you reverse the gear. This back-and-forth method may be time-consuming, but not nearly so time-consuming as getting yourself free if you become stuck.

6. Washboard roads are common in the desert. Driving on these roads can be frustrating and jarring. One method used to smooth the ride on this type of road is to increase speed. A vehicle traveling at about 45 miles per hour rides smoother than a vehicle traveling at 15–20 miles per hour. However, this increased speed sacrifices some control over the vehicle. You may easily lose control on such a road before you realize what is happening; slamming on the brakes tends to cause a further loss of control.

7. Rocky roads are very hard on a vehicle, particularly on the tires. Take it easy, drive slowly and carefully, watch the road, and attempt to miss as many rocks as possible, particularly those with sharp points and edges.

8. Move slowly, if in doubt about the road ahead; stop, get out, check the road on foot. Check clearances, for high centers may rupture oil pans. Gas tanks can be punctured on some vehicles. Overhangs may cause driving wheels to become suspended above the ground.

9. Soft sand is probably the most common barrier found in the desert. If you encounter sand, look for an alternate route. If none is available, get out and check the sand; determine if it is somewhat solid and coarse or is soft and fine. If you decide to attempt a crossing, remember that standard, narrow tires are swallowed in sand faster than oversized tires—larger tires have a broader "footprint," hence increased flotation. You can increase these footprints by deflating your tires to some extent. Do not deflate them, however, unless you have at your disposal the means to pump them back up again. When determining whether to go across the sand, determine how far you must go to solid ground, and logically determine whether you can make it if you use a burst of speed. If you decide on this course of action, don't change your mind in the middle of the operation. Slowing down at that point is likely to slow you to a full stop and a state of being stuck.

10. Regardless of how much driving experience you have had, you will undoubtedly find yourself stuck at some time, if driving in the desert. Getting unstuck is not a serious problem if you have come prepared. First determine where the nearest solid ground is. Do not try to power yourself out, because you will only power yourself into your own ditch. (Remember that a stuck four-wheel-drive vehicle is stuck

twice as badly as a two-wheel-drive vehicle.) The minute you feel you have lost traction, stop. If you are with another vehicle, its driver will probably be able to pull you out with a tow chain.

If yours is the only vehicle and some simple shovel work combined with pushing by the vehicle's occupants is insufficient to free you, more complete measures will have to be undertaken. First jack up the buried wheel or wheels. Watch that the jack does not slip off the pad. Be sure to block the unjacked tires with rocks so the vehicle does not roll. Dig the wheel out, and make a gradual ramp for the wheel to climb up. When these steps are accomplished, lay the sand mats (pieces of heavy wire mesh, boards, or sturdy carpet about four feet or longer by twelve inches wide) down under the wheel, and extend one end in the direction in which you will drive. If you do not have sand mats, you may improvise; use bushes, sticks, stones, even cool cushions from your vehicle's seats. Let your vehicle down. Release some air from the tires, both front and rear (only if you have a pump with which to reinflate them). Ideal tire pressures vary but, as an average figure, nine to twelve pounds is about right. Check to make sure the undercarriage is clear and will not high-center. You are now ready to ease out—put emphasis on the *ease*. This method of jacking up one or two tires, if necessary, should get you out. If it does not, try again with your vehicle unloaded.

11. In general, desert driving requires experience and good judgment. Do not abuse your vehicle. Concentrate on your driving, and avoid placing unnecessary stresses upon your vehicle when covering difficult terrain.

In no way is this chapter meant to discourage or frighten the novice desert enthusiast. Most of the precautions extended are simply common sense reduced to print. In any habitat (including cities)—and the desert no more than any other—one is advised to follow certain survival rules which apply to meeting the conditions presented there. If one follows basic rules and uses common sense in desert exploration, one has provided a degree of insurance for a pleasant, safe trip. The benefits to be reaped from successful, hassle-free desert exploration are very great. Enjoy the desert. Respect it. Share responsibility for it. Consider the motto, "take nothing but pictures; leave nothing but tracks, and place these very carefully."

Checklist: Suggested Items for Vehicular Maintenance and Repair

GENERAL DESERT TRAVEL

spare tire (mounted and inflated)
tire iron and lug wrench
jack
jumper cables
fan belt
radiator hose
heater hose
tool kit (including crescent wrench, set open-end wrenches, pliers, and both regular and Phillips screw-drivers)
oil
water
emergency flares

REMOTE DESERT TRAVEL

All of the above items, except that two spare tires, two jacks, and two tire irons should be included
two platforms for the jacks (twelve-inch squares of heavy plywood)
two sand mats
tire repair kit
spark plug tire pump
spark plug wrench
fuel pump
radiator stop leak
hydraulic fluid
gasket sealer
siphon hose
bailing wire
box assorted screws, nuts, bolts
electrical equipment (including fuses, set of points and condenser, spark plugs, roll electrical tape, electrical wire)

fire extinguisher
shovel
tow chain, or at least fifty feet of ¾-inch nylon rope
gas can, at least five-gallon, full
water can, at least five-gallon, full
gloves
axe

CHAPTER XI

Man, Heat, and Dehydration

THE DESERT'S most extenuating environmental conditions
are ordinarily those produced by heat and aridity. These two
factors are of vital concern to those people whose survival in
the desert is in question, as too many individuals learn each
summer in our southwestern deserts. For just as the plants
and animals of the desert must adapt their bodies and/or
life-styles—either morphologically, physiologically, instinctively, or cogitatively—to survive in heat and aridity, so
must the animal called man. Of these four means, only the
last—use of intelligence—is applicable for *Homo sapiens*.
When faced with a desert survival problem, man, so long
removed from coping with life on a mere survival basis, often
fails to recognize physical limitations in regard to heat tolerance and moisture need. Today, due to the increased frequency with which man lives in, works in, or visits the
desert, deaths and accidents in which heat and dehydration
play a role are increasingly frequent; yet most such incidents
could be avoided through proper preparation, knowledge of
the human body's limitations, and intelligent use of survival
techniques.

Not until World War II were complete and extensive
physiological studies done on man in the desert. The American Armed Forces were fighting in some of the most ex-

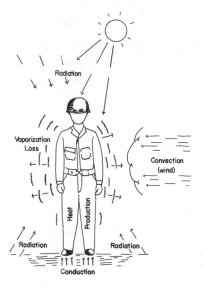

[FIG. 81.] Man's total heat gain balanced by his evaporative heat loss.*

*Reprinted from *Physiology of Man in the Desert*, courtesy of E. F. Adolph.

treme desert areas of the world, requiring the determination of how much water a fighting or working man required and what limitations heat placed upon him. Through exhaustive, basic research conducted at that time by Dr. E. F. Adolph, Professor Emeritus of Physiology at the University of Rochester, and his associates, we now know rather precisely what happens to man as he becomes dehydrated and how best to prevent this condition.

The human body gains heat through four major means: (1) direct radiation from the sun and reflected radiation from the ground and sky; (2) convection in which the air molecules carry heat to the skin; (3) conduction through body contact with surface areas, such as the ground; and (4) the production of metabolic heat by the body itself. The body picks up heat in any environment in which the ambient temperature exceeds that of the surface of the body, or at approximately 92° F. and above. The body's heat gain must be reduced when it reaches a certain level, or fever ensues, leading ultimately to death if it is not dissipated. Man's tissues and organs function properly over only a narrow range of temperature, with approximately 107° F. the maximum limit. Evaporative cooling of the skin and adjacent areas by evaporation of sweat produced by the more than two million sweat glands distributed over the human body is the body's primary heat-reducing means. The inner core of the body is cooled when its heat is transferred to the blood, which is then directed to the cooler peripheral body areas adjacent to the skin.

This evaporative cooling is efficient but costly in terms of water loss; it is particularly costly where heat is intense and water supplies are limited. Water lost from the body through sweating must be replaced; if it is not, dehydration and attendant complications ensue. Approximately two-thirds of the human body is composed of water, and the body needs it all, state Adolph and his associates. As one becomes dehydrated, the blood becomes more concentrated, and the blood flow becomes inadequate, partially because the blood volume has been reduced. In turn, this retarded blood flow

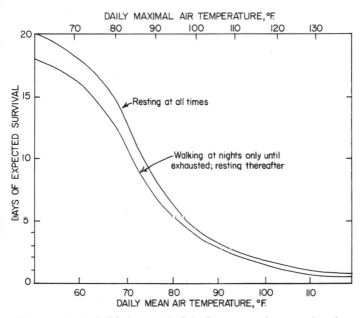

[FIG. 82.] Probable limits of a dehydrating man's survival in the desert when he has no water to drink.*

*Reprinted from *Physiology of Man in the Desert,* courtesy of E. F. Adolph.

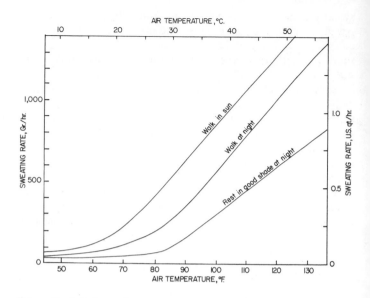

[FIG. 83.] Relation between average sweating rates and prevailing air temperatures in the desert.*

*Reprinted from *Physiology of Man in the Desert,* courtesy of E. F. Adolph.

causes the body's inner core temperature to continue to rise. Adolph and associates report that as dehydration occurs, pulse rates and rectal temperatures increase; breathing is faster; some numbness and tingling are apparent; and low morale and sleepiness may occur. As dehydration progresses, breathing is difficult; nausea and gastrointestinal upsets occur; loss of appetite and difficulty in muscular movements are apparent; the individual becomes emotionally unstable. By the time a person has lost water equivalent to 5 to 6 percent of body weight, he or she often shows signs of exhaustion and may become unable to walk and carry on ordinary activities. At an 8 percent deficit, the flow of saliva has nearly ceased. At 10 percent, people cannot be expected to cooperate among themselves. If the water loss reaches 12 percent of body weight, circulation is so impaired that an explosive, deep body heat rise is likely to occur, leading to death. In cooler environments, man may endure greater water deficits; he will become gradually weaker, dying at a deficit of 20 to 25 percent.

Man in the heat of the desert is usually partially dehydrated much of the time. This condition, known as voluntary dehydration, is especially prevalent between meals. Voluntary dehydration occurs because the sensation of thirst is not always present, even under partial dehydration. The deficits tend to be replaced during meals and over leisure hours. Because voluntary dehydration does occur, one who is subjected to desert heat should, to a certain extent, force himself to drink if water is available even though he is not thirsty. Any water which is not needed will eventually simply be excreted. The body can go into debt for water to a slight extent—about 1 to 3 percent of the body weight—without too drastic an effect. Any greater dehydration, however, tends to produce low morale and other early symptoms of dehydration.

Since desert air is ordinarily very dry, sweating rates can be deceptive. The skin may appear dry when actually the sweating rate is high; perspiration is being rapidly evaporated without remaining for any length of time on the skin's surface. By holding his hand over his arm for a few minutes and then removing it, one can see that a quantity of sweat is pouring out at all times when the body is undergoing heat stress. The body produces approximately eighty calories of heat per hour through its metabolic activity. Dissipation through sweating of this heat gain alone requires five ounces of water each hour. In high desert temperatures, man accumulates heat from other sources also. Adolph and associates measured sweating rates of man in various activities in the desert. They found that a man walking at the rate of approximately 3.5 miles per hour in the sun with an air temperature of 100° F. lost an average of one quart of water in perspiration each hour! Under identical environmental conditions, the same man driving a vehicle lost ¾ quart, while the man resting in the shade lost a mere ¼ quart, or one cup. In other experiments, the researchers determined the daily water needs for men undertaking various activities in the desert on days with a daily mean temperature of 90° F. Those men who were inactive and remained in the shade required approximately five to six quarts of water; those moderately active in the sun required approximately seven

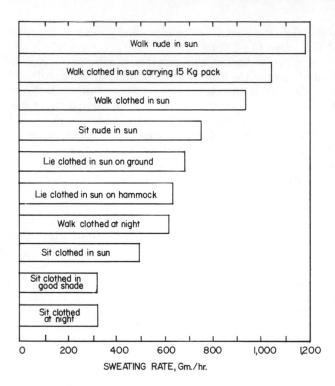

Walk nude in sun

Walk clothed in sun carrying 15 Kg pack

Walk clothed in sun

Sit nude in sun

Lie clothed in sun on ground

Lie clothed in sun on hammock

Walk clothed at night

Sit clothed in sun

Sit clothed in good shade

Sit clothed at night

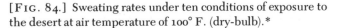

0   200   400   600   800   1,000   1,200

SWEATING RATE, Gm./hr.

[FIG. 84.] Sweating rates under ten conditions of exposure to the desert at air temperature of 100° F. (dry-bulb).*

*Reprinted from *Physiology of Man in the Desert,* courtesy of E. F. Adolph.

to eight quarts; and those working strenuously in the sun required approximately nine to ten quarts. Men on maneuvers in vehicles in the desert when the maximal air temperature was 102° F. were reported to drink an average of six quarts of water per twenty-four hours; men working in the sun at the same temperature drank a maximum of twelve quarts in twenty-four hours—and the researchers called attention to the fact that desert temperatures are often much higher than 102° F., with a consequent greater water need. The studies also determined that a man *resting in shade* during the hottest month, July, in a part of our most extreme southwestern desert country, Death Valley, would require nine quarts of water per day for maintenance alone. They projected survival statistics for a man *resting in the shade, doing no walking, and having no water* under various shade temperature conditions. Days of expected survival at shade temperature of 120° F. was two; at 110° F., three days; at 100° F., five days; and at 90° F., seven days. These and similar findings obviously have profound implications for the desert hiker.

Dehydration prevention measures are simple: (1) Imbibe amounts of water sufficient to equal those amounts lost through sweating, and/or (2) reduce sweating to a minimum. The individual facing an emergency survival situation in the desert may often find the first alternative impossible due to lack of water; the second may be difficult to practice, although not impossible. If some water is available, use of the

TABLE 1.

Days of expected survival in the desert under two conditions*

Condition	Max. daily shade temps., °F.	Available water per man, U.S. quarts					
		0	1	2	4	10	20
	120	2	2	2	2.5	3	4.5
	110	3	3	3.5	4	5	7
	100	5	5.5	6	7	9.5	13.5
No walking	90	7	8	9	10.5	15	23
at all	80	9	10	11	13	19	29
	70	10	11	12	14	20.5	32
	60	10	11	12	14	21	32
	50	10	11	12	14.5	21	32
	120	1	2	2	2.5	3	
	110	2	2	2.5	3	3.5	
Walking at night	100	3	3.5	3.5	4.5	5.5	
until exhausted	90	5	5.5	5.5	6.5	8	
and resting	80	7	7.5	8	9.5	11.5	
thereafter	70	7.5	8	9	10.5	13.5	
	60	8	8.5	9	11	14	
	50	8	8.5	9	11	14	

*Reprinted from *Physiology of Man in the Desert,* courtesy of E. F. Adolph.

Man, Heat, and Dehydration

two means in intelligent conjunction is advised. Adolph and his associates established certain general guidelines for survival under conditions of water shortage in the desert, with the primary maxim that each ounce of sweat a person can cheat the body from expending is an ounce of water gained for the body. For people as much as for plants and animals, the difference between life and death may at times hang on the precarious balance of a mere few ounces of moisture. Adolph and associates advise that if some water is available in an emergency situation, a fully hydrated man who decides to walk during the daytime should carry two gallons of water for every twenty miles he expects to cover. If he walks at night, he should carry one gallon for every twenty miles. A healthy, hydrated man can walk ten miles in three to four hours during a summer day in the desert without water supplies before he dehydrates to the point of exhaustion. However, if the distance to be covered is more, the basic rule of the desert should be obeyed: Walk only at night. Without water and walking only at night, a man can expect to cover no more than twenty to twenty-five miles in average summer weather before dehydration collapse—that is, however, obviously

TABLE 2.

Attainable distance before occurrence of limiting water deficit*

Daily mean temp., °F**	Number of miles, if the transportable water supply per man, in U.S quarts, is:				
	0	1	4	10	20
40	170	190	260	400	640
50	170	190	260	400	640
60	130	150	200	310	490
70	90	100	140	210	340
80	45	50	70	110	170
90	20	25	35	50	80
100	15	18	20	30	50
110	9	10	15	20	30
120	7	8	10	15	25

*Reprinted from *Physiology of Man in the Desert,* courtesy of E. F. Adolph.
**About fifteen degrees below maximal.

more than twice the distance he could expect to walk during daylight hours. Night walking should be started about nine or ten in the evening and continued until sunup to make use of the coolest hours.

The individual who does not walk or otherwise exert himself but stays in one location and follows general rules for reducing sweating expends approximately half or less the amount of water in sweat as does the man walking during the day. As do many animals, man should utilize the micro-environment most beneficial to him. A resting man should make use of the most complete shade available. If possible, while resting he should be elevated from the ground. Ground-surface temperatures may reach 160° F. or higher, and the first few inches of air above that surface are also superheated. Removing oneself to a level just above this may place the body in air having a temperature thirty or more degrees lower. Insofar as possible, one should also stay shielded from winds which increase evaporation of sweat and contribute to body heat gain through convection.

To remain clothed is exceedingly important. Contrary to much popular belief, the retention of clothing has been proved to help slow down the sweating process, by preventing perspiration from evaporating so fast that only a part of its cooling effect is used by the body. In addition, clothing insulates the body against heat gain by radiation and convection by reflecting much of this incumbent energy. For reflective purposes, white clothing is ideal. Under no circumstances should the clothing be so tight as to interfere with the evaporative cooling of the body. Thus the optimal clothing would be made of thin, loosely woven white cloth to allow air circulation. A hat is very important in the desert. Through the use of a simple, lightweight hat, the heat gain and attendant loss of water from the head and neck area are greatly reduced. The ideal hat is one, such as a man's straw hat, that projects well up off the head and allows air circulation. Clothing and a hat are also important in protecting the body from the direct rays of the sun which can burn even a darkly tanned skin quite easily and quite severely. In the desert sunlight, the person who removes his trousers, shirt, and hat subjects the body to a heat gain equivalent to a rise in air temperature of ten Fahrenheit degrees—certainly a convincing reason for remaining fully clothed under conditions of stress. Research determined that a person walking nude in the sun at a temperature of 100° F. had a sweating rate approximately *four times* that of a person sitting clothed in good shade.

When faced with a water emergency problem, keep your mouth closed; to prevent unnecessary evaporation of moisture from the mouth, refrain as much as possible from talking and do not smoke. If water is not available or is very limited, eat little or nothing, as digestion of food requires water; also refrain from ingesting salt, which increases water need. Do not drink urine, blood, or salt water, all of which may intensify thirst and none of which will serve as useful moisture sources for the body. Do not drink alcoholic beverages; the body processes alcohol as a food, and water is required in the process. In emergency situations in which vehicles are involved, radiator water may be available. However, in most cases today, this water contains coolants or similar agents with a basic ingredient of alcohol. Drinking water containing these agents can cause severe stomach cramps, pain, and possible death. Radiator or other polluted water and urine can be used for other than drinking, however. Spread the liquid over the skin or use it to soak clothing; it serves briefly to reduce the body's sweat needs for evaporative cooling.

If one is preparing to walk to seek rescue, often one has some water available at the location of departure—be it water carried in a plane or auto or that in a waterhole. If water is available, the person preparing to walk should forcefully overdrink, thereby using the stomach as an auxiliary canteen capable of carrying one to two quarts of extra water. Originally thought to be detrimental to the human system, this forced drinking has been proven to be beneficial in survival situations. Another fallacy which has been dispelled relates to the amount of water an individual should carry when attempting to walk to find help. Formerly, the disadvantages of strain placed on the individual by carrying a large supply of water were believed to outweigh the advantages of the water itself. Not so, for water in an amount equal to one-third a man's body weight can be carried with only a 32 percent increase in effort. The cost in sweat of carrying water was found to be less than 1 percent per hour of the supply carried. Each extra quart carried and consumed can increase the hiker's expected attainable distance by five to seven miles in average summer weather. Lack of suitable containers probably most commonly limits the amount of water that can be carried.

Rationing one's water over an extended period of time does not increase one's survival time, as was once believed. Although one's morale may be boosted by knowing that the canteen is full, this knowledge does nothing for the body's physiological condition. Water in the stomach does a better job than water in the canteen. When one experiences thirst, the minimum amount of water necessary to quench that thirst should be drunk. In some cases, individuals have died of heat and dehydration while water remained in their canteens, so assiduously did they ration their scant supplies.

The human body expends a certain amount of water under certain conditions. It cannot be trained to do with less, nor can it be tricked into believing it is receiving water when it is not. Thus Adolph and associates found that the old trick of placing a pebble in the mouth might help an individual psychologically but certainly not physiologically.

Studies revealed that sweating rates of individuals are approximately proportional to two-thirds of the power of the body weight. Hence a 200-pound person sweats approximately 30 percent faster than a 130-pound person. This fact has practical applications for a party in difficulty in the desert. If a group of people is stranded with no water or only a very limited supply, and decides to send a member on foot for help, theoretically a larger person can endure longer in this quest if no water is available; however, if some water is available, a smaller person can make the same amount of water go further.

Water is vital to the human body. Neither heroics nor wishing will substitute for it. Plan your desert outings carefully, and be prepared with an adequate water supply. But if an emergency situation arises—if you are stranded in the desert due to an airplane crash or a disabled vehicle or are lost afoot—consider all factors of your situation carefully. Particularly consider your water supply or nonsupply, and ask yourself: How long can I survive if I stay where I am? What are the possibilities of my rescue in this location? How long can I survive if I walk? How far can I expect to walk? How far might I need to go to increase my chances of rescue? Answer yourself truthfully; you cannot deceive your body physiologically. Remember that a man at rest loses only half as much water as the man who walks. And since the rate of dehydration often determines survival time, the solution to your problem takes very careful consideration. Your life may well depend on your decision.

CHAPTER XII

Potentially Dangerous Desert Animals

WHEN LANDS hosting fearsome, dangerous, and venomous animals are mentioned, the desert is often popularly ranked second only to the tropical jungles as depicted in the late, late show. This classification is unwarranted. The desert does contain a few species which are *potentially* dangerous to man. Most of these animals will not bother you if you provide them the same courtesy. In no way should their presence in the desert deter the outdoor enthusiast; but the hiker, camper, or backpacker who fails to take certain precautions against startling, upsetting, or damaging either himself or the animals that fall into this category, through an unneeded confrontation, is foolish and irresponsible. In addition to the potentially dangerous desert animals, we will also note some animals often considered to be dangerous which are not.

Centipede

Their name indicates a hundred legs; however, centipede species vary in the number of legs they have. They are at least many-legged, with each pair of legs arising from a separate body segment. A large pair of poison claws, ap-

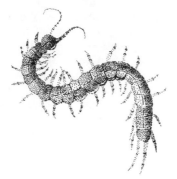

FIG. 85. The giant desert centipede, *Scolopendra heros*, may attain a maximum length of 8 inches. It can inflict a painful, but not serious bite, if handled or molested.

pendages of the first trunk segment, are used in obtaining food. Over 3,000 described centipede species of varying sizes and colors—including yellow, red, blue, and combinations of these—are distributed throughout the world in both temperate and tropical climates; centipedes are certainly not unique to the desert. The most impressive species present in the southwestern desert country is the giant desert centipede, *Scolopendra heros,* which occurs in Mexico and many of the southern states of the United States, including Georgia, Alabama, Kansas, Texas, and Arizona. *Scolopendra heros* may reach a maximum length of eight inches, has twenty-one pairs of legs, and varies in color from olive to brown. The last, or anal, pair of legs is modified for pinching or grasping. Prey may be attacked and grasped by these prehensorial legs; the head is then rapidly curved backward and the venom claws are embedded in the prey, which is held immobile by other pairs of legs until the venom takes effect. Food consists of insects, spiders, worms, and similar material. Individual centipedes are solitary and nocturnal. They spend much time under stones and bark and in holes in the ground, preferring some moisture. In the desert they are observed primarily in the summer months, at night, and particularly after the moisture brought by summer rains has triggered insect abundance.

Desert centipedes may bite people who handle them or with whom they come into accidental contact, as they might

Potentially Dangerous Desert Animals   189

in bedding left on the ground. The bite is reported to be a "painful inconvenience," but is ordinarily no reason for major concern. Application of an antiseptic to the bite is indicated to combat infection. If the animal has run across the skin, the many sharp-tipped claws may scratch the human skin, causing irritation and bacterial infection. Some centipedes, although certainly not all, have repugnatorial glands located on the ventral side of each body segment or on certain of their legs. These glands are capable of emitting an irritating acid; debate exists as to whether or not the desert centipede drops any such material into the scratches. It is probable that these are minor wounds which have simply occurred in the animal's efforts to escape the thin-skinned human with whom it has unfortunately come into contact.

Millipede

The nonvenomous millipedes superficially resemble centipedes. Their name implies that they are thousand-legged, which they are not; like the centipede, they are many-legged. They have one pair of legs per body segment; however, at some point in evolution, their segments fused in sets of two, so that they now appear to have two pairs of legs per segment. As a group they vary in size, but the millipedes commonly seen in our southwestern deserts are approximately four to six inches in length. These species are dark brown, more often black, in color; they are in general herbivorous, eating decomposing plants, and primarily nocturnal. They are not particularly fast moving and may, if threatened, roll up into a neat ball, rather well enclosed in the hard tergin covering their dorsal surface. They possess repugnatorial glands on each trunk segment; the chemical excreted from these glands varies from species to species and may include aldehydes, quinones, and phenols. Certain species have been identified as possessing hydrogen cyanide. Some have been reported to have secretions caustic to the skin; however, these reports are not from species in our area.

Millipedes dwell primarily in moister habitats than the

F IG . 86. Millipedes of the southwestern deserts are 4 to 6 inches long, dark brown to black in color, and herbivorous. They are nonvenomous, but do excrete a substance which may temporarily stain the hands of human handlers.

desert. They are seen in the dry desert environment after the summer rains; they emerge then from under rocks and debris and from retreats in the ground in great numbers, and, by our standards and perhaps by their own as well, appear to revel in the moisture. At this time, children are likely to find that handled desert millipedes excrete from their repugnatorial glands a substance which temporarily stains the hands yellow-brown and gives them an unpleasant odor. These animals are essentially harmless. To rub the eyes with hands soiled by their secretion is not advisable, however. If the secretion does enter the eye, wash the eye with large amounts of water; contact a physician if discomfort is present.

Whip Scorpion, or Vinegaroon

Whip scorpions belong to the class Arachnida (the scorpion, spider, mite, and tick class). Within it, they compose a separate small order, Uropygi; its members are also referred to as uropygids. These uropygids are certainly among the more menacing in appearance of the desert arthropods, yet they are not venomous. As a group, whip scorpions are found throughout tropical and semi-tropical parts of the world. Some, such as *Mastigoproctus giganteus*, which occurs in the North American desert, live in dry environments, but most species prefer a moister habitat. *Mastigoproctus giganteus* ranges in the southern United States from the east to west coasts. It is one of the large species, up to approximately 2½ inches in length. Dark gray to black in color, it normally walks on the last three pairs of long, jointed legs, using the first, even longer pair in a sensory–tactile function. The *pedipalps* (anterior appendages, lying on each side of

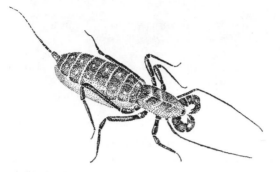

FIG. 87. The whip scorpion, or vinegaroon, *Mastigoproctus giganteus,* may reach approximately 2½ inches in length and is dark gray to black. Though it appears ferocious, it is actually harmless to man.

the mouth) are extremely stout and heavy; they form formidable pincers used in seizing prey, which consists of small invertebrates. From the last segment of the abdomen arises a long, thin posterior appendage which is moved or whipped from one position to another, varying from straight up to straight back to a variety of intermediate positions. Neither it nor the jaws contain any substance of danger to man. When irritated, the animal elevates the end of the abdomen and sprays the attacker with a fluid secreted from a pair of large anal glands. In *M. giganteus,* this secretion is reported to be 84 percent acetic acid and 5 percent caprylic acid. When sprayed on a fellow arthropod, the caprylic acid effectively paves the way for the entrance into the arthropod victim's body of the acetic acid. The fluid may irritate human skin. Its repugnant odor is due to the acetic acid; hence the animal's common name, vinegaroon. Whip scorpions are nocturnal, hiding in retreats during the day; in the desert, they are seldom seen except during the warm summer rainy season. Some species do not mature until three years of age and may engage in courtship dances before mating. The female secludes herself in some retreat during egg laying. She remains there with the eggs attached to her body until they hatch and the young have undergone several molts; shortly after their dispersal, she dies.

Sun Spider, or Solpugid

The sun spider (*Eremobates sp.*), like the vinegaroon, is an arachnid. It belongs to the order Solifugae, which includes approximately 800 tropical and semi-tropical species, with more than 100 species occurring in the southwestern United States. Many prefer an arid environment and are common in warm deserts of the world where they hide under stones or in crevices or burrow underground. Their tendency to have diurnal habits has earned them their common name, sun spider; a second name, wind spider, refers to their running speed.

Sun spiders are often light in color and may reach a length of 2¾ inches. They have two body sections. The first portion appears to be composed almost entirely of large pincers; the second is a fused abdominal section. Their most remarkable features are the two enormous *chelicerae* (anterior appendages), each composed of two pieces which together form a pincer; these pieces articulate vertically. The first pair of legs is often held aloft or in front of the animal; they are used as tactile organs. The animal moves by means of the remaining three pairs.

Solpugids have voracious appetites and feed on all types of small animals. They are nonvenomous and obtain food by seizing it, then killing it and ripping it apart with the chelicerae. Sun spiders are totally harmless to man; they are in fact helpful in destroying insects and certainly do not deserve the unwarranted fear man often feels toward them.

Fig. 88. The sun spiders, or solpugids, *Eremobates sp.*, are approximately 2 to 3 inches in length. Nonvenomous, they are not only harmless to man but are helpful as destroyers of insects.

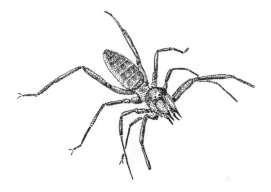

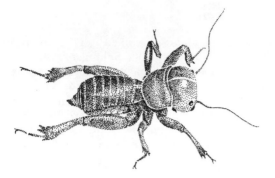

FIG. 89. The Jerusalem cricket, *Stenopelmatus sp.*, is a harmless, interesting insect up to 2 inches in length. It has often been erroneously considered dangerous to man and animals.

Jerusalem Cricket

A totally harmless but impressive-appearing insect found in the desert as well as in other areas is the Jerusalem cricket, *Stenopelmatus sp.* These insects are shy and nocturnal in habit, usually golden to dark brown in color, approximately 1½ to 2 inches in length, and have large, smooth, rounded heads. The Navajo Indians reportedly apply to these insects a fitting common name which translates as "Old Man Baldhead." The top of the head has markings which, with imagination, can be seen to resemble a smiling face; hence another common name, "Baby Face." Since their legs are adapted for tunneling in sandy soil, the Jerusalem crickets are also sometimes referred to as sand crickets. Jerusalem crickets, like the sun spiders, are sometimes referred to as "Nina de la Tierra," or "Child of the Earth." Like a good many other unusual-looking animals, this one has suffered from a poor reputation, completely unfounded and perpetuated by superstitious, uninformed individuals who have in the past blamed this innocuous little insect for even the deaths of cattle and horses. In actuality the Jerusalem cricket's only protection against man, cow, or horse is its nipping jaws. This insect is not a true cricket, but a member of an insect family separate from, but closely related to, the family which includes the true crickets.

FIG. 90. Velvet ants are actually mutillid wasps. Often brightly colored, the females are wingless. As with other wasps, their sting can be painful.

Velvet Ant

Velvet ants are not ants; rather, they are wasps of the family Mutillidae and are often referred to as mutillid wasps. The males have wings, but the females are wingless and may be seen running over the ground in the summer. They are interesting and often striking in appearance; many have long, fuzzy hair over much of the body, and they are often brightly colored, varying from red, yellow, and orange, to white, or occasionally displaying combinations of colors. The females seek cocoons of other wasps, or sometimes of bees, which are located in the ground. In each cocoon they deposit an egg, then reseal the cocoon. The young mutillid wasp uses the pupa within the cocoon as its food and undergoes its own development in that location.

The velvet ants possess a powerful sting. Their often-bright color pattern is thought to serve as warning coloration, advertising their power to potential predators. Their stings have earned them the exaggerated common names of "cow-killers" and "mule-killers." They are not stock killers. But even man should observe their warning colors and take heed—watch, but do not touch, these wasps.

The desert is home to many other kinds of wasps, and to a rather bountiful array of ant and bee species. As in any other area where these insects abound, care should be taken, for one's comfort, to avoid being stung. Certainly for the individual known to be supersensitive to their venom, as is occasionally the case particularly in regard to bee venom, caution should be practiced, including medical consultation as to measures to be taken, if stung.

Kissing Bug

Kissing bugs, *Triatoma sp.*, are also commonly known as cone-nosed bugs, assassin bugs, bellows bugs, and walpai tigers. They are members of the family Reduviidae. Several species are present in the Southwest; they are similar in appearance to box elder bugs. One-half to one inch in length, these insects have an elongated cone-shaped head. Their mouth parts are of the piercing and sucking type and are folded beneath the head when not in use. Kissing bugs can be of concern to man; they may produce a painful venomous bite and are carriers, at least in some parts of their range, of a serious illness, Chagas' Disease.

Kissing bugs feed on the blood of their hosts, which may include man. Normally they live in rodent nests, particularly those of pack rats. By piercing and sucking, they feed on the rodents' blood. In early and midsummer, they often invade homes, particularly those located on the deserts' edge around cities. This invasion is particularly likely where pack rat nests occur close to habitations. The kissing bugs hide in crevices and cracks of houses, emerging at night to feed on the blood of their sleeping human victim. The severity of the bite varies according to the susceptibility of the victim. Normally, a hard welt ½ to 3 inches in diameter develops. More sensitive individuals may develop extensive swelling of the affected member, and some experience systemic symptoms such as nausea, rapid heart action, and increased rate of respiration.

In southern Mexico and South America, *Triatoma* is host to a small flagellate microorganism which can, in its extended stage, cause Chagas' Disease in humans. Symptoms of the disease are often delayed for long periods. The parasite may eventually invade the human blood system and migrate into tissues, commonly those of the heart, spleen, and lymph nodes. No cases of Chagas' Disease have been

FIG. 91. The kissing bug, *Triatoma sp.* (½ to 1 inch in length), produces a painful venomous bite as it pierces human skin and consumes blood. In the early summer, these insects may invade and be serious pests in homes located in the open desert.

recorded in the United States. However, the same or a very similar trypanosome which causes Chagas' Disease has been found in kissing bugs and small animals in the southwestern United States.

The human sleeper may be bitten by the kissing bug without being aware of it. Often, however, the sleeper is awakened by itching or pain; a normal reaction is to slap at the insect and scratch the bite. The kissing bug often defecates as it bites; the trypanosome is carried in this material. If this defecated material is already present on the victim's skin, or if the victim smashes the bug, releasing the material on himself, and then scratches the bite, he will thereby rub feces, which may carry the trypanosomes, into the wound, possibly infecting himself. The trypanosome also can be contracted if rubbed into the eyes or mucous membranes. Therefore, do not smash the offending insect on your body, and wash well the bite and surrounding area to remove any feces.

Tarantula

The tarantula is the desert's largest spider, with a leg span of six to seven inches. Heavy-bodied, hairy, dark brown to black in color, the various species which are found in our desert areas are classified in more than one genus. They have often been needlessly feared and killed by man. In North America, tarantulas are not confined to the desert but are also found in other habitats; their eastern limit in the United States is the Mississippi River. They are, however, especially plentiful in the Southwest.

Tarantulas live singly in burrows from which they venture for short distances for hunting, quickly retreating underground if threatened with danger. Their primary food consists of insects and other arthropods; in captivity they will eat mice and lizards, as they may also in the wild. They tend to suddenly jump or pounce upon their prey, subduing it by injecting venom with their fangs. Digestive juices are then poured into the victim's body, and the liquified nourishment is sucked into the spider's body.

Tarantulas are extremely long-lived. They do not reach sexual maturity until approximately ten years of age. Females have a tendency to eat their mates, if possible, and the males' longevity record following sexual maturity is not a good one, due to both this factor and the fact that many of the males fall prey to predators in their search for mates. Females, which do not roam to the extent of the males, may live up to twenty-five years. Immature males and females are virtually indistinguishable until their last molt, when the males become apparent—they are darker than the females, who are often also heavier-bodied. The female lays her eggs on a silken sheet which she then forms into a bag. Sometimes moving the bag from one location to another in the burrow, the mother watches over her eggs for as long as seven weeks until the spiderlings emerge. The young soon leave to establish their solitary burrows. They suffer a high mortality rate; ultimately, probably only one or two of the original group will survive.

Much of the year tarantulas are seldom or never seen by human observers. Summer is their most active period, when they tend to be nocturnal. They may also be observed after showers on moist, overcast summer days. Most often the tarantulas are observed crossing roads, and at night their eye shine may be seen reflecting in the car lights. Unfortunately a good many of the big spiders are killed by automobiles as the unsuspecting, long-legged creatures move slowly and deliberately across the blacktop. Other enemies include rodents, birds, lizards, and some snakes which will eat them. In its defense against such predators, the tarantula may tilt its body backward, displaying its fangs in a defensive attitude. Additionally, tarantulas have one unique feature—the fine hair on their abdomen is very irritating. If being attacked, as by a small mammal, the tarantula will work its hind legs rapidly and scrape loose a small cloud of the fine abdominal hair, brushing it at the intruder. When these hairs come into contact with the mucous membranes of the eyes or nose of mammals, a disagreeable irritation results, and this diversion will often give the tarantula time to escape the predator.

FIG. 92. Hairy, dark brown or black, the tarantulas in our deserts are unnecessarily feared. They are mild-mannered, and their bite is approximately equal to a bee or wasp sting where man is concerned. Some may have a leg span of 6 or 7 inches.

One major predator of the tarantula is the tarantula hawk. *Pepsis* is a large, dark metallic blue, often orange- or red-winged, digger wasp, which uses the adult tarantula as a food source for its young. The female tarantula hawk searches for and finds an adult tarantula, usually a female (preferred because of her larger size), and paralyzes it with its sting. The tarantula hawk has a regular routine for the paralyzing process. She mounts the spider and, bending her abdomen under the ventor of the tarantula, envenomates the prey. A series of stings may be necessary to completely subdue the prey. Once the spider is subdued, the Pepsis wasp drags the spider—eight to ten times her own weight—to a burrow or hole. There the wasp lays an egg on the tarantula. The spider, paralyzed but not dead, will provide the wasp's young with a source of fresh food for the entire larval period.

Tarantulas have in the past been inappropriately attributed with lurid attacks on unsuspecting people and animals; indeed a common name for them in Mexico, where they often were believed to be dangerous to horses, has been "Areno de caballo" (horse spider). The tarantulas in the North American desert areas are, in fact, virtually harmless to anything of horse, human, and even much smaller size. They do have venom but, for man, a tarantula bite is considered to be about equal in strength to a bee or wasp sting. The tarantulas actually are quite tractable. They are kept as pets by some individuals and can ordinarily be handled readily; the spiders will normally walk on the human hand or up an arm with no problem suffered by either human or spider, provided the spider is not confined in its actions or grabbed—which, after all, is better than a human could be expected to do if it were being handled by a spider many times its size!

Black Widow Spider

"Black widow" is the common name for several species of spiders of the genus *Latrodectus*. Spiders of this genus have an almost worldwide distribution in tropical and temperate regions. They are found in every state in the continental United States and in portions of Canada, although they are more common in the southern than in the northern portions of the United States. They are one of the most easily recognized and best-known of our North American spiders, and are among the most venomous spiders known.

Man, when bitten by a black widow, experiences local pain. The spider's venom is neurotoxic. Symptoms include sweating, congestion of the face and eyes, salivation, nausea, vomiting, feeling of apprehension, severe muscular cramps, boardlike rigidity of the abdomen, abnormally high blood and spinal fluid pressures, changes in the electrocardiogram, and pain settling in the abdomen and legs. Progression of symptoms is rapid, but the effects begin to regress

FIG. 93. Widespread in distribution, the black widow spider, *Latrodectus sp.* (approximately 1 inch in length), occurs throughout much of the temperate and tropical world. It is retiring and unaggressive, but extremely venomous; antivenin is available. These spiders are common around abandoned buildings, in piles of debris, or in undisturbed dark corners of garages and storage buildings. An adult female is readily recognized by the red marking on her abdomen, easily noted as she often hangs upside down from her web.

after several hours. Poisoning may be fatal to small children or to people with hypertension or coronary problems. Antivenin is available. Frequently the human victim has not seen the spider and does not realize the cause of his illness. Errors in diagnosis are sometimes made; the removal of the victim's appendix is one common mistake! Fatal cases are rare. One researcher found that for the ten-year period from 1960 through 1969, 344 deaths from bites and stings of venomous animals were reported for the United States. Of this total, only four were reported as caused by black widow spider bites. (By way of comparison, 122 deaths were reported in the same period as a result of wasp and bee stings combined.)

Black widows spin their webs in crevices, under logs, in abandoned rodent holes, and in similar locations. They are less spiders of the desert environment than of man's environments, often being found in old buildings, wood piles, and dark corners of garages and attics. You are, in fact, much more likely to encounter them around residences in the desert than in the desert wilderness.

A remarkable dimorphism is present in the sexes of the

black widow; only the larger, dark females produce sufficient venom to be dangerous to man. Females are fairly large, and a deep shiny black in color. A globular abdomen displaying a red hourglass marking on its ventral surface makes the female easily identifiable. Males are much smaller, gray, variously striped or spotted, and do not carry the red marking. The black widow spins a rather messy-appearing, ungeometric web in which prey is trapped. These spiders are solitary and active primarily at night. The females spin egg cocoons, white or light gray in color; the 300 to 500 eggs they contain hatch in approximately thirty days.

Although potentially very dangerous, these spiders are retiring and unaggressive, probably normally biting a human only when the victim brushes against the spider or a similar contact is made.

Brown Recluse Spider

Spiders of the genus *Loxosceles* are distributed fairly widely in the United States; several species are represented, particularly in the southern and western states. These small to medium-sized spiders, approximately $5/16$ inch in body length, are dark brown to fawn color, with a darker, violin-shaped mark on the upper side of the cephalothorax. This mark gives rise to one of their common names, "violin spider." As with the black widow spiders, the recluse spiders are most abundant around manmade structures.

This spider possesses a hemolytic venom. When bitten, a person may feel little or no discomfort or may have a local stinging pain. Within a few hours, a hemorrhagic blister appears at the site and gradually increases in size. Over a period of days, the affected area centered about the bite becomes gangrenous, tissue sloughs off, and a draining ulcer forms. The ulcerous condition may continue to spread outward, destroying adjacent tissue due to the fact that the toxin remains in the tissue at the site for a long period. Physicians may find it necessary to excise the bite area to remove the infecting source, after which the ulcer begins to heal. If left unchecked, the ulcer may continue to grow to a size several inches in diameter. In some cases the victim may have chills, fever, aching, a generalized skin rash, and nausea. Death is

FIG. 94. Recluse spiders, *Loxosceles sp.* (approximately ⁵/₁₆ inch in length), are also known as violin spiders after the darker marking on the upper side of the cephalothorax. These spiders possess a hemolytic venom. Their bite may produce a serious ulcerous condition which spreads outward from the site of the bite.

rarely associated with the bite of the brown recluse. No antivenin is available.

As with the black widow, this spider is retiring, and man's encounters with it are often connected in some way with moving stored materials, bundles of unused clothing, and piles of debris, or otherwise disturbing the spider and its large irregular web. Ordinarily the primary problem associated with the bite of this spider is that of the ulcer. Its bite does not present an emergency situation, inasmuch as several hours may elapse before the first symptoms appear. Such a bite is, however, a situation to be handled by a physician.

Gila Monster and Mexican Beaded Lizard

Worldwide, only two known species of venomous lizards exist. The two species are members of the same genus and are similar in appearance. The Mexican beaded lizard, *Heladerma horridum,* occurs only in Mexico; its range in the Pacific drainage from the state of Chiapas northward into southern Sonora is such that it barely touches the Sonoran

Desert's southern portions. Basically the Mexican beaded lizard is not a desert inhabitant.

The Gila monster, however, is primarily a desert species, occurring in extreme southwestern Utah, the southern tip of Nevada, southwestern New Mexico, Arizona, and Sonora. A rather typical habitat for it is the saguaro forest.

The Gila monster, *Heloderma suspectum,* is heavy-bodied, with an almost cylindrical body. The head is large, somewhat flattened, and equipped with strong jaws; it terminates in a rounded snout. Out of the generous-sized mouth flicks, snakelike, a black tongue. The animal has a large sausagelike tail which serves as a fat storage organ, changing from plump to depleted according to the animal's condition. The legs are short and appear set too far apart to support the lengthy body. The feet have strong curved claws. Average adult length (body plus tail) for the Gila monster is 14 to 18 inches; a specimen of 20 inches has been reported. The Mexican beaded lizard is larger, a specimen 32 inches having been recorded. These two lizard species are covered over their dorsal surface with small, round, closely set scales. The Gila monster is patterned with contrasting markings of orange, pink, or yellow, and black; the Mexican beaded is similarly mottled and blotched in terms of yellow and black. The combination of rounded scales and irregular color pattern give these lizards a general effect of Indian beaded work.

Gila monsters are dormant during the coldest months, diurnal in moderate temperatures, and primarily nocturnal during the hottest months. Their irregular color pattern serves in dim light to conceal them. Against a dark background, the black portions of the pattern blend, and the light markings appear to be sticks, rocks, or the like. On a light background, the reverse occurs. The Gila monster retreats to burrows of other animals, digs its own, or enters pack rat nests or natural cavities. It is most common on the lower slopes of desert mountains, ranging onto the outwash plains, and may also be found in canyons and along washes where water, which it appears to need during its active period, may be available. Three to eleven eggs are produced by the mature female after the summer rains have begun. These eggs are buried about five inches deep in sand or soft soil. Gila monsters are thought to live to an age of twenty-

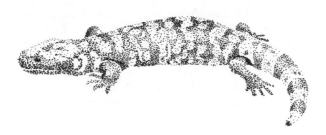

FIG. 95. The Gila monster, *Heloderma suspectum,* is one of the only two venomous lizards in the world. This lizard may reach a maximum length of 20 inches, is patterned with orange, to pink, to yellow, and black, beaded-looking scales. If cornered or handled it may bite, chewing its venom into the victim. The bite of a Gila monster should be considered a serious medical emergency.

five to thirty years. Their food consists of bird and reptile eggs and small mammals, such as young rabbits and rodents, which are killed by means of the lizard's venom.

The neurotoxic venom of these two lizard species is produced in modified salivary glands in the lower jaw. The venom is not injected by means of fangs, but is free flowing and is chewed into the wound by the grooved teeth. The Gila monster is famous for its tenacity; it hangs on tightly when biting. Modified teeth which draw the venom by their capillary action quickly become bathed in the venom and, as the lizard continues to chew, increasing amounts of venom enter the wound. To disengage the reptile from its victim as quickly as possible is thus important.

No human deaths appear to be uncontestably attributable solely to the bite of the Gila monster. Deaths have occurred in connection with such bites but, in all cases, such deaths appear to have been complicated by alcoholism, debility, or similar conditions. Symptoms and their severity following a bite are varied and depend upon many factors, such as the quantity of venom received, which depends somewhat upon the number of teeth engaged in the bite and the length of time they were engaged; the size of the lizard; the physical condition and size of the victim; and other variables. Symptoms following a minor bite have been reported as consisting of local pain, prolonged bleeding at the site, and sometimes nausea and faintness. More severe bites may cause severe pain, profuse bleeding, initial shock, anxiety, swelling, perspiration, and edema. In extreme cases labored breathing, cyanosis, fever, swelling of the tongue, and paralysis have been reported.

Two other lizards are sometimes confused with the Gila monster. The nocturnally active gecko is occasionally thought to be a young Gila monster, and the chuckwalla—a large, rock-inhabiting, primarily vegetarian lizard—is confused with the adult Gila monster. Neither the gecko nor the chuckwalla have the beaded scales of the Gila monster, and neither is venomous.

The Gila monster deserves neither name—monster nor *suspectum*—nor does the beaded lizard deserve *horridum*. All of these names simply continue to contribute to a popular misconception and fear of these exceedingly interesting animals. They are not numerous and, unless they are caught, handled, or cornered, they make every attempt to avoid man. These lizards are somewhat deceptive, often appearing sluggish and slow moving. If teased, cornered, or forced to bite, they then exhibit agility and speed, being capable of rapidly twisting the head about and grabbing the victim with unexpected rapidity, singleness of purpose, and tenacity. Many of the reported Gila monster bites have occurred as a result of human handling of the lizards (some of the alcohol-

FIG. 96. The chuckwalla, *Sauromalus obesus,* is a large (5½ to 8 inches, snout-to-vent length), heavy-bodied, herbivorous lizard. Creosote bush is its staple food. The chuckwalla inhabits rocky sites, basking on top of the rocks, and wedging itself into crevices among the rocks when threatened.

accompanied bites have taken place in this situation), and bites by captive animals have occurred through cloth bags.

The Gila monsters pose almost no threat to the person who avoids them or simply observes them from a respectful distance. If a bite does occur, however, it is to be considered potentially dangerous, and immediate medical help should be obtained. We wish also to note that the Gila monster is *protected by law* in the state of Arizona. These lizards are not to be killed, and they cannot be caught, sold, or kept as captives without a special permit. This law, passed in 1952, is certainly a commendable example of environmentally protective legislation.

Scorpions

Scorpions are members of the class Arachnida and are the oldest known terrestrial arthropods; they can be traced back to the Devonian period, more than 266 million years ago. Scorpions are found in many of the tropical, subtropical, and desert areas of the world, and about 800 species have been described worldwide. All scorpions are venomous; some are of great danger to man. In the North American deserts, lethal species are few, but of importance.

Scorpions are eight-legged and have long anterior pedipalps greatly enlarged to form a pair of pincers for capturing prey. The preabdomen consists of seven segments. A postabdomen of five segments terminates in a bulbous base and sharp, curved barb that injects the venom hypodermically. This postabdomen, or "tail," is articulated, allowing movement to the side or up over the body, bringing the barb beyond the head. In stinging, the scorpion raises the tail over the body, curves it forward, and, with a stabbing motion, envenomates the prey. The pedipalps alone are generally used to subdue the prey; however, if difficulty is met, the prey is held by the pedipalps and envenomation is accomplished by use of the barbed tail. Scorpions are predacious in nature and eat spiders, beetles, flies, grasshoppers, worms, centipedes, sun spiders, black widow spiders, and sometimes other scorpions. Inasmuch as the principal purpose of the venom is to paralyze small invertebrate prey, the strength of the toxin in most species is not powerful

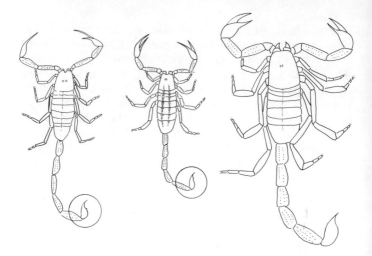

FIG. 97. Note the comparative sizes of two scorpion species. The two smaller specimens are *Centruroides sculpturatus*, a potentially lethal species. The center scorpion, with darker body stripes, was formerly considered a separate species, *C. gertschi*. At the far right is the larger, nonlethal, giant hairy scorpion, *Hadrurus arizonensis*. Average adult size of the *Centruroides* is 2 to 3 inches; for *Hadrurus* it is approximately 4 to 6 inches.

enough to cause great danger to man. The sting of many nonlethal species is often equated to that of a yellow jacket or hornet.

Scorpions are secretive, usually hunting for prey at night. They are commonly found under loose bark on trees; in lumber piles, brick stacks, and firewood; under rocks; in abandoned buildings; in garages and attics; under houses; and in crevices. Their presence in shoes and bedding is not unknown. Scorpions require water and may be attracted to habitations for this reason. Dr. Herbert Stahnke, an authority on scorpions, states that any constantly moist place is very likely to attract scorpions.

In the United States scorpions are more widespread than one might presume, being distributed over three-fourths of the nation. Approximately forty species occur in the continental United States; in the state of Arizona alone, approximately twenty species occur. Scorpions range across the southern states from Florida to California; they occur as far north as Washington and Montana and have been collected in southern Canada. In general they are not found in the New England and Great Lake states. Florida and California have the most species. In the deserts under discussion, Arizona, southern California, Baja California, southwestern New Mexico, and Mexico have lethal species.

Lethal scorpions which may be encountered in the North American deserts belong to the single genus, *Centruroides;* for the most part, only the single species *sculpturatus* occurs in the range outlined. Formerly, a second species, *gertschi,* was also recognized; this species is now considered to be a form of *sculpturatus.*

Because its venom is potentially lethal, the desert dweller or hiker should be able to identify *C. sculpturatus.* Unfortunately, to complicate the problem, *C. sculpturatus* is not the largest nor most imposing of the scorpions in its range, nor is it brightly marked, as is the black widow spider. It is quite small by comparison to the giant hairy scorpion, *Hadrurus arizonensis,* one of the impressive, large, nonlethal scorpions of the Southwest. Dr. Stahnke presents the following points for identification: (1) *C. sculpturatus* is yellowish or greenish-yellow to straw color over the entire body. The former *C. gertschi* is of the same coloration but also displays two irregular blackish stripes on the upper surface. (2) In size, *C. sculpturatus* range from ½ inch in length at the time they leave the mother to an average adult length of 2 inches, although certain individuals may be almost 3 inches when fully developed. (3) These scorpions are "slender." The adult female's body at its greatest width is not wider than ⅜ inch; the male's is only ¼ inch or less. (4) The adult female's "tail" may be slightly more than $1/16$ inch in diameter; the male's is even more slender. (5) The pincers are very slender, about six times as long as the broadest part. (6) Most importantly, *C. sculpturatus* possesses a subaculear tooth. This very small tooth, or *tubercle,* at the base of the stinger may be discernible to the naked eye if it is silhouetted against the light, or may be seen with a hand lens.

Although the only lethal species of scorpions which occur in the North American desert area belong to the genus *Centruroides,* this genus also includes nonlethal species. Most, although not all, members of this genus, whether poisonous or not, display the subaculear tooth. The only

FIG. 98. A subaculear tooth is found at the base of the stinger of species of *Centruroides*. A hand lens may be necessary to determine its presence. This tooth, or tubercle, is one aid in identifying the lethal species, *C. sculpturatus;* however, in some areas additional species of *Centruroides*, nonlethal but bearing the tooth, may be present.

species of *Centruroides* in Arizona is *sculpturatus*. Thus if one is stung by a scorpion in Arizona which is identified as possessing the subaculear tooth, one is able to positively identify the species as *sculpturatus* and the sting as potentially dangerous. In other states, where nonlethal subaculear-toothed *Centruroides* occur, this determination is not valid.

One behavioral feature also helps to differentiate *C. sculpturatus*. Nonlethal species are sometimes known as "ground scorpions"; they are often found on the ground or substratum. *C. sculpturatus* reacts negatively to gravity and is more often found clinging to the underside of its covering. Thus *C. sculpturatus* is often found hanging from the underside of rocks, boards, and the like. Keep this fact in mind when moving materials or picking up rocks. Stings commonly occur when people pick up objects without checking the underside and inadvertently touch or press the scorpion with their hands.

The study of *C. sculpturatus* and the nonlethal species (perhaps in a natural history museum) is recommended homework for desert enthusiasts; the differences between them are easy to note. One common name for *C. sculpturatus*, slender scorpion, notes one of its identifying characteristics. Another, bark scorpion, refers to its penchant for clinging to the underside of loose bark on tree trunks and limbs. This name denotes another trait that is advisable for the human firewood-gatherer to remember.

For the desert explorer, *C. sculpturatus* is the primary lethal species which must be considered in the North American deserts; however a scorpion with a notorious reputation is found in the area about Durango, Chihuahua, particularly in the city. Durango is in a marginal, borderline position in regard to the Chihuahuan Desert. Currently this Durango scorpion is classified as *C. suffuses*. Dr. Stahnke reports, however, that much intergrading occurs between the various *Centruroides* species and that *suffuses* may prove to be a form of *sculpturatus*. In appearance, it closely resembles the banded form of *sculpturatus* (the former *C. gertschi*). *C. suffuses* may well be prevalent in the city of Durango due to the scorpion's search for moisture; in its search, it invades homes. The infamous "durango" scorpion was reported as responsible for 1,608 deaths in that city between 1890 and 1925.

Dr. Stahnke computed the total number of deaths in Arizona due to scorpion stings for the years 1929 through 1948, and found it to be sixty-five, or the cause of approximately 68 percent of the deaths due to venomous animals. (During that same time period, fifteen people died in Arizona from rattlesnake bites.) Dr. Robert E. Arnold, author of a book on treatment of injuries inflicted by venomous animals, computed the total number of deaths due to scorpion stings in the entire United States for the years 1960 through 1969 to be six; four of these occurred in Arizona. The sting of a *C. sculpturatus* obviously can be lethal, particularly to young children, the elderly, or adults with hypertension. Antivenin is available.

Symptoms which follow a scorpion sting also aid in differentiating the lethal from the nonlethal. Reaction to the nonlethal sting is largely localized at the site with pain, swelling, and discoloration of the immediate tissues; in some cases, pain extends up the affected extremity. The sting of the lethal species may cause immediate severe pain at the site; this pain soon recedes; swelling and discoloration *do not* occur. Instead, the reaction is systemic, the venom being a convulsant neurotoxin (affecting the nervous system and leading in some cases to convulsions). The sting site tingles, prickles, and becomes hypersensitive. The presence of this sensation at the site proves one more means of identifying the sting of *C. Sculpturatus*. In testing, give a gentle tap to the sting site. If the patient immediately draws away, the sting is very likely to have been that of *C. sculpturatus*.

Symptoms which develop following a *C. sculpturatus* sting include the following: A numbness travels up the affected extremity. Tightness develops in the throat; the tongue has a thick feeling; the victim may drool and exhibit a fever and breathing difficulties. Great restlessness develops, which can lead in severe cases to convulsions. Even after recovery, the original site of the sting often remains hypersensitive for from several days to a week, and a slight bump will start tingling or painful sensations in the area.

Avoiding Unnecessary Confrontations with Scorpions

1. Remember that the potentially lethal species, *Centruroides sculpturatus,* tends to cling to the underside of objects, such as rocks, logs, bark, and the like. Again don't put your hands where you can't see. The common name, bark scorpion, advises you to be somewhat cautious about grabbing firewood without first checking for scorpions.

2. Scorpions need a certain amount of moisture and may be attracted to damp spots.

3. Learn to tell the difference between the lethal and nonlethal species.

4. The age-old rule has been to shake your shoes out before putting them on in the morning if they've been on the ground. We've never known anyone who found a scorpion by doing so, or failed to find one by not doing so, but shaking out your shoes doesn't hurt anything, may make you feel more secure, and will at least get rid of any gravel in them. Anything left lying on the ground which can provide a hiding place for scorpions may harbor them. We recommend rolling up or elevating your bedroll above the ground when it's not in use—at least, inspect and shake it out before you crawl in if it has been in a location where scorpions may have had access to it.

5. As with rattlesnake bites, the sting of a *Centruroides sculpturatus* will often affect small children more severely than adults. Take proper precautions for them. Don't frighten children, but teach them precautions. A common way in which children sustain *C. sculpturatus* stings is by picking up rocks and inadvertently touching the scorpion clinging out of sight on the underside.

FIG. 99. The western or Arizona coral snake, *Micruroides euryxanthus* (average of 15 to 20 inches in length), produces venom dangerous to man. However its small mouth size prevents it from easily biting a human. This coral snake has alternating rings of red, cream and black, each red ring bordered by the cream colored rings; all rings of color completely encircle the body, and the snout is black.

Arizona Coral Snake

The coral snakes are members of the family Elapidae which includes the cobras, kraits, mambas, and other notorious Old World members. In the United States, two distinct genera of coral snakes occur: the *Micrurus fulvius*, or eastern coral snake, approaches the Chihuahuan Desert on its eastern borders but does not enter it; in Arizona, extreme southwestern New Mexico, and extending south into Mexico is found the western or Arizona coral snake, *Micruroides euryxanthus*, which is further subdivided into three subspecies.

The highly venomous eastern coral snake is a large reptile, up to almost four feet in length. Fortunately the Arizona coral, although also highly venomous, is very small and retiring and is seen only occasionally. Average adult size of the Arizona coral is fifteen to eighteen inches, although one individual of twenty-two inches has been recorded. The snake's body has a diameter not much greater than that of a pencil. The snake is strikingly beautiful. Shiny, waxy-looking, and appearing almost as though it were painted with enamels, the Arizona coral is marked by alternating, bright rings of red, white or cream, and black. Several other brightly colored harmless snakes are often confused with the Arizona coral, including the long-nosed snake, the Sonora mountain kingsnake, the California mountain kingsnake, and the shovel-nosed snake. To differentiate the Arizona coral from these look-alikes is relatively simple, for only in the coral snake do the rings of color completely encircle the body. Also the red rings on the coral snake are always bordered by yellow or whitish rings, unlike all the harmless species with the exception of one, the Organ Pipe shovel-nosed snake. The old rhyme "Red and yellow kill a fellow/ Red and black, venom lack" serves as an aid in differentiating the color pattern of the Arizona coral. The coral has a black snout which also helps to differentiate it from some of its look-alikes.

Arizona coral snakes are secretive and nocturnal, retiring to sandy burrows or rock cover much of the time. They live in a variety of arid and semi-arid regions within their range, including scrub, grassland, and the plains and lower mountain slopes within the desert; they appear to be partial to rocky desert areas with sandy soil. The Arizona coral has one peculiar trait which is also displayed by certain hook-nosed snakes. If annoyed or molested, it everts its cloacal lining, producing an audible, sharp popping sound. Its food is thought to consist primarily of small lizards and snakes.

The bite of the large eastern coral snake may prove fatal to human beings. No deaths have been reported from the bite of the Arizona coral snake, and very few bites have been reported. In keeping with its body size, the mouth of the Arizona coral is small. Additionally these snakes have fixed, erect fangs (unlike the rattlesnakes). These fangs are necessarily short; otherwise they would project beyond the snake's lower jaw. The opening through which the venom flows is not at the tip of the fangs, but rather at a higher level on the front face of the fang; for venom to be released from the fang opening into the victim, the fang must penetrate to a certain depth. Additionally, the snake "chews" the venom into the victim. All of these factors prevent the coral snake from easily injecting venom into a human subject.

Only three envenomations by the Arizona coral snake have been recorded. In all three cases, the coral snake was being handled by the victim. All reported immediate, but not severe, pain at the site, persisting from fifteen minutes to a period of several hours. Weakness, drowsiness, and nausea occurred within several hours. Prickling and tingling occurred at the site and in nearby tissue. Symptoms disappeared within twenty-four hours.

The venom of these snakes is essentially neurotoxic. No antivenin has been developed for the Arizona coral snake, although one exists for the larger eastern coral.

Rattlesnakes

The rattlesnakes are a diverse and extremely interesting group of New World venomous snakes which have developed as their first line of defense the rattle which is attached to the tail and which serves in essence as a warning to creatures that might injure the snake. As an evolutionary device, the rattle has great significance, and while still useful in a warning context today, certainly must have been even more significant in the past in the areas once shared by the rattlesnakes and large hoofed animals, such as the buffalo.

All rattlesnakes are venomous, and all rattlesnake bites should be considered of *serious significance* with proper measures immediately instituted (first aid measures are discussed in Chapter XIII). Rattlesnakes as a group are easily identified by the presence of the rattle. However, a rattle-less rattlesnake has evolved on certain islands in the Gulf of California. Also, at birth rattlesnakes have but a single pre-button or button. It is the first of the loosely articulated rings which will form the rattle, but inasmuch as these very young individuals have but a single segment, no rattle sound is produced. Be advised, however, that even these young *do* possess venom.

Rattlesnakes are found only in the New World, where they occur from southern Canada southward to Argentina and range from sea level to near timberline. The majority of species are found in arid and semi-arid areas but some occur in marshes and forests. Through evolution, they have differentiated and vary greatly in size, color, patterns, and venom type and toxicity. All belong to the family Crotalidae and are classified as belonging to the genus *Crotalus* (twenty-seven species, sixty-two subspecies) or *Sistrurus* (three species, seven subspecies). Of these thirty species and sixty-nine subspecies of rattlesnakes described, eleven species or a total of seventeen subspecies are found in Arizona. With more species than any other state, Arizona is the center of radiation; as one moves away from the hub, less and less diversity is apparent. New Mexico has seven species; California, six.

In the United States, the rattlesnakes display extreme variations in size. The largest is the eastern diamondback, *Crotalus adamanteus,* which may in exceptional cases reach eight feet in length; second largest is the western diamondback, *C. atrox,* of the southwestern United States and Mexico, a resident of the desert areas we are considering. It may occasionally reach seven feet in length. Dr. Laurence M. Klauber, authority on rattlesnakes, stated that the western diamondback is probably a greater hazard to man and domestic animals than any other snake in North America. The smallest species, members of the *Crotalus* genus, inhabit the mountains and are among the smallest of all rattlesnakes. The species of *Sistrurus* are relatively small; *S. catenatus,* known as the massasaugua and found in some of the more eastern portions of the southwestern desert country, seldom reaches more than thirty inches in length.

Rattlesnakes are known as pit vipers because they possess heat-sensing pits at the anterior end of their snouts, located between the eyes and nostrils. The pits are capable of sensing radiant body heat from nearby potential prey and are a valuable sense organ. Rattlesnakes' sense of smell is good, their sense of sight moderately good, and they receive both airborne and earthborne sound frequencies. These snakes have hinged fangs, which are folded upward and stored along the upper jaw when not in use. As a rattler prepares to strike at prey, the mouth is opened widely, the fangs move forward. The two fangs have a slight backward curve. They sink into the victim's flesh and act as hypodermic needles, injecting venom which flows in hollows through them from the venom ducts to an exit point near the tip of the fang. The fangs are immediately retracted, and the snake withdraws. The entire action is carried out with great rapidity. Dr. Charles Shaw, former Curator of Reptiles and Assistant Director of the San Diego, California, Zoo, states that rattlesnakes have the most highly developed venom-injecting mechanism of all snakes.

Although very effective in defense, the venom is actually more a means of subduing prey to be used for food. The venom originates in modified salivary glands and also acts as a digestive agent once it is injected into the prey, which

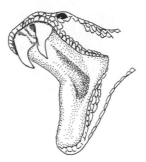

FIG. 100. Pit vipers, the group including the rattlesnakes, have the most highly developed mechanism of venom injection among reptiles. The mouth opens widely; the large, hollow fangs in the upper jaw swing forward from their folded, resting position; the fangs stab and inject venom in the prey in one rapid, deft move.

certainly accounts for some of its destructive properties when injected into a human victim. To state exactly the symptoms that will follow a rattlesnake bite is difficult due to the many species of rattlesnakes; the variations in makeup and strength of the various species' venoms; the size of the snake and hence amount of venom available to be injected; the amount of venom that the snake actually injects (in some cases, no envenomation occurs, or only a limited amount); the site of the bite; age, size, and condition of the victim; activity following the bite; first aid administered; and so on. In general, rattlesnake venom is *neurotoxic* (toxic or acting like a poison in regard to nervous tissue); *hemorrhagic* (tending to cause hemorrhage); *thrombogenic* (tending to produce thrombus, or blood clot); *hemolytic* (inducing the liberation of hemoglobin from red blood cells); and *proteolytic* (producing hydrolysis of proteins with formation of simpler and soluble products, as in digestion).

Symptoms which have been reported include the following: pain at the site; rapid occurrence of swelling and discoloration; swelling from the tip of an extremity which reaches the trunk in approximately twenty-four hours. (The rate of the advancement of the swelling and the amount is felt to be an indication of the seriousness of the bite.) Weakness and giddiness, respiratory difficulty, nausea and vomiting, circulatory disturbances, sometimes numbness and tingling of the face, lips and other parts, and double vision and temporary blindness have also been reported. Dr. Henry P. Limbácher, a physician who has written on rattlesnake bite, and Dr. Charles H. Lowe, Professor of Zoology at the University of Arizona, state that death is most apt to occur in the second twenty-four hours, and is generally a result of respiratory and circulatory failure.

In comparison to venoms of other rattlesnakes, that of the Mohave rattlesnake, *C. scutulatus*, displays a very high concentration of the neurotoxic factor. Dr. Lowe states that the Mohave has a "unique" venom with neurotoxic elements for which no specific antivenin has been developed and that the bite of a Mohave is potentially much more serious than that of a western diamondback, a species with which it is sometimes confused. It is important, therefore, that desert enthusiasts learn to identify the Mohave, the bite of which may be much more dangerous than that of most other rattlesnakes. The Mohave's range includes southern Nevada, eastern California, much of Arizona, extreme southwestern New Mexico, and thence southward to Puebla near the southern termination of the Mexican plateau. It is therefore found in much of the Chihuahuan, Sonoran, and Mohave Deserts. Adults reach a length of two to four feet. Among the key distinguishing factors for Mohaves are *sharply outlined diamonds or hexagons* on its back (whereas the western diamondback's similar markings tend to be flecked and obscure). The Mohave's tail has alternating dark and light rings with the *light rings wider* than the dark ones. Slanting backward from the snake's eye toward the corner of the mouth is a dark streak which is bordered by light scales. Mohaves often, but not always, tend to have a green cast to their coloration. Their basic color varies from olive green to an occasional brown or yellowish. The Mohave is often found in open country where there is a sparse growth of mesquite or creosote bush; it occurs from sea level to 8,000 feet.

H. M. Parrish, Vice President of Health Affairs at the University of South Dakota, writing in 1963, stated that Arizona has the highest rate of snakebite fatality in the United States, and that about fifty rattlesnake bites were recorded annually in southern California at that date. Dr. Herbert Stahnke, formerly a professor at Arizona State University, reported that for the years 1929 through 1948, fif-

FIG. 101. The Mohave rattlesnake, *Crotalus scutulatus* (24 to 50 inches long), displays well-defined, light-edged diamonds down the back and tail with contrasting light and dark tail rings, the dark rings narrower than the light rings. Its ground color is a greenish-gray.

teen fatalities due to rattlesnake bite occurred in Arizona (during the same period, sixty-four died from scorpion stings). Dr. Laurence M. Klauber, formerly Consulting Curator of Reptiles for the San Diego Zoo, in a 1971 publication, estimated that in the United States as a whole between 6,000 and 7,000 persons are bitten annually by rattlesnakes, and that annual fatalities from such bites in the United States now average about ten a year. He thus concluded that the mortality rate is below 1 percent.

Rattlesnakes are dangerous. Proper precautions should be taken to avoid being bitten, and a bite should be considered an emergency situation. However, worry regarding them should not preclude enjoyment of the desert. As the foregoing statistics show, a desert hiker/camper is in less danger from rattlesnakes in the desert than he is from members of his own species on the highway while traveling to that desert.

Avoiding Unnecessary Confrontations with Rattlesnakes

The experienced desert hiker/camper/backpacker respects rattlesnakes as a part of the animal community and for the ability they have to inflict a dangerous bite. These individuals realize that their chances of sustaining such a bite are very small and their chances of recovery very great (estimated mortality rate from rattlesnake bite in the United States is somewhat less than 1 percent, or approximately ten deaths annually). All would agree, however, that such a bite is to be avoided if at all possible. Certain precautions can be exercised to reduce the risk of serious encounters with rattlesnakes. Observing these precautions becomes second nature to experienced desert hikers.

1. Wear protective clothing—boots and long pants—while hiking and after dark around camp (that is, don't leave camp for a bathroom break ill-protected at a time when rattlers are most likely to be moving about).

2. Keep your eyes open. Look where you step and where you put your hands. Never put your hands or feet where your eyes can't see. Estimates suggest that well over 90 percent of rattlesnake bites occur on the extremities.

3. Use a flashlight when walking in the desert and around camp on warm nights. Rattlesnakes do occasionally come into camps (no doubt unintentionally, or they may have been there first and you just didn't notice), notwithstanding human movement, noises, bonfires, and so on.

4. When walking, keep to clear areas as much as possible; most of the desert's surface is open, making this rule easy to follow. Rattlesnakes tend to rest under low plants and under or next to rocks, logs, debris, and the like.

5. Go around, rather than over, large rocks, logs, and the like, if possible. If not, step on top of the object first to make sure a snake is not resting next to it on the far side. Check the surrounding area before sitting down on a log or rock.

6. Resting rattlesnakes often coil themselves neatly and compactly, sometimes partially embedded in soft sand. Their coloration aids them well in blending into their background. The experienced hiker becomes adept at spotting the characteristic shape of a coiled snake.

7. Be careful in climbing rocky cliffs. Do not place your hands on a ledge above your eye level. Do not bring your face up to the same level as, and within striking distance of, a ledge which you have been unable to check by sight—snakes may be present.

8. Find a cleared area when crawling under a fence.

9. When moving logs, stones, and the like, you may want

to use a stick or hook to turn over the object first to check for snakes and scorpions underneath. Gather firewood in the daytime when the surroundings are clearly evident.

10. Learn what rattlesnakes occur in the area and what they look like.

11. Remember that rattlesnakes are found in a variety of habitats, including the higher elevations of desert mountains. They range to 11,000 feet in the western United States and up to 14,000 feet in Mexico.

12. Become familiar with the habits of rattlesnakes. In hot weather, they will primarily be active nocturnally, but may also be encountered while resting in shade under logs and the like during the day. They are likely to be found in areas where tumbled rocks, debris, abandoned buildings, and building material give them cover. They spend the winter denned up, often in caves or smaller rocky niches, and may sun themselves outside these on warm days, or are numerous in the surrounding area in spring and fall as they move toward or away from these locations. In cold weather, rattlesnakes are inactive, but even on cool days they may occasionally be unexpectedly encountered as they sun themselves in a warm, protected location. We found a sunning rattlesnake just inside the spacious entrance to a hole on a cool February day, and one of us was struck at by a rattler on a cold, windy Thanksgiving Day when the snake was in the process of sunning in a protected niche out of the wind.

13. Remember that rattlesnakes do not always rattle before striking.

14. The advice often given is that if you hear a rattlesnake rattle close to you, stand still, locate the snake, and then move away; rattlesnakes will not chase you, and a calm, slow retreat is less likely to frighten or startle the snake into striking. (Admittedly, such advice is easier to give than to follow. One's natural reaction to the sound of a nearby rattle or the sight of an uncomfortably close rattlesnake usually is to jump—which may prove to be a successful maneuver or may cause problems, such as falling down, frightening the snake into striking, or conceivably, but not likely, jumping into another snake, if you are in a denning area.)

15. Realize that you are responsible for young children you take into rattlesnake country. Do not unduly frighten them, but teach them proper precautions at an early age and

oversee their activities while they are in the desert. Because of their smaller body size, children are more seriously affected by a rattlesnake bite than are adults. To place children on cots or in a tent at night for sleeping is wise, if danger of rattlesnakes is present at that particular time and place.

16. Do not kill rattlesnakes unless they are in the immediate vicinity of homes or in other areas where they are a real threat. If one is killed, bury it or otherwise completely destroy it.

17. Do not handle dead rattlesnakes nor allow children or dogs to do so. Reflexes allow the "dead" snake to inject poison for some time. The person or dog who handles a rattlesnake's head can be injected with the poison by inadvertently "stabbing" himself with the fang; more than one person has been bitten by a "dead" rattlesnake.

18. Respect rattlesnakes, but do not live in fear of them. Our family of four has been enjoying desert hiking and camping for more than twenty years. During that time we have encountered probably about a hundred rattlesnakes. Of those, two have struck; both missed. The single bite sustained by any of our four family members was received while handling the live snake in a scientific study. Which leads to the last precaution: Do not attempt to catch or handle live rattlesnakes!

Copperhead Snake

The copperhead, *Agkistrodon contortrix,* is present in portions of the Chihuahuan Desert. This snake, like the rattlesnakes, is a member of the family Viperidae and subfamily Crotalinae. The copperhead, too, is a pit viper, and is dangerously venomous, but the copperhead does *not* have rattles. The subspecies of the copperhead most likely to be encountered in the North American desert range is the Trans-Peco copperhead, *A. c. pictigaster.* It is found primarily in west Texas and attains an average maximum growth of two feet. Its ground color is a light hazel brown. It is marked by broad, straight-edged crossbands of a coppery brown; these bands have narrow dark borders.

When alarmed, copperheads rapidly vibrate their tails and, although they lack a rattle, they may produce a noise by

FIG. 102. The copperheads, *Agkistrodon sp.* (2 feet in length, for the subspecies found in the desert), like the rattlesnakes, are members of the pit viper subfamily. The copperhead is found in only one of the four North American deserts—the Chihuahuan.

beating a tattoo with the tail against vegetation or the ground. The copperheads should be treated with the same respect as their rattlesnake relatives; the copperhead's bite is similar in effect and severity.

Rear-fanged Snakes

In addition to the venomous snakes already noted, a few small, venom-producing, rear-fanged snakes exist within the geographical range we are considering. All have a poorly developed venom-introducing means in which venom flows down grooves in enlarged teeth at the back of the upper jaw. The snake must "chew" with these fangs to embed them in the victim to allow entry of the venom; inasmuch as the mouths of all these species are small, these snakes find it difficult or impossible to envenomate man. Charles Shaw states that the venom of these species found in the American West is probably not powerful enough in the small quantities that would be obtained by a bitten man to harm him and that the effect would probably be no more serious than a bee sting. One of the authors, having been bitten as a child by a lyre snake while handling it, can attest that that particular bite caused no reaction whatsoever. These snakes should be considered essentially harmless to man and interesting. They include the black-headed snakes, *Tantilla sp.;* vine snake, *Oxybelis aeneus;* lyre snake, *Trimorphodon bis-cutatus;* and night snake, *Hypsiglena torquata.*

The potentially dangerous animals of the desert should not be feared; in no way is the information given about them meant to induce fear. Rather it is hoped that the desert appreciator will *respect* these animals. Keep in mind that they should be respected not only on the basis of their potential danger to you, the human, but also—and primarily—on the basis that they are living things, each an important part of the ecosystem in which they live. True, some of them may be potential killers, but certainly none of these species is so successful in this regard as another desert dweller known as *Homo sapiens*.

CHAPTER XIII

First Aid in the Desert Environment

IN GENERAL the desert backpacker and camper risks incurring the same types of injuries as the person engaged in the same activities in other habitats: cuts, abrasions, sprains, fractures, and the like. However, the desert outdoorsman is particularly prone to two additional types of possible problems—those related to heat and dehydration, and the bites and stings of some of the desert's fauna.

We strongly recommend that all teens and adults who have not previously done so take a good first aid course. Knowledge thus gained may prove invaluable, not only in the out-of-doors, but also in the home and city.

First Aid Kit

Whenever camping or backpacking, carry a good first aid kit with you. Check it before leaving home; replace any missing items or prescription drugs which are out of date. The following list suggests the items it should contain. Tailor the kit to your needs, depending upon any particular medical problems you or your companions may have. Confer with your physician regarding any prescription drugs either you or he feel you may need. *Be sure to carry a good first aid booklet in the kit.*

SUGGESTED ITEMS FOR FIRST AID KIT

first aid booklet
snakebite kit (ideally, each individual in the party should have one; when hiking, don't leave the kit in your vehicle; take it with you)
tweezers (pointed tips, good quality, particularly helpful for removing spines)
needles
small magnifying glass or hands lens (good for other things as well as first aid)
scissors
razor blades
oral thermometer

Band-Aids
roll of one-inch-wide gauze
roll of two-inch-wide gauze
gauze pads, three inches square, individually wrapped
roll of one-inch adhesive tape
Q-tips
sterile cotton or cotton balls
safety pins
moleskin
Ace bandage

water-purifying tablets
salt tablets
liquid antiseptic
ammonia inhalent
aspirin or other analgesic tablets
laxative

prescriptions (consult with your doctor as to needs and uses)
    antibiotic tablets

antibiotic salve

anti-diarrhetic medicine

pain-killing drops to be used in case of eye injury

pain-killing drugs for emergencies

medications related to prevention of sunburn and/or treatment of severe sunburn

medicines for special needs, such as allergies or the like

Mouth-to-Mouth Resuscitation

This chapter will discuss only the specialized aspects of desert-related first aid, with one exception: mouth-to-mouth resuscitation. All individuals should know how to use this important life-saving technique, which may serve them well in any environment. If you find yourself with another person who has stopped breathing, immediately prepare the victim for mouth-to-mouth resuscitation:

1. To establish air exchange as *rapidly* as possible is important for the individual who has stopped breathing. Irreversible damage occurs within four to six minutes when the brain cells are deprived of their oxygen supply.

2. With victim on his back, place your face close to his. Look, listen, and feel for air exchange.

3. If no air exchange is apparent, immediately roll the head on its side; using your finger, quickly sweep the patient's mouth clear of foreign objects or material.

4. Roll the head back to its original face-up position.

5. Tilt the patient's head backwards as far as possible so that the front of the neck is stretched tightly.

6. Hold the nostrils closed by pinching them with your thumb and finger. Seal your mouth on the victim's mouth and blow a breath into the victim's lungs, watching to see that the victim's chest rises—a confirmation that air exchange is taking place.

7. Place your head close to the victim's to determine if you can hear air escape from the victim's nose and mouth.

8. If no exchange is taking place, you may need to accentuate the stretch of the neck to get the tongue out of the way. In order to pull the tongue as far forward as

possible, insert your thumb between the patient's teeth and, with your fingers under his chin, pull the jaw forward.

9. Apply mouth-to-mouth resuscitation:
   a. Maintain maximum extension of head as just described.
   b. Pinch patient's nose shut with your thumb and forefinger.
   c. Take a deep breath, open your mouth wide, and place it over the mouth of the patient, making a tight seal.
   d. Blow your full breath into the patient's mouth until you can feel the resistance offered by his expanded lungs and see his chest rise. (Each breath should provide about two pints of air, or approximately twice the amount of air in a normal breath.)
   e. Remove your mouth to allow patient to exhale.
   f. The process of blowing into the mouth, followed by exhale of air from the patient's lungs, should be repeated twelve to fifteen times a minute and increasingly more often, up to twenty times per minute, for an infant.
   g. As the size of the victim decreases, so does the amount of air delivered, until an infant receives only puffs of air from your cheeks. With an infant or small child, place your mouth over both the nose and mouth of the patient.
   h. The mouth-to-mouth resuscitation should be continued until the victim revives, or until trained personnel are available to assume care of the patient.

10. Mouth-to-mouth resuscitation, once initiated, should not be prematurely terminated, for patients have been known to revive after hours of mouth-to-mouth resuscitation.

Heat-Related Illnesses

As we have discussed, the desert's warm climate requires the human body to cool itself more frequently for greater periods of time than in most other climates. Man in the hot desert environment cools his body primarily by means of evaporation of perspiration from the body's surface. Therefore, the maintenance of adequate water input and salt intake is of the utmost importance. E. F. Adolph and A. H. Brown state that man in a temperate climate loses two to three liters of water per day, half of it in urine. In the desert, losses range as high as eleven liters daily, up to 90 percent of it through perspiration. Douglas H. K. Lee, writing in *Adaptation to the Environment*, provides even higher figures: eight to twelve liters of water daily in sweat; one liter as urine; and .75 liter from the respiratory tract. All of the body parts do not lose water equally; the blood serum concentrates more than twice as much as the liquids of other parts of the body. Thus plasma and blood volume diminish greatly; the heart's stroke volume diminishes; stress is placed on the entire circulatory system; and an accelerated pulse rate and elevated body temperature result. Additionally, quantities of sodium chloride are lost from the body in the sweat, causing further body complications.

Man can acclimatize to the *heat* to some extent; that is, his body makes adaptive changes over a period of time when continuously or repeatedly exposed to heat stress. A man whose body has so adapted is thus able to work longer and more efficiently under hot conditions than can a newcomer. Body mechanisms in this process may include a decrease in heat production (as elimination of nonessential movements), increase by the body of blood volume and extracellular body fluid during the early acclimatization period; gradual drop in pulse rate; reduction of the chloride concentration in sweat; and finally an ability to some extent to physiologically "tolerate" or "put up with" distresses that were very unwelcome and upsetting when first encountered.

For the most part, individuals in the desert, especially those acclimatized to the heat, need not take salt tablets or otherwise supplement their salt intake beyond the amount desired with their food. Individuals involved in moderate to heavy labor in heat, however, may, even if acclimatized, feel the need to consume some extra salt. The outdoorsman who suddenly subjects himself to strenuous exercise in the heat, particularly if he is not acclimatized, may need extra salt. Douglas H. K. Lee recommends that the sedentary, acclimatized individual in a hot, dry environment need take no additional salt beyond that provided by a normal diet; the acclimatized individual in a hot, dry environment undertaking moderate to heavy labor may need to add seven grams of salt to his normal intake; the unacclimatized individual undertaking heavy labor in the same environment may need to add fourteen grams of salt to the normal diet; and an unacclimatized individual undertaking moderate to heavy work in a very hot environment may need twenty-one grams more salt than is provided by his normal diet.

The disorders related to heat stress are derived from a deficiency of salt or water or both. They result from an imbalance in intake as compared to output in the commodity of sweat.

1. **Heat cramps.** Heat cramps may affect people engaged in strenuous or semi-strenuous activities in hot environments. Loss of large quantities of sweat creates an imbalance in the electrolyte ratio. If salt intake is insufficient to remedy this imbalance, heat cramps may occur. At times these cramps may result from drinking iced drinks too fast or in too-large quantities. Prevention includes sufficient ingestion of extra salt—either with food, water, or as tablets—whenever heavy work is to be carried out in heat.

SYMPTOMS OF HEAT CRAMPS

a. Muscle cramps in legs and abdomen
b. Pain accompanying cramps
c. Faintness
d. Profuse perspiration

FIRST AID MEASURES FOR HEAT CRAMPS

a. Remove patient to cool place.
b. Give patient salted drinking water (one teaspoon salt to one quart water).

c. Apply manual pressure to the cramped muscles.
d. Remove patient to hospital if more serious problems are indicated.

2. **Heat exhaustion.** Heat exhaustion also occurs in individuals involved in strenuous activities in hot environments. The body, in its attempt to lose heat, transports quantities of blood from the body core to the vessels in the skin. The pooling of the blood in the peripheral vessels combined with the amount pooled in the lower extremities when standing sometimes provides an insufficient blood return to the heart and brain, thus leading to physical collapse.

SYMPTOMS OF HEAT EXHAUSTION

a. Weak pulse
b. Rapid and usually shallow breathing
c. Generalized weakness
d. Pale, clammy skin
e. Profuse perspiration
f. Dizziness
g. Unconsciousness

FIRST AID FOR HEAT EXHAUSTION

a. Remove patient to cool place.
b. Keep patient lying down.
c. Remove as much of patient's clothing as possible.
d. Administer cool water in which some salt has been dissolved for drinking.
e. Remove body heat by convection, but do not chill.
f. Remove to medical help if any more serious problem is indicated.

3. **Heat stroke.** Heat stroke is a *true emergency* and, if prompt action is not taken, the victim may die. Heat stroke is a catastrophic disturbance of the heat-regulating mechanism of the brain. It is associated with high fever and collapse, and may result in convulsions and unconsciousness. Heat stroke is often related to direct exposure to sun, poor air circulation, age (over 40), poor physical condition, alcoholism, and obesity. Symptoms of heat

stroke are very different from the preceding two conditions, for in heat stroke the skin is *hot* and *dry*.

SYMPTOMS OF HEAT STROKE

a. Sudden onset of condition
b. Hot, flushed, dry skin
c. Dilated pupils
d. Full and fast pulse
e. Breathing fast at first, graduating to shallow and faint
f. Early loss of consciousness
g. Muscle twitching possibly leading into convulsions
h. Body temperature elevated to 105° to 106° F. or higher

FIRST AID FOR HEAT STROKE

a. Remove patient to cool place.
b. Remove as much clothing as possible.
c. Assure an open airway (see the discussion of mouth-to-mouth resuscitation earlier in this chapter).
d. Reduce body temperature promptly by dousing body with water or, if possible, by wrapping patient in wet sheet, or both.
e. If cold packs or ice and means to make an emergency substitute are available, place these under the arms, around the neck, at the ankles, or other locations where blood vessels lie close to the skin.
f. Protect the victim from injury, such as tongue biting, if convulsions occur.
g. Transport to a medical facility immediately.

Desert Dehydration

Dehydration often plays a role in heat-related illnesses. However, an individual may also die of non-heat-related dehydration. A characteristic series of desert dehydration symptoms occur at a series of water deficits, based on a percentage of the victim's body weight. In its early stages dehydration acts mainly by reducing the blood volume, often promoting heat exhaustion. Dehydration in its later stages causes disturbances of cell functions, which reinforce one another with progressive deterioration of the individual's body. Until an irreversible point has been reached, dehydration is usually readily rectified by replacement of the body's water. A person active in the desert can suffer from early stages of dehydration, reducing his ability to work well or maintain a positive emotional state, without being fully aware that dehydration is affecting him other than that he is perhaps suffering a degree of thirst. Thirst becomes apparent at approximately a 2 percent loss of body weight, or even earlier.

According to Adolph and associates:

1. A 1 to 5 percent loss of body weight due to dehydration produces:
   a. Thirst
   b. Vague discomfort
   c. Economy of movement
   d. Anorexia (lack of appetite)
   e. Flushed skin
   f. Impatience
   g. Increased pulse rate
   h. Increased rectal temperature
   i. Sleepiness
   j. Nausea

2. A 6 to 10 percent loss of body weight due to dehydration produces:
   a. Dizziness
   b. Headache
   c. Dyspnea (labored breathing)
   d. Tingling in the limbs
   e. Absence of salivation
   f. Cyanosis (bluish skin caused by deficient oxygenation of blood)
   g. Indistinct speech
   h. Inability to walk

3. An 11 to 20 percent loss of body weight due to dehydration produces:
   a. Delirium
   b. Spasticity
   c. Swollen tongue
   d. Inability to swallow
   e. Deafness

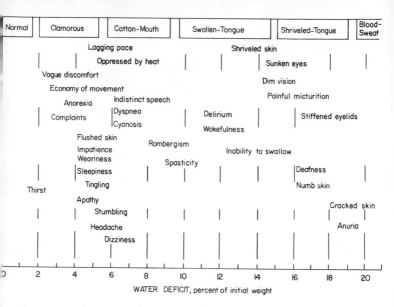

[FIG. 103.] Signs and symptoms characteristic of desert dehydration.* Each sign is located at the water deficit at which it is usually first noted.

*Reprinted from *Physiology of Man in the Desert*, courtesy of E. F. Adolph.

    f. Dim vision
    g. Painful urination
    h. Shriveled skin
    i. Numb skin
    j. Bloody cracked skin
    k. Anuria (absence or defective excretion of urine)

Dehydration Exhaustion

Dehydration exhaustion occurs at a 5 to 10 percent deficit.

SYMPTOMS OF DEHYDRATION EXHAUSTION

1. Vague discomfort
2. Feeling of heat oppression

First Aid in the Desert Environment

3. Restlessness
4. Sleepiness
5. Inclination to sit or lie down
6. Muscular fatigue
7. Rising body temperature
8. Accelerated pulse
9. Tingling limbs

Experimentally, subjects suffering from dehydration exhaustion, when given all the water they wanted, usually drank copiously. Given sufficient water, these men regained their initial body weight in twenty-four hours or less. They suffered no obvious aftereffects from their dehydration. Adolph, *et al.*, state that a man can undergo a water deficit so extreme as to be unable to walk or stand, yet will recover his walking ability within a few minutes after receiving water, with almost complete recovery in six to twelve hours.

At a 12 percent loss, an individual cannot recover without assistance, and a person dehydrated to this point, Adolph and associates state, must be given water intravenously, intraperitoneally, by stomach tube, or through the rectum.

Death occurs at a 15 percent to 25 percent body-weight loss, those occurring at the higher deficits in cool atmospheres. In hot environments, death occurs at a lower percentage of weight loss and is probably due to heat stroke.

FIRST AID FOR SERIOUS DESERT DEHYDRATION

a. Provide water for patient.
b. Prevent overheating of patient.
c. Transport to a medical facility.

Cactus-Related Problems

The cylindrical joints of the cholla cactus may at times pose a problem for the unwary desert explorer. These spine-studded joints are easily removed from the plant by simply brushing against it or are particularly plentiful on the ground beneath the plant where pants legs and footwear may pick them up. So readily do these joints attach themselves to animals and humans that one species is known as the "jump-

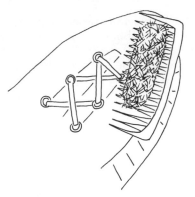

FIG. 104. To remove cactus joints easily, insert the teeth of a comb between the cactus and the impaled object. Pull the comb upward and outward.

ing cholla." Jump it does not, but to the impaled individual it may seem to have done so. If one attempts to remove these joints from his body or clothing by use of bare hands, he simply transfers the problem to the hands. Attempts to remove a joint with a stick may be successful, or may simply roll the joint into an adjoining portion of the victim. The simplest means of removal is that using an ordinary pocket comb. Insert the teeth of the comb between the cactus and the individual or object impaled. Holding one end of the comb, flip the joint *outward, away from you,* being careful not to toss it against an onlooker.

Cactus spines can cause rather intense pain, which may persist for several minutes or longer. For example, after slipping and falling while descending a mountain and in the process having firmly embedded the spines of a cholla joint in one hand while breaking the fall, one of us can state that the pain radiates up the arm and persists for a half hour or more in a severe case. Medical help is ordinarily not needed unless a person has been severely impaled in many parts of the body, as in a major accident, or if numerous spines are broken off in the body.

Prickly pear cacti have, in addition to the usual spines, very tiny hairs or spines called *glochids,* which are difficult or impossible to see once embedded in the human skin. These glochids are not dangerous, but are very annoying.

The minute tips of glochids protruding from human skin cause irritation when rubbed or touched. The afflicted skin area can be rubbed with sand; the glochid tips are thus broken off, reducing the constant irritation; the flesh-embedded glochid portions are gradually dissolved by the body.

Prevention is the best cure for cactus spine problems.

Sunburn

Sunlight is intense in the desert. Do not underestimate it or overestimate your skin. Even possession of a tan is not total insurance against sunburn, for tanned skin may burn if exposure is sufficiently intense and prolonged. Be prepared to prevent sunburn with preparations of your choice or based on your doctor's recommendation. Prevention is certainly best, but just in case—also be prepared with medication to treat sunburn.

Special Rules for First Aid Treatment of Various Poisonous Bites and Stings

In all of the following first aid treatments in which ice, constriction, incision, and suction are recommended, follow these rules.

1. **Ice.** In this book, the use of ice for any first aid treatment refers to use of ice packs or, where these are not available, the use of ice separated by cloth from the skin itself. We do *not* advocate cryotherapy, a treatment in which the afflicted body part is immersed directly in ice or ice water. This ligature and cryotherapy treatment was earlier accepted as a partial treatment for scorpion and rattlesnake envenomation. It has been found to be dangerous, in that it promotes serious tissue destruction and has led in some cases to the necessity for amputation. One study of twenty-seven cases in which extremities were lost following venomous snakebites revealed that in twenty-three of these cases cryotherapy had been used in excess of twelve hours.

Ice can retard, to a certain extent, the body's absorption and circulation of venom. Its use may thus help delay a part of the immediate problem while the patient is rushed to medical help. It is of some help, also, in numbing pain at the site.

REMEMBER IN REGARD TO USE OF ICE

a. *Do not use ice directly on the skin. Do not immerse the body part in ice, ice slush, or ice water.*
b. When using ice, have cloth layers between the ice and the body.
c. Remove the ice periodically, for example five to ten minutes on, followed by five minutes off; repeat; and so on.

2. **Constriction.** Where constriction or use of a constricting band is suggested in first aid treatment, we are *not* advocating the use of a tourniquet. A constricting band, when used, should be placed two to three inches above the bite—that is, between the bite and the heart. Its purpose is to restrict the flow of venous blood and lymph but *not* to restrict arterial blood flow. A distal pulse, signifying arterial circulation, should be present in the extremity at all times and should be monitored. The constricting band should be loose enough to allow insertion of a finger or pencil-sized object between the band and the body part. If swelling progresses up a limb, advance the constricting band above the swelling.

Improper use of a band can be dangerous; applied too tightly, thereby restricting arterial flow to the area beyond it, it can cause severe tissue damage. Use of a constricting band is most useful while incision and suction are being implemented. After this period it appears that the band may soon be discarded. Experimentally, use of a constricting band for a total of an hour or longer has been found to cause considerable tissue damage.

REMEMBER IN REGARD TO USE OF CONSTRICTION

a. Use a constricting band, not a tourniquet.
b. Arterial flow of blood should not be restricted. Check for distal pulse; monitor it.
c. Advance constricting band to point above swelling, if swelling progresses up limb.

3. **Incision.** Incision of a venomous bite, combined with suction, can be an important first aid measure for Gila monster, rattlesnake, and copperhead bites. When incision and suction are done promptly and well, as much as 20 to 50 percent of the venom may be removed; however, dangers exist when making indiscriminate incisions.

REMEMBER IN REGARD TO MAKING INCISIONS

a. Use a cutting instrument that has been sterilized—wipe the instrument with antiseptic or hold it over a flame (a match flame will suffice). Use iodine, alcohol, or the like to clean skin area to be cut.
b. Make a *small, longitudinal incision over each fang mark.* The incision should be *parallel with the long axis of the bitten limb. Do not cut across the limb.*
c. Incisions should be approximately ¼ to ⅓ inch in length, and not more than ⅛ to ¼ inch in depth.
d. No additional incisions should be made.
e. Making incisions involves the danger of cutting nerves and blood vessels, particularly on the hands, wrists, neck, ankles, head, and groin. If in doubt, do not make a bad situation worse by causing further damage through first aid incisions.

4. **Suction.** When suction is advised, use suction devices which accompany snake bite kits, if available. If necessary, suction can be done by mouth. The human mouth is loaded with bacteria which may infect the incision; therefore the suction devices are preferable. In suctioning by mouth, suck and spit continuously. Venom is not dangerous if swallowed. If the person performing mouth suctioning has open sores in the mouth, some small amounts of venom may be absorbed; this minor problem presents only small risk.

REMEMBER IN REGARD TO USE OF SUCTION

a. Apply suction with suction device, if available.
b. If mouth suction is used, suck and spit continuously.
c. Continue suction for at least thirty to sixty minutes.

Black Widow Bite

SYMPTOMS OF BLACK WIDOW BITE

1. Two tiny red marks identify site of entrance of chelicera.
2. Severe local pain becomes increasingly severe within about thirty minutes.
3. Pain spreads through the body, settling in abdomen and legs.
4. Other symptoms may be nausea, vomiting, sweating, feeling of apprehension, salivation, muscle spasms, breathing difficulties, abnormally high blood and spinal fluid pressure.
5. Coma may result in thirty minutes after bite.

FIRST AID FOR BLACK WIDOW BITE

1. Ice may be used at the site.
2. Keep patient quiet.
3. Transport patient to medical facility immediately (antivenin is available for administration by medical personnel).

Brown Recluse Spider Bite

SYMPTOMS OF BROWN RECLUSE SPIDER BITE

1. Little or no pain is felt at site; patient may not be aware initially of bite.
2. Painful, red area may develop at site a few hours after bite.
3. Within two or three days, necrosis of site may occur.
4. Other symptoms which sometimes occur include headache, chills, nausea, vomiting, fever, and generalized skin rash.

FIRST AID FOR BROWN RECLUSE SPIDER BITE

No first aid measures are needed. A physician should be seen promptly if a bite occurs, or if an individual suspects from evident symptoms that one may have occurred.

Scorpion Sting

All scorpions are venomous, and all can produce a sting that will be accompanied by some degree of pain. Human reaction to the sting of some of the nonlethal species consists of a sharp burning sensation lasting from a few minutes to half an hour. The stings of other species produce pronounced swelling, with or without slight discoloration; yet other species' venoms may cause a highly discolored swelling and a burning sensation. With some of these venoms, pain may travel some distance from the site of the sting, as from a hand as far as the armpit. Local application of ice may provide some relief. Unless the victim displays an unusually severe reaction, the pain produced by these ground scorpion stings is usually approximately equal in intensity to a wasp or bee sting. Basically, symptoms resulting from stings of the nonlethal species can be classified as localized and not systemic. Exactly the opposite occurs with the sting of the lethal species, *Centruroides sculpturatus. The potentially dangerous* C. sculpturatus *sting may cause initial pain, but no swelling or discoloration at the site. Symptoms for* C. sculpturatus *are primarily systemic.*

SYMPTOMS OF *Centruroides sculpturatus* STING

1. Pain at the time of the sting
2. Prickly, tingling, numbness at site which may progress to other portions of the body
3. Tightness of throat
4. Difficulty in speaking
5. Extreme restlessness
6. Respiratory difficulties
7. Drooling
8. Hypertension
9. Gastric distention
10. Possible convulsions
11. Blindness

FIRST AID MEASURES FOR
Centruroides sculpturatus STING

1. Use ice on site immediately and continue to do so while seeking medical aid; ice seems to be particularly be-

neficial for treatment of scorpion stings.

2. Keep patient as quiet as possible.
3. Transport immediately to medical facility. (A specific antivenin is produced for treatment of the sting of *C. sculpturatus* by Antivenin Productions Laboratory, Arizona State University, Tempe, Arizona. Supplies of this antivenin are stocked in specified hospitals and clinics throughout Arizona.)
4. If possible, the scorpion should be captured in order that positive identification of the species involved can be made.

Gila Monster Bite

The bite of a Gila monster is potentially dangerous. However, this reptile's bite is a natural defensive mechanism; most bites to humans have occurred when the lizards were being teased or handled, which should never be done.

SYMPTOMS OF GILA MONSTER BITE

1. Local pain
2. Prolonged bleeding
3. Initial shock
4. Anxiety
5. Rapid swelling
6. Nausea and vomiting
7. Fever
8. Swelling of tongue
9. Labored breathing
10. Paralysis

FIRST AID FOR GILA MONSTER BITE

1. Remove the lizard from the bite as rapidly as possible, as the lizard continues to chew venom into the victim while it remains attached. It may be difficult to disengage the reptile, which hangs on tenaciously once it has obtained a firm grip. Its jaws may be pried open with pliers, etc. A strong tasting or smelling liquid (as alcohol, chloroform, gasoline) may be poured into its mouth, or a flame may be applied to the lizard's jaw.

(Refrain from using the gasoline and flame methods in conjunction!) Do not waste time, however, and if other means fail, simply forcefully pull the lizard off the victim, even at the expense of laceration to the site.
2. Apply a constricting band.
3. If lacerations have resulted from the bite, apply suction to these areas to aid in removal of the venom.
4. If puncture wounds are visible, make an incision directly over each site where a tooth penetrated.
5. Apply suction.
6. Keep the patient quiet.
7. Patient should be encouraged to drink water.
8. An ice bag may be used.
9. Patient should be transported to a medical facility immediately.

Copperhead Bite

First aid measures are the same as those for rattlesnake bite.

Rattlesnake Bite

Severity of rattlesnake bite is dependent upon many factors including size of snake; amount of venom injected (bites are occasionally received without injection of any venom); species of snake; location of bite; depth of bite; age, size, and physical condition of victim (due to their smaller size, children are often in more danger from rattlesnake bite than are adults); individual susceptibility to bite; activity of victim following bite; first aid treatment; medical aid received.

Rarely, bites are received directly into a blood vessel, in which case generalized systemic symptoms—changes in heartbeat and respiration, shock, unconsciousness and the like—may occur almost immediately. However, in the majority of cases the venom is injected under the skin and usually not to any great depth into muscle, thus providing a good chance for removal of a certain quantity of the venom through shallow incisions in the skin. Additionally, approximately 98 percent of the bites are estimated to occur on the extremities where use of constricting bands, incision, and suction are often possible.

SYMPTOMS OF RATTLESNAKE BITE

1. Pain at site
2. Rapid onset of swelling and discoloration which extend toward the heart (This swelling may extend from the tip of an extremity to the trunk in approximately twenty-four hours. The amount and rate of advancement of swelling is an indication of the severity of the bite.)
3. Weakness and giddiness
4. Respiratory difficulty
5. Nausea and vomiting
6. Low blood pressure, thready pulse
7. Subnormal temperature
8. Numbness and tingling of face, lips, other body parts
9. Double vision, blindness
10. Death, if it occurs, is most likely during the second twenty-four hours and is usually a result of respiratory or circulatory failure.

FIRST AID FOR RATTLESNAKE BITE

1. *Do not panic.*
2. *Keep patient quiet.*
3. *Immobilize bitten part,* if possible. If not, keep movement of bitten limb to a minimum; muscular action increases the spread of the venom. Keep bitten body part below level of heart, if possible.
4. Some authorities believe that if the victim can be rapidly moved to a hospital or doctor for professional treatment, this should be done and no first aid administered. However, many bites are sustained some distance from medical help; then, the following first aid measures should be considered.
5. *Apply constriction.*
6. *If determination is made that the victim was definitely bitten by a rattlesnake and that envenomation has occurred, immediately carry out incision and suction.*
7. If some doubt exists as to whether the patient was bitten by a venomous snake, or whether or not en-

venomation has occurred, watch the bite for the first three to five minutes. If during this time pain occurs and swelling appears at the site, assume that envenomation by a poisonous snake has occurred and consider incision and suction. *Pain* and *swelling* at the site are signs of a rattlesnake bite. The bite of a nonpoisonous snake or a poisonous snake which has not injected venom will not produce swelling.

8. If some distance from vehicle, transport victim by litter, if possible. Prevention of as much activity on the victim's part as possible is important.

9. Keeping patient as quiet as possible, rush to medical aid. (The antivenin available for medical use is a horse serum; it is imperative that medical personnel test patient for reaction before administration.)

10. If bite is on hand or arm, remove rings, bracelets, or the like before swelling makes their removal difficult.

11. If possible, before leaving the field capture the snake (if capture can be accomplished without incurring another bite). The victim should not attempt capture; such activity will be deleterious. If a companion can capture the snake, species identification may prove important to the doctor. Due to its size and abundance, the western diamondback, *Crotalus atrox,* is considered the most dangerous of the western rattlesnakes. However, the sidewinder, *Crotalus cerastes,* although small, has venom of high toxicity. The tiger rattlesnake, *Crotalus tigris,* has venom considered very toxic. The venom of a Mohave rattlesnake, *Crotalus scutulatus,* is particularly dangerous; additionally, this snake attains a good size and is capable of delivering a quantity of venom. Much greater amounts of antivenin and more intense treatment may be required for the Mohave snakebite victim. *Do not take chances on a second bite* being sustained by the victim or companions in capturing the snake. *Do not delay first aid measures or transport of the victim* by taking time to capture the snake.

12. The victim's state of mind is important. Neither he nor his companions should assume the worst. A high percentage of untreated victims of rattlesnake bites recover. With application, without panic, of in-

telligent first aid measures, followed by medical services as promptly as possible, chances for recovery from rattlesnake bite are approximately 99 in 100, and those, you must admit, are good odds.

CHAPTER XIV

Desert Survival Skills

IN ANY DESERT EMERGENCY, decide on an intelligent course of action to be taken. Give yourself time to think this situation out calmly and rationally. Talk to yourself, if you are alone, to help restore calmness. If you are in a group, discuss your situation with one another. To let one person take charge may be the best plan. Consider all possibilities open to you. In deciding upon a plan, *consider all alternatives in terms of physiological cost*. Once a decision is made, set your plan into action and stick with it unless additional unforeseen factors make it necessary and truly advisable to change it.

The Vehicle in an Emergency

When a survival situation must be faced, very often a vehicle or aircraft is present. If you have any hope that rescue operations may be undertaken, remaining with the machine is considered the best plan. If you have a contact who knows where you were going and when you were to return, *as you should have,* rescue should be imminent. A vehicle is easier for the rescuers to see than is an individual. Additionally, the vehicle provides many advantages and resources important to survival and rescue. Take stock of the resources you have. Determine how to use them effectively.

1. Food or water supplies, or both, may be present in the vehicle.

2. The mirrors (rearview and side) may be used for hand-held signaling devices.

3. Seat covers, upholstery, cool cushions, and so forth may be used to provide shade or may serve in many other ways.

4. Seat cushions may be removed from the vehicle. Sit or lie on them in shade, elevating the body above the high surface temperatures.

5. Floor mats may serve a variety of purposes.

6. The glove compartment may provide matches, maps, and other papers for starting fires. Often it holds a flashlight, which can be used for night signaling.

7. Tools may be used for many purposes, such as digging, breaking open barrel cacti, obtaining gas from car for starting fires.

8. Hub caps may be used for digging, signaling, and as containers for use in solar stills.

9. The tires can be burned as signals.

10. Oil from the engine is useful in producing quantities of black smoke in signal fires. Oil may also be used under the eyes to reduce glare, or on the lips to prevent cracking. (Do not cover large body areas with oil, for this covering prevents evaporative cooling.)

11. Gas is useful in building fires. It can be siphoned from the gas tank, or fittings around the engine may be loosened, allowing the gas to drain into a container or onto rags or pieces of upholstery.

12. The cigarette lighter may be used in starting fires. (This technique is somewhat difficult, and very fine, dry tinder is needed.)

13. Sparks to be used in starting fires may be obtained from the vehicle's battery.

14. Dismounted headlights, powered by the vehicle's battery, can be used to signal at night.

15. Flares are often carried in vehicles; use these for signaling.

16. The vehicle provides shade outside in which to rest during the day and protection within during cooler night temperatures.

17. The vehicle may, and should, hold a first aid kit.

18. Radiator water may be drunk if you are sure no antifreeze or coolant has been added to it. If it is not pure, it may be spread on the skin, or clothes may be soaked in it to aid in body cooling.

Leave your vehicle and hike to help only if you feel there is no hope of rescue in your present situation; or you know exactly how far and where to hike for certain rescue, and you know you have sufficient water to take you to your destination. Refer to the figures and tables on water needs in Chapter XI. Do not underestimate your water needs nor overestimate your ability to survive dehydration. Remember that in average summer weather a healthy hydrated man can walk approximately ten miles per gallon of water during the day and approximately twenty miles per gallon at night. If water is available, carry all you can with you. If you decide to walk to help, leave clear, obvious signals or notes as to the route you are intending to follow in order that rescuers may follow you if necessary.

Direction-finding

In determining direction in your hike to help, you should always have a compass with you in the desert and know how to use it before you arrive there. Additionally, you should have maps of the area in which you are hiking or camping. You should make a consistent habit of noting landmarks in your camp and as you hike. The openness of the desert's terrain grants excellent visibility of the many landmarks, provided by the numerous low mountain ranges. These ranges are distinctive, if one takes the time to study them and get them firmly in mind. Their appearance changes with variations of light and shadow during different times of day and as you change your location and angle toward them; take these factors into consideration.

You *should* have compass, maps, and the like. If you are without a compass, confused regarding directions, and must hike to help, use common sense to determine direction.

1. The sun rises in the east (depending upon the time of year and your distance north of the equator, the sun will rise a little to the north or the south of true east), and it sets in the

west (again, a little to the north or south according to the season). With your right hand to the morning sun and your left to the setting sun, you are facing north. In the desert, most days are sunny; the sun's location and movement are easily observed.

2. During the day you can use a watch to determine direction, if the watch is set on actual sun time, not daylight savings. Hold the watch on a horizontal plane. Point the hour hand at the sun. SOUTH will be located in the smallest angle between the symbol 12 and the hour hand.

3. If the day is cloudy, hold a stick upright on the center of the watch. Align the faint shadow the stick will cast over the hour hand. NORTH will be halfway through the small angle between the shadow and the symbol 12.

4. East can be determined during midday hours by use of a shadow. Select an object at least three feet in height which will cast a shadow with a definite projection. On the ground, mark the point where the shadow tip is located. After fifteen minutes, mark the shadow tip again. Draw a line from the first mark through the second mark. This line points EAST.

5. At night you can locate Polaris, the North Star, which is never more than approximately one degree from the Celestial North Pole. Locate the Big Dipper. The two stars, called the pointers, located on the outer edge of the bowl of the Dipper (the portion of the ladle farthest from the handle), point almost directly to the nearby North Star. The North Star is thus opposite the open top of the Dipper.

6. If you are walking toward help and there is any possibility of becoming disoriented while resting, mark your direction of travel with rocks, equipment, or the like before falling asleep.

Walking Out

If you are walking to help, walk toward a known travel route, an inhabited area, or, if nearby, toward the coast. Walk slowly and steadily. Rest approximately ten minutes out of each hour. When resting it is often advisable to prop your feet up, unlace your boots. Adjust or change your socks, which become compacted after a period of hiking; feet may then begin to shift in the boots, causing blisters. Even dirty socks will provide a good change as they are likely to be less compacted after having been given a "rest."

While walking, be alert to signs of water, food, civilization, or rescue efforts. If possible, be prepared to signal to rescuers with mirror, flashlight, firearm, whistle. Unless in your specific situation you have reason to believe differently, it is normally considered best to move downhill toward lower elevations in your search for help. If you find a road, it is advisable to stay on it; by following this sign of civilization, your chances of reaching help should be much improved.

Remember that night walking is most economical from the standpoint of water. However, also remember that walking in the early evening and morning when there is some light is advantageous in certain ways. You have less chance of missing possible water, food, or signs of human habitation when some light is available. Also with improved vision, your chances of avoiding accidents are improved. Remember that in the summer the cooler night hours are the favored times for rattlesnake activity. Watch for snakes insofar as possible, and take precautions (for example, check before you sit down to rest, and so on).

When walking, take the easiest route; avoid obstacles if possible. Attempt to go around steep gullies and hills. If you must ascend a steep incline, zig-zag up, for a straight assault exacts a greater cost in sweat and energy. When climbing, place your entire foot on the ground; when descending an incline, bend your knees and take your time. Do not use undue speed which may cause loss of control. Falling or a similar accident will only compound the problems you already face. If possible, avoid walking for long distances in sand, as this walking is most fatiguing. If you must hike over sand, place your body weight well forward and keep your knees bent. If it is necessary to travel through dunes, follow the firm valley floors between the dunes as much as possible.

Distance in the desert is deceptive. Do not overestimate your ability to reach a particular point which can be seen in the distance. It is recommended that one unfamiliar with this desert-distance deception estimate the distance to a point and then multiply the figure by three for a more accurate estimate. Underestimating distance can be dangerous; so, too, can underestimating your ability to cope and falling prey to panic.

Desert Survival Skills

Basic Survival Techniques

Certainly whether resting while hiking toward help or while awaiting rescue, follow all suggestions which will serve to prolong your survival time:

1. Remain quiet. Undertake no unnecessary activity or movements.

2. Take advantage of the coolest microclimate available to you—rest in shade, elevate yourself several inches above the ground surface.

3. Avoid strong breezes, if possible, as these unnecessarily increase evaporation of perspiration and heat gain from convection.

4. Remain clothed. Wear a hat if available, or improvise one. Wear colored glasses if available. If not, and glare bothers you, improvise slit goggles, or blacken under eyes with small amounts of engine oil or soot.

5. Drink water as needed to prevent fuzzy thinking and serious dehydration. Remember it is the water in your body that will save your life, not the water in your canteen. Ration your sweat, not your water.

6. Do not drink urine, blood, or sea water. Use urine on skin or clothing to provide cooling. If near the coast, soak clothing in sea water for cooling.

7. Do not eat unless water supplies are available; if limited water supplies are available, consume carbohydrates, rather than proteins.

8. Do not take salt tablets unless water supplies are adequate.

9. Do not talk any more than necessary. Do not smoke, and keep your mouth closed to prevent evaporation of moisture.

10. Do not substitute alcohol for water. Its use not only results in fuzzy thinking which can be extremely dangerous in an emergency situation, but also requires large amounts of water for the alcohol's digestion. (In July, 1964, five men in an Arizona labor camp, drinking wine on a Sunday afternoon when the temperature was 119° F., died from a combination of exposure to high temperature and humidity levels plus alcohol consumption. That same year, four other men died in Arizona under similar circumstances.)

Signals

Take any feasible signal measures available to help rescuers find you. These may be either sound or sight signals. In signaling, three is the number signifying an emergency.

Sound signals include the following:

1. If you have a firearm, you can signal with three evenly spaced shots. Do not fire indiscriminately, and do not fire unless you think someone is in the area. If hunters are shooting in the area, three shots may not be recognized as a call for help. In this case, if you believe people are in the vicinity, fire after dark when no hunter would be firing.

2. Banging on metal provides a far-reaching sound. You can improvise; for example, you can hit a hub cap with a tool.

3. Yelling or calling is not advised unless searchers are close, as a large amount of energy is required.

4. A whistle is a very good sound signal. It can be heard for a long distance and is an unusual, attention-getting sound in the wilderness.

Sight signals are the most effective to employ. Many types might be used:

1. Every hiker should carry a signal mirror which can be used in an emergency. A regular small mirror can be used; however, a signal mirror which is made to be sighted through the center is best. This type is used by the Armed Forces and may be obtained through surplus stores. Made of metal or glass, it is small, lightweight, and may save your life. It is considered to be one of the most effective means of signaling.

When using a signal mirror, sight through the hole, holding the mirror about three inches in front of your face. Sight toward the target, as a plane's cockpit, looking in the mirror reflection for the spot of sunlight shining on your face. At this point, adjust the angle of the mirror until the spot of sunlight lines up with the hole. When you have done this, your flashes will be directly on target. This method can be used to signal searchers on foot, in vehicles, or in aircraft many miles away. The signal is amazingly intense, almost blinding. Once you have targeted in on a plane's cockpit, flash the plane periodically, but do not keep the light flashing into the cockpit constantly as it can seriously interfere with the pilot's ability to see.

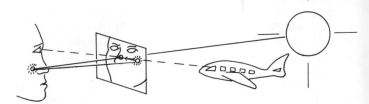

FIG. 105. Hold the signal mirror in front of your face. Sight the target through the hole. The spot of light coming through the hole will fall on your face or shirt and be reflected on the rear of the mirror. Adjust the mirror until the light spot in the mirror disappears through the sighting hole while you continue to sight your target through the hole.

The foregoing method works well if the angle from the sun to the target is ninety degrees or less. If it is more than ninety degrees, the following method must be employed: In slightly outstretched hand, hold the mirror at an angle so that it catches the sun. A light spot will fall on the palm of your hand. Sight the target through the hole, then adjust the angle of the mirror so that the reflection of the light spot on your hand coincides with the hole in the mirror and disappears. This method may be used when the sun is as much as approximately 180 degrees away from the target.

The only disadvantage in using an ordinary mirror is that perfect sighting is more difficult to accomplish. By holding your hand in front of the mirror and catching the reflected light, you can get a general idea of where the flashes are most intense and can adjust your aim by catching the reflected light on your surroundings. You may be able to scratch off a small portion of the mirror backing to allow a sighting hole. Many women carry mirrors in their purses and mirrors attached to vehicles can be used when a signal mirror is not available. A tin can lid can also be employed; in this it is simple to punch a sighting hole through the center.

To flash a mirror along the horizon consistently throughout the day is advisable in an emergency situation, even though the effort may appear to be futile. The energy required is little, and the flashes seen for great distances may well attract attention. Flash toward the sound of an aircraft, even though you may be unable to see the plane itself.

2. If you have a flashlight, use it to signal at night, if you have reason to believe that rescuers are nearby. Dismount vehicle lights and use these for night signaling when it appears their use may be effective. Remember your battery power is limited.

3. Raise the hood and trunk of your vehicle to signal trouble.

4. Make your site as obvious as possible. Spread objects around that are not in use—blankets, tarps, extra clothing, parachutes, and so on.

5. You may wish to use the International Ground–Air Emergency signals. Make these signals in a large size on the ground. Use available materials—strips of blanket, aluminum foil, parachute, rocks, and the like. Those signals most commonly needed are the following:

a. Require doctor—use a single straight line, as I
b. Unable to proceed—use X
c. Need food and water—use F
d. Am proceeding in this direction—use arrow pointing in direction taken
e. All is well—use LL
f. No—use N
g. Yes—use Y
h. Not understood—use two of the capital letters L, back to back

THE SIGNAL FIRE

All of the foregoing signals are effective in their own right; however the signal fire is used more often than any other. Both the bright blaze and the smoke it emits have chances to attract attention. If possible, maintain three fires in a triangle—the recognized distress signal. In an emergency situation have a fire prepared for lighting, if possible, or keep a fire going to which material may be quickly added. In some parts of the desert, long-lasting fuel may be difficult to find, and one should weigh the energy required and the possible value to be derived from a constant large fire as opposed to a small fire which can be increased if rescuers are thought to be in the area. At best, as a minimum measure when awaiting rescue, keep a plentiful supply of fuel around and keep at least coals burning at all times.

If the country in which you are situated is generally dark colored, attempt to build a fire which gives off a light-colored smoke. If you are in light-colored country, try to get a dark-colored smoke. Very black smoke probably has the best visibility, especially to aircraft. Green branches, if available, can be collected and thrown on hot coals or flames when great amounts of light-colored smoke are desired. If you are stalled with a vehicle, one of the best fuels for smoke signals is your spare tire. By pouring engine oil over the tire and igniting it, you should be able to produce a large amount of billowing black smoke visible for many miles.

A signal fire may also consist of a bucket of sand soaked with gasoline and lit (very carefully) when possible rescuers are in the vicinity.

You should always carry waterproof matches with you. However, if you do not have these, alternatives are possible. In order to start a fire with a spark or series of sparks, prepare tinder carefully. Tinder should consist of very fine, very dry, readily flammable material, such as the underbark of the cottonwood tree, bird or mouse nests, small dry grass, frayed bits of cotton cloth, or the like. When building any fire, start with tinder, then work your way up through a series of increasingly larger sticks until you reach the size you need for your particular purpose.

1. Start your fire with a cigarette lighter, if any member of your party has one.

2. Use the cigarette lighter from your vehicle.

3. Damp wooden matches can usually be dried by stroking them twenty to thirty times through the dry hair on your head.

4. Bright sunlight can be directed through a hand lens or other magnifying glass from your first aid kit, or any convex lens, to start a flame.

5. If you have a live storage battery in your vehicle, you can produce a spark from it. Direct this spark into fine tinder.

6. Use flint and steel to strike a spark. The steel is struck against flint or agate. Iron pyrites may be substituted for steel. If you have no flint, find a piece of hard rock from which you can strike sparks when it is struck with steel (use a

knife blade, tool, or the like). Strike with a downward scraping motion so that the sparks fall on the tinder placed below them. As the tinder begins to smolder, fan or blow it gently until a flame is present.

7. Two rather difficult fire-making methods—the use of the hand drill or the fire plough—require practice to perfect. Both methods depend on friction to ignite tinder. The equipment for both must be constructed of dry woods, such as yucca, cottonwood, and willow.

   a. The apparatus for the hand drill method consists of a drill and a base fire board. The drill is usually eighteen to twenty inches long and tapers at one end. The tapered end is the upper end; the larger end rests on the fire board, which is placed flat on the ground surface. Place the palms of your hands together over the tapered end of the drill and rub them together with a constant downward pressure. Your hands will gradually work their way down the drill. Pass them back to the top each time. Tinder should be placed around the friction point on the fire board. After a period of time, the friction should build enough heat to ignite the tinder.

   b. In the fire plough method, a groove from six to eight inches long and just wide enough for the fire stick is cut into the flat fire board. Place the fire board at an angle to the ground surface; you might, for example, prop the upper end on your bent knee. Hold the fire stick; while bearing down on it, move it back and forth in the groove. This process will build up a powder which collects at the end of the groove. Finally the friction should cause a spark which will ignite the powder.

Finding Water

If you are stranded in the desert, regardless of the circumstances, your foremost concern is very likely to be water. A good general rule to follow in emergency situations is: *If you have a sufficient water supply, or if you have found a water source, stay where you are and await rescue.* However, if your water supply is very low or absent and rescue seems far distant, your decision may be to attempt to locate a source of water. Hopefully, you will have a good map of the area which will designate probable water. Lacking this, other possibilities may be explored. Remember in all cases, however, that the energy and moisture required to search or dig for water must be determined to be small in comparison to the expected reward.

1. Tanks which hold water for varying lengths of time are found in almost all desert areas. These basins are natural rather than manmade. Located in the bottoms of stream and arroyo beds, they are usually hollowed out of rock; however, dirt tanks may also be present. Tanks are essentially depressions in the bed which are impermeable to water. Hence, as it rains and the arroyos or washes become active, these tanks fill with water. The water may be retained for varying periods of time, particularly if the tanks are partially protected by being located in shade, or in some other way. Some members of the animal population of an area stake their lives on these tanks where they occur; using them as a water source; normally they are fairly dependable water sources. Tanks can be located in a number of ways, but usually a combination of methods is best. First, scan the land for 360 degrees. Because the desert land is open, one can determine the slope of the land and ascertain where the main drainage is located. As the smaller streambeds converge, the size of the common drainage gradually increases. In the larger runoff channels, the water has often eroded its path down to the bedrock, which is the perfect material for forming the tanks. By following these major streambeds downhill, you have a good chance of finding a tank.

Since local animals depend on these water sources, many animal trails lead to or from these natural cisterns. Watch for trails and follow them. The correct direction can be determined by finding a junction of two trails; follow the direction indicated by the arrow formed by the joining of the two trails. Birds flock to these waterholes; listen for their calls or watch their flights in the early morning and evening hours. Doves often fly toward water in the early morning and evening; quail tend to fly toward water sources in the late afternoon and away from them in the morning.

2. Animal trails and bird flights may also lead you to man-made watering sources. Watch always for windmills

FIG. 106. For some months following a rain, in occasional locations water may be found by digging at the base of rock cliffs, particularly lava cliffs.

and also for watering troughs to which ranchers may haul water by vehicle for their stock.

3. In some cases, water may be found at the base of cliffs either on the surface or not far underground, for some time following rains. Occasionally springs may be located; lava and limestone tend to have larger springs than other types of rocks. Limestone caverns often contain pools or dripping springs. Be careful not to venture past the cavern's lighted areas as you can easily become disoriented.

4. Moisture often condenses at night on cool objects, such as metal or stones. This moisture may be collected just after sunup, for example, by soaking it up in a handkerchief and wringing it out. Airplane wings or similar surfaces may provide such moisture. If you possess a piece of canvas, scoop out a depression in the ground, cover the bottom with the canvas, and line the basin with pebbles taken from about a foot below the surface (which are less dry than those found on the ground surface). Dew may collect on the rocks during the night and trickle down onto the canvas. (Consider carefully, though, the energy and moisture required to prepare this dew trap in relationship to expected returns.)

Desert Survival Skills

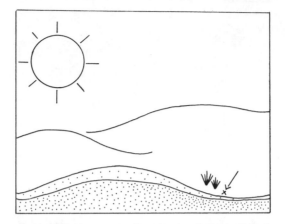

FIG. 107. When digging for water in sand dunes, pick the lowest point between dunes. Along a beach, dig in the first depression behind the first sand dune. The top sand layer may be underlain by wet sand. If you hit wet sand, dig no deeper, for below the fresh-water layer may be one of salt water. Prepare a hole in the damp-sand layer and wait for water to seep in.

5. Look for indicator plants which grow only where they can obtain water supplies. Sycamores, cottonwoods, willows, hackberry, tamarisk, and cattails are examples. You may have to dig to find the moisture.

6. If you are along a sandy beach, either on the seashore or along a dry lake, the best place to dig for water is in the first depression behind the first sand dune. This spot is the most probable place for rain water to collect. If you hit wet sand, cease digging; if conditions are right, water will seep out of the sand into the hole you have dug. The primary water is usually fresh; however, if you dig deeper, the lower water may contain salt. If you are among the sand dunes, rain water will collect in the lowest point between the dunes. At these points, dig down three to six feet; if the sand becomes damp, continue digging. However, if in lower layers the sand becomes dry, you have passed the water-bearing layer and should discontinue digging.

7. If you locate mud flats, find the lowest point and wring out any damp mud in a cloth to collect water. Check the

THE DESERTS OF THE SOUTHWEST

water to determine its salinity. If it is too disagreeable, do not drink it.

8. Small upwellings of fresh water occur along some beaches. Occasionally these upwellings are found on the Gulf of California coast where underground fresh water floats above salt water. Where the fresh water is exposed, a *pozo,* or "coyote well," is formed. Animals take advantage of these "wells," as can man if he locates them, although the water tends to be rather saline. Pozos are small, often consisting of a small basin only a few inches in diameter. These "wells" are often surrounded by a small ring of green succulent vegetation, which helps one to identify such a site.

9. If you come upon a dry desert streambed, dig at the lowest point on the outside of a bend in the bed. At this point, water sinks and accumulates as the stream dries up. Watch for damp spots in dry streambeds and dig there. Watch also for holes dug in streambeds by coyotes seeking water. Often water seeps into these holes, and man as well as coyotes and other animals can benefit from the water source.

10. If you locate an open water supply such as a tank or the like, *purification of the water is always advisable.* If it is

FIG. 108. If you are digging for water in a dry streambed, dig at the lowest point on the outside of a bend in the channel.

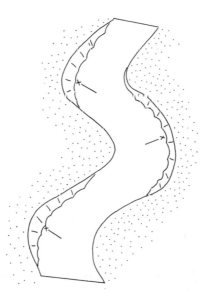

dirty, strain it through a cloth. Purify it by boiling it for five minutes; by using two halazone tablets to one quart of water (let stand thirty minutes); by using two to three drops of tincture of iodine per quart of water (let stand for thirty minutes); or by adding two to four drops of household bleach per quart of water. Admittedly, in a desperate situation, the above methods may be unavailable to you, and the water, polluted or unpolluted, may be literally your life-saver.

11. Certain desert plants may constitute an important source of emergency moisture. Particularly the cacti, which soak up moisture supplies as sponges would when moisture is present, may be important to man. The barrel cactus of the Southwest desert country has helped many a stranded person to survive. Several species are present, depending on the area you are in. These cacti are globular to short cylindric in form, and usually unbranched, although a few species produce a clustered group of several stems. Barrel cacti are heavily spined, and some species have in each cluster a main spine that is strongly hooked, closely resembling a large fishhook. Moisture does not simply flow out of this cactus. The best means of obtaining moisture from the barrel cactus is to break the cactus open, using a heavy knife, rock, or tool, such as the jack in your vehicle. The pulp inside, which holds the moisture, may be pulverized to obtain the liquid (use tool, rock, or the like), or you can chew on the pulp extracting the moisture and then spitting out the residue. Do not swallow the pulp; it can make you ill. Smaller plants tend to contain the most moisture. These cacti are "accordion-pleated" to allow for expansion with water supply. A well-filled plant with its pleats expanded will contain more moisture than a shriveled, tightly pleated specimen. The barrel cactus is the only one from which acceptable moisture in any quantity can be obtained. The saguaro, although large, does not contain potable moisture.

All desert cacti fruit is edible. The fruit of some species remains on the plant for considerable periods. The fruit often contains a great deal of moisture and is strongly recommended as a source of both food and water.

The immature flower stalks of the yucca and sotol plants contain moisture. These stalks are present only briefly during the year, however. (Do not confuse them with the dead and dried flower stalks which often remain attached to the

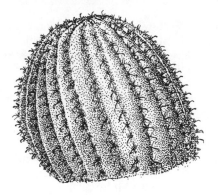

FIG. 109. Depending upon the species, certain barrel cacti, *Ferocactus sp.*, may reach 9 to 12 feet in height, although most species range from 2 to 4 or 5 feet tall. These cacti are usually solitary, unbranched, and globular to short cylindric in form. In an emergency, they can be cut open by man and the inner pulp mashed to obtain the moisture it contains.

plants for a considerable time.) When no flower stalks are present, the main stalks can be split open and the pith used in the same manner as that of the barrel cactus to obtain very limited moisture.

12. If the materials are available, you may wish to construct one or more solar stills for obtaining water. Essentially, the solar still is a simple device which can distill drinkable water, using as its source soil, fleshy plants such as cacti, or polluted waters such as body waste. The functioning pieces of the solar still are a piece of clear plastic film about six feet square and some type of fairly broad-mouthed container with which to collect water. The solar still is constructed by scooping out a bowl-shaped hole in the soil. The hole should be about thirty-six to forty inches in diameter and about eighteen to twenty inches in depth. Dig the sides down straight at first, then taper them to the center to provide a slanting ledge on which to place plant material. At the center of the hole, dig a small, deeper depression approximately the size of the container. Place the container securely in this bottom-most part. The container may be a pan, bucket, hub cap, or the like. A trough may be dug around part of the perimeter of the still, at about mid-depth, as a site in which to place polluted water. Lay the plastic

sheet over the top of the cavity and hold it in place with a rim of rocks and soil. In the center of the plastic, place a small-sized rock (no larger than your fist). The rock, weighting the plastic down in the center, causes an inverted cone of plastic to be formed, with the tip of the cone directly above the container. With sunlight shining through the plastic, water is evaporated from the soil and from materials placed in the still; the air becomes super saturated and water condenses on the underside of the cooler plastic. The drops of water then flow to the low point of the cone and drip into the container below. (If the plastic is very smooth and slick, you may need to roughen it a bit by rubbing it with sand or some other abrasive so that the water drops are not shed from its surface above the tip of the cone.)

The plastic must be held firmly against the ground surface by the ring of sand, soil, and rocks so that no moisture is allowed to escape from the still. Each time the plastic is removed, a half hour to an hour or longer is required, once it is replaced, to get the still into operation again. Therefore, do not remove the plastic any more frequently than is absolutely necessary. The use of a plastic tube 4 to 6 feet in length, ¼ inch in diameter, as a part of the still is helpful. Securely place one end of the tube in the water container (if you have tape, tape it in place). Bring the other end of the tube to the ground surface and out beyond the edge of the plastic and dirt rim. Use this tube as a straw for sucking the moisture up from the container without disturbing the distillation process. When the plastic tube is not being used to remove water, tie the end of it shut or otherwise seal it.

The location of the still is important. If the soil is going to be your only source of water, the still is best placed in a streambed or depression in which rain water collects, so that you are making use of the soil with the highest water concentration. In general, a clay-type soil is usually better than a sand type, as clay normally holds more water for longer periods. Following long dry spells, the water yield from soil alone may be quite small. If cactus or polluted water is to be used as the still's primary source of moisture, the still can be placed in almost any convenient spot. However, always make sure its location receives maximum sunlight. Be very careful that polluted water, cactus parts, or soil do not touch the inner portion of the plastic sheet or the collection con-

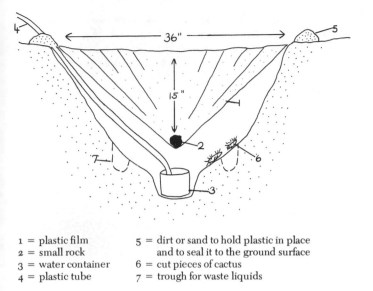

1 = plastic film
2 = small rock
3 = water container
4 = plastic tube

5 = dirt or sand to hold plastic in place
    and to seal it to the ground surface
6 = cut pieces of cactus
7 = trough for waste liquids

FIG. 110. In the solar still, water from the soil, plant parts, human waste, and other materials condenses on the underside of a plastic film and drips into the container. Water can be sucked up through the plastic hose to avoid disturbing the condensation process.

tainer, polluting the water. When using succulent plant material, be sure the plants have been chopped open to some extent. In the still, do *not* use radiator water which contains chemical contaminants.

Finding Food

The need for food in a survival situation is far less pressing than the need for water. If water is in short supply or lacking, one should eat nothing; digestion of food intensifies the need for water. Man can survive a mere few days without water; he can survive for several weeks without food—not, admittedly, entirely in comfort. In actuality, a man undergoing a water deficit usually does not feel hungry.

Consider always the physiological costs involved in the search for food. Consider whether the use of energy and moisture in attempts to obtain food is more feasible than to do without the food. Inasmuch as this chapter is concerned with survival in an emergency situation in the desert, and not with wresting a living from the desert wilderness, we will explore which foods may be most easily available for use on a short-term basis.

PLANTS AS FOOD

1. All of the cactus fruits are safe to eat. Some fruits break open, and their contents can be easily removed (as the saguaro). Others can be singed over a flame to remove spines, then peeled and eaten. Even the old dried up cactus fruits contain seeds which can be pulverized (using stones) to form a powder to be eaten plain or mixed with water to form *pinole*. The Indians used seeds in this manner; they ground them using two stones—the large, base rock called a *metate* and the hand-held, smaller grinding rock, or *mano*. These worn rocks are often found lying in the desert where last abandoned by their Indian owners many years ago.

2. The new young pads of the prickly pear cactus can be eaten raw or boiled.

3. The night-blooming cereus, *Cereus greggii*, resembles a cluster of weathered sticks and grows close to larger trees and bushes which give it support and protection. This cactus has a large bulbous, turniplike, edible root which may weigh almost fifty pounds. Unfortunately these plants are not particularly plentiful and are difficult to locate, for their stems are sprawling and inconspicuous, often partially hidden by the nurse plant.

4. The leguminous, bean-bearing trees comprise a large group of plants from which edible food sources may be gathered. The honey and screwbean mesquite trees and the palo verde, ironwood, and acacia trees are the principal Southwest desert members of this group. These trees are all small, bearing large crops of bean pods, which can be boiled and eaten when green and tender (or eaten raw in limited quantities when green). The dry mature beans, like the cactus seeds, are hard and must be ground. The resultant meal can be cooked with water for a gruel or formed into

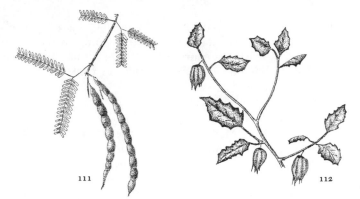

FIG. 111. Mesquites, *Prosopis sp.*, range from shrub to tree size. The seeds and the seed pods, which do not split open, provide an important food source for animals, as they once did for man also.

FIG. 112. Ground-cherry, *Physalis fendleri*, is a plant of the southwestern mesas, found above 3,000 feet. It is a widely branched, straggling plant, 1 to 2 feet in height. As the fruit develops it is covered by the thin, papery, fine-toothed calyx. The round, yellow, many-seeded berry is edible, raw or cooked.

cakes and baked. These beans, especially those of the mesquite trees, were a staple of life for many Southwest Indian tribes.

5. The basal central heart of the agave plant can be baked in hot coals in the ground and eaten. The agave heart was a staple for certain Indian tribes in times past, particularly in Baja California. To extract the heart from these plants, dig a pit, and produce sufficient coals to cook this food item is a somewhat major operation.

6. The green flowering stalk of yucca may be chewed on for its sugar and moisture content.

7. Nuts of the jojoba shrub may be eaten.

8. If one is on the edge of the desert, bordering other environments, other types of food may be available. For example, dandelions and cattails may be found near moisture or piñon nuts may be gathered at the higher elevations.

9. The ground-cherry, or tomatillo, *Physalis pubescens* and other species, grows in open areas throughout the west on moist to medium-dry ground from sea level to 8,500 feet.

Each fruit is contained in a distinctive "Chinese lantern"-type covering. The plant is leafy and vining, with flowers from yellow to white to purple. The fruit is usually present in the fall. It may be eaten fresh, dried, or cooked.

WHAT NOT TO EAT

When in doubt about the suitability of a plant as food, do not consume it. Many plants are poisonous; no single or group of criteria identifies them. Entire volumes have been written on both the edible and the inedible plants. A large percentage of the plant species have yet to be tested by modern man as to their edibility. Two general rules are often given regarding wild plant foods.

1. If possible, boil plants that are at all questionable; the elevated heat breaks down many toxins.

2. Test cooked plants by holding a small portion in your mouth for a few moments. If a burning, nauseating, or bitter taste develops, do not eat the food.

Certainly neither rule is foolproof; a good many exceptions may be found to both, and the exceptions can prove deadly. Certain definite rules regarding our North American desert wild plants can be given:

1. Avoid all plants with milky sap, such as the milkweeds. These plants are poisonous.

2. In the Southwest, avoid plants with bright red seeds; these are the coral bean plants, *Erythrina flabelliformis,* a spiny shrub or sometimes a small tree up to fifteen feet in height. In early summer, the branches are leafless, but adorned with brilliant red flowers. In mid-summer, the plant bears nearly triangular leaflets. In late summer and fall, it displays thick pods, six to ten inches in length, which split open to display the bright red, poisonous seeds. Later these fall and are found on the ground.

3. Avoid mushrooms unless you can positively identify the edible species.

4. Avoid nightshade (horse nettle, or wild potato), *Solanum sp.* This wide-ranging plant is common along roadsides. It is a member of the potato family; the plant, with grayish leaves and purple or yellow flowers, closely resembles its cultivated potato relative. It is poisonous.

5. Avoid locoweed (milkvetch, rattleweed), *Astragalus*

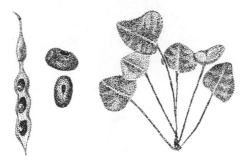

FIG. 113. The coral bean, *Erythrina flabelliforma*, is a small or medium-sized shrub, which may reach tree size in Mexico. The bright red seeds produced in 6- to 10-inch-long pods are extremely poisonous.

FIG. 114. Nightshade, *Solanum sp.* (up to 3 feet in height), is a low shrub, common along roadsides, which somewhat resembles the potato plant. Its flowers are purple. Some species are spine-covered; others are not. An alkaloid, solanin, may be present in leaves and unripe fruit, making them poisonous.

sp. This genus is wide-ranging, with many species. The plants are four to twelve inches tall, members of the pea family, and have white to purple flowers. Some species contain selenium and are poisonous.

6. Avoid Jimsonweed (sacred datura, thornapple), *Datura meteloides*. This conspicuous, coarse herb forms a large spreading clump. It produces many large, fragrant, white flowers; the fruit is a round pod armed with prickles. Jim-

FIG. 115. Locoweed, milkvetch, or rattleweed, *Astragalus sp.*, is a widespread member of the pea family. It grows 4 to 12 inches in height and has white to purple flowers. These plants often contain selenium, making them poisonous.

FIG. 116. Jimsonweed, sacred datura, or thornapple, *Datura meteloides,* is a large, spreading, coarse herb with many large, funnel-shaped white flowers. The fruit is round and prickle-studded. Datura, which contains atropine, is very poisonous. May reach a maximum of 4 feet in height, usually lower.

sonweed is very dangerous; it contains scopolamine and atropine which block the autonomic nervous system. Its effect may include acute thirst, difficulty in swallowing, and failure of the sweat glands with a consequent dangerous rise in body temperature. The eyes dilate, causing near blindness and pain; delirium, hallucinations, and hyperexcitability occur; with enough of the drug, convulsions leading to death are a distinct possibility. Unfortunately, this plant is occasionally used as a hallucinogen. Recently, during a single summer month in Tucson, nine people were hospitalized after partaking of the leaves or drinking tea brewed from the plant.

ANIMALS AS FOOD

In a survival situation, almost every animal may be considered edible if properly prepared. However, obtaining wild animals for the purpose of eating is not as easy as the Hollywood director or many wilderness survival books depict it, although it is not impossible. Many survival books describe deadfalls, snares, and very elaborate designs to kill, injure, or capture game. These methods often work more readily in the forest than in the desert. The openness of the terrain, the lack of resources for construction, and a scarcity of large game make these methods less successful in the desert. Some of these trapping techniques may prove successful, if suitable construction materials can be found, at an isolated tank or waterhole to which a number of animals are drawn for water.

Birds may be caught at a waterhole or where seeds have been sprinkled to attract them by using a monofilament fishing line. Attach one end of this very fine line to a stationary object. Take the remainder of the line, about twenty-five feet in length, and place it in a loose tangle on the ground. Hopefully, the birds will become entangled and can be captured by hand.

Sometimes a noose may be fashioned out of string and laid around an animal's hole or burrow. When the animal begins to emerge, the string can be jerked to, hopefully, noose it.

In an emergency situation, if you have a firearm, you may be able to obtain game with it; rabbits are a good possibility. Make sure of your shots in order to save ammunition, which may also be useful for signaling.

Many of the desert's most common animals—such as lizards and snakes—are small. A slingshot can be valuable for killing or stunning them. Even rocks thrown by hand may provide good results for small game.

If you do obtain animals, beware of certain problems:

1. Some animals, particularly rabbits, may occasionally carry tularemia, a disease transmittable to man. If an animal acts sickly or its liver appears to be spotted, do not eat the animal.

2. Rabies is a problem at times in the desert; bats, in particular, carry it. Avoid being bitten by bats if you are attempting to capture or handle them (a practice not to be recommended). Also be aware of the very occasional wild animal which shows absolutely no fear of man, indicating that it may be suffering from rabies (though not *all* animals that fail to run from man are rabid).

3. Some toads have glands in the skin; when dogs mouth certain species—for example, the large Colorado River toad—they may become very ill. Skin frogs before eating them; do *not* eat toads.

4. In some of the higher desert country and adjacent to it, as in northern Arizona and New Mexico, the rodent population in summer occasionally harbors fleas which are carriers of plague.

5. A few animals have scent or musk glands which will taint the meat unless they are carefully removed immediately after killing. Skunks are particularly difficult for this reason. The peccary provides excellent meat, but the scent gland located on the back near the rump should be removed immediately after killing.

6. Insofar as possible, avoid allowing the hair of an animal to come into contact with the meat. Hair may cause the meat to have a strong taste.

7. Avoid caterpillars with hairs. Some hairs cause a skin reaction if handled; some are poisonous if eaten.

ANIMALS SUITABLE FOR FOOD

1. Small mammals, such as rabbits, pack rats, kangaroo rats, mice, ground squirrels, and the like.

2. Larger mammals, such as bobcats, foxes, coyotes, badgers, raccoons, ring-tailed cats, coatimundis, peccaries, deer, antelope, bighorn sheep, and porcupines. (Where it occurs, the porcupine can provide a good source of food; slow moving, it is easy to kill.)

3. Birds of all kinds are edible (although the vulture may be offensive); dove and quail are particularly excellent eating, and are attracted to waterholes where their capture may be possible.

4. Bird eggs, regardless of the stage of embryo development, are good.

5. Lizards are all edible. Beware of the Gila monster's bite, however, and take no chances with this lizard. A particularly good lizard to procure in an emergency situation is the chuckwalla. A large lizard, it lives among jumbles of rocks. When frightened, it dashes into rock crevices where it inflates itself with air, making it impossible for enemies to extricate it. However, Indians solved the problem, as can the individual in an emergency situation, by holding onto a protruding tail or leg while stabbing the chuckwalla with a sharp stick, puncturing its air sac, thereby allowing extraction of the lizard's body from the crevice.

6. Snakes of all species are good to eat. Do not take a chance on being bitten by a rattlesnake while attempting to procure it as food. If a rattlesnake is to be used for food, *carefully* cut off its head and bury it; eat only the remainder of the reptile.

7. The desert tortoise may be difficult to locate, but is easy to capture and provides good meat in an emergency.

8. Insects are nourishing food, despite preconceived ideas people may have about using them as food. Grubs found in rotten wood and in and under rocks, hairless caterpillars, and large grasshoppers at times are quite plentiful and fairly easy to obtain.

9. Sea life may be obtainable in the parts of the Sonoran Desert which border the Pacific Ocean or the Gulf of California. For those facing an emergency situation along the desert coast, many resources are available from the sea itself, either through the tide pools, fishing, or land life (such as birds) which derives its living from the sea.

Meat may be cooked on a stick over a fire; it may be wrapped in green leaves or aluminum foil (if these are available) or given a mud coating, then buried with hot coals and baked. Foil may also be used to improvise pots and the like for cooking. Water and food can be heated in a cardboard or other flammable container as long as the water level is kept high and static and low heat is used (the portion of the container which is above the water level may burn). Any extra meat can be preserved by making it into jerky. Take fat-free meat, cut it into thin strips several inches in length, hang it in the sun for two or three days until completely dried. The jerky will keep indefinitely as long as it is dry, and may be eaten dry, soaked, or cooked. Meat may also be preserved by sand-drying. Cut meat into strips, wipe it dry, and bury it about six inches deep in dry sand until it is completely dried.

Relatively few people are ever actually required to face an emergency-survival situation in the desert. With respect for the desert and the conditions it imposes, and with proper preparation for enjoyment of the arid land, one is far safer exploring the desert than exploring many American cities. Advice for the desert enthusiast is *Do not get caught in an emergency situation if preplanning and good sense can avoid it.* But if you do find yourself in trouble, remember:

1. *Do not panic.*
2. *Think. Your brain is your greatest asset.*
3. *Neither underestimate nor overestimate either desert conditions or your abilities to cope with them and the situation in which you find yourself.*
4. *Consider all alternatives from the standpoint of physiological costs.*
5. *Follow the rules for survival.*
6. *Do not give up.*

One should depend on preparation and intelligent action in desert exploration, rather than miracles. But when only sheer determination remains and the object is survival, don't discount the miraculous, backed by resolve.

May you never need desert survival information. May all your desert exploration be "rewarding travel in an unfrequented land."

SUGGESTED REFERENCES

Adolph, E. F. and Associates. *Physiology of Man in the Desert.* New York: Hafner Press, 1969.

Arnold, Robert E. *What To Do About Bites and Stings of Venomous Animals.* New York: Macmillan, Inc., 1973 (hardcover); Collier Books, 1973 (paperback).

Aschmann, Homer. *Central Desert of Baja California: Demography and Ecology.* Manessier, 1967.

Benson, Lyman. *The Cacti of Arizona.* Tucson: University of Arizona Press, 1974.

Benson, Lyman and Robert A. Darrow. *The Trees and Shrubs of the Southwestern Deserts.* Tucson: University of Arizona Press, 1976.

Brown, G. W., Jr. *Desert Biology: Special Topics on the Physical and Biological Aspects of Arid Regions,* vol. 1. New York: Academic Press, 1968.

Coyle, Jeanette and Norman C. Roberts. *A Field Guide to the Common and Interesting Plants of Baja California.* New York: Natural History Publishing Company, 1976.

Dodge, Natt N. and Jeanne R. Janish. *Flowers of the Southwest Deserts.* Southwest Parks and Monuments Association, 1973.

Ferris, Roxana. *Death Valley Wildflowers.* Death Valley Natural History Association, 1962.

Findley, Rowe. *Great American Deserts.* Washington, D.C.: National Geographic Society, 1972.

Fletcher, Colin. *The New Complete Walker.* New York: Alfred A. Knopf, Inc., 1974.

Humphrey, Robert R. *The Boojum and Its Home.* Tucson: University of Arizona Press, 1974.

Jackson, Donald Dale and the editors of Time-Life Books. *Sagebrush Country.* New York: Time-Life Books, 1975.

Jackson, Donald Dale; Peter Wood; and the editors of Time-Life Books. *The Sierra Madre.* New York: Time-Life Books, 1975.

Jaeger, Edmund C. *Desert Wild Flowers.* Stanford: Stanford University Press, 1969.

Jaeger, Edmund C. *Desert Wildlife.* Stanford: Stanford University Press, 1961.

Jaeger, Edmund C. *The North American Deserts.* Stanford University Press, 1957.

Johnson, William Weber and the editors of Time-Life Books. *Baja California*. New York: Time-Life Books, 1972.

Kirk, Donald R. *Wild Edible Plants of the Western United States*. Healdsburg, California: Naturegraph Publishers, 1970.

Kirk, Ruth. *Desert: The American Southwest*. Boston: Houghton Mifflin Company, 1973.

Klauber, Laurence M. *Rattlesnakes: Their Habits, Life Histories, and Influence on Mankind,* 2 vols. Berkeley: University of California Press, 1973.

Krutch, Joseph Wood. *The Desert Year*. New York: The Viking Press, Inc., 1963 (paperback).

Krutch, Joseph Wood. *The Forgotten Peninsula*. New York: William Sloane Associates, 1961.

Krutch, Joseph Wood. *Voice of the Desert*. New York: William Morrow & Co., Inc., 1955 (paperback).

Larson, Peggy Pickering. *Deserts of America*. Englewood Cliffs: Prentice-Hall, Inc., 1970.

Leopold, A. Starker and the editors of Life. *The Desert*. New York: Time Incorporated, 1961.

Leopold, A. Starker. *Wildlife of Mexico: The Game Birds and Mammals*. Berkeley: University of California Press, 1957.

Little, Elbert L., Jr. *Southwestern Trees: A Guide to the Native Species of New Mexico and Arizona*. U.S. Department of Agriculture, 1950.

Lowe, Charles, ed. *The Vertebrates of Arizona*. Tucson: University of Arizona Press, 1964.

Miller, Alden H. and Robert C. Stebbins. *The Lives of Desert Animals in Joshua Tree National Monument*. Berkeley: University of California Press, 1964.

Nesbitt, Paul H., Alonzo W. Pond, and William H. Allen. *The Survival Book*. New York: Funk and Wagnalls Inc., 1969 (paperback).

Niethammer, Carolyn. *American Indian Food and Lore*. New York: Collier Books, 1974 (paperback).

Peterson, Roger Tory and Edward L. Chalif. *A Field Guide to Mexican Birds*. Boston: Houghton Mifflin Company, 1973.

Peterson, Roger Tory. *A Field Guide to Western Birds*. Boston: Houghton Mifflin Company, 1961.

Phillips, Allan, Joe Marshall, and Gale Monson. *The Birds of Arizona*. Tucson: University of Arizona Press, 1964.

Ryan, R. Mark. *Mammals of Deep Canyon; Colorado Desert, California*. The Desert Museum, Palm Springs, California, 1968.

Schmidt-Nielsen, Knut. *Desert Animals: Physiological Problems of Heat and Water*. New York: Oxford University Press, 1964.

Shaw, Charles E. and Sheldon Campbell. *Snakes of the American West*. New York: Alfred A. Knopf, Inc., 1974.

Shreve, Forrest and Ira L. Wiggins. *Vegetation and Flora of the Sonoran Desert,* 2 vols. Stanford: Stanford University Press, 1946.

Small, Arnold. *The Birds of California.* New York: Winchester Press, 1975.

Stebbins, Robert C. *A Field Guide to Western Reptiles and Amphibians.* Boston: Houghton Mifflin Company, 1975.

Sutton, Ann and Myron Sutton. *The Life of the Desert.* New York: McGraw-Hill Book Company, 1966.

INDEX

Tularemia, 270
Turkestan Desert, 27, 28

U

Uma notata, 52, 58, 59, 144
Uric acid, 63
Urine, 63, 69
Urocyon cinereoargenteus, 101
Uropygids, 191
Urosaurus graciosus, 144
Uta stansburiana, 88, 145

V

Varnish leaf acacia, 123
Vegetation: in definition of desert,
    30, 75–76; as water source, 56
Vehicle maintenance, 176–177
Velvet ants, 195–196
Venom, *see* Antivenin; Bites;
    Stings
Verdins, 103, 111
Vinegaroon, 191–192
Vizcaino region, 142–143
Voles, 88, 101
Vulpes macrotis, 125
Vulpes velox, 101

W

Washboard roads, 174
Washingtonia filifera, 103, 134,
    135
Water: as erosion factor, 23; needs
    of plants, 36–49; needs of ar-
    thropods, 53–54; for evaporative
    cooling, 64–65; in camping, 162;
    from radiators, 186; and forced
    drinking, 186; rationing, 187;
    finding, 255–263; purification of,
    259–260
Water-savers, 42–44

Water-spenders, 42, 44–46
Water-table-tapping plants, 45
Welles, Ralph and Florence, 95,
    97–98
Wells, 259
Went, Frits, 39–40
Western diamondback snake, 244
Whip scorpion, 191–192
Whistle, 164
White bursage, 131
White Sands National Monument,
    120
Willows, 103
Winds, 21–23
Winter fat, 78, 79
Winter precipitation, 34–35
Wolf, 126
Woodpeckers, 107, 109
Wormwood, 79
Wren, Bewick, 109
Wren, cactus, 146
Winter torpor, 110

X

Xantusa vigilis, 106–108
Xerophytes, defined, 37

Y

Yucca, Mohave, 104
Yucca brevifolia, 101
Yucca night lizard, 106–108
Yuccas, 101–102, 104, 118–120; as
    water source, 260–261; for food,
    265; mentioned, 76, 117
Yucca schidegera, 104
Yucca valida, 142
Yuma, Ariz., 16–17, 19, 135

Z

Zenaida asiatica, 64
Zenaidura macroura, 63, 89, 103